TLACAELEL
REMEMBERED

THE CIVILIZATION OF THE AMERICAN INDIAN SERIES

TLACAELEL
REMEMBERED

❀

MASTERMIND OF THE
AZTEC EMPIRE

SUSAN SCHROEDER

UNIVERSITY OF OKLAHOMA PRESS : NORMAN

Also by Susan Schroeder

Chimalpahin and the Kingdoms of Chalco (Tucson, 1991)

(co-ed. and co-trans.) *Codex Chimalpahin*, 2 vols. (Norman, Okla., 1997)

(co-ed.) *Indian Women of Early Mexico* (Norman, Okla., 1997)

(ed.) *Native Resistance and the Pax Colonial in New Spain* (Lincoln, Neb., 1998)

(co-ed.) *Annals of his Time: Don Domingo de San Antón Muñón Chimalpahin Quauhtlehuanitzin* (Stanford, Calif., 2006)

(co-ed.) *Religion in New Spain* (Albuquerque, 2007)

(co-ed.) *Chimalpahin's Conquest: A Nahua Historian's Rewriting of Francisco López de Gómera's* La conquista de México (Stanford, Calif., 2010)

(ed.) *The Conquest All Over Again: Nahuas and Zapotecs Thinking, Writing, and Painting Spanish Colonialism* (Brighton, England, 2010)

Library of Congress Cataloging-in-Publication Data
Name: Schroeder, Susan.
Title: Tlacaelel remembered : mastermind of the Aztec Empire / Susan Schroeder.
Description: Norman, OK : University of Oklahoma Press, [2016] | Series: Civilization of the American Indian series volume 276 | Includes bibliographical references and index.
Identifiers: LCCN 2016014429 | ISBN 978-0-8061-5434-3 (hardcover)
ISBN 978-0-8061-9222-2 (paper) Subjects: LCSH: Tlacaelel, active 15th century. | Aztecs—Biography. | Statesmen—Mexico—Biography. | Aztecs—History. | Indians of Mexico—History. Classification: LCC F1219.75.T42 S37 2016 | DDC 972/.01—dc23
LC record available at https://lccn.loc.gov/2016014429

Tlacaelel Remembered: Mastermind of the Aztec Empire is Volume 276 in The Civilization of the American Indian Series.

The paper in this book meets the guidelines for permanence and durability of the Committee on Production Guidelines for Book Longevity of the Council on Library Resources, Inc. ∞

CONTENTS

ILLUSTRATIONS

PREFACE

The discovery in 1978 of the ruins of the Aztec *templo mayor* in the heart of Mexico City's *centro histórico* merely served to confirm what everyone had known all along: the capital of Mexico Tenochtitlan was indeed as grand and extraordinary as the written histories of ancient times revealed. Ongoing excavations demonstrate how very cosmopolitan and sumptuous the polity was.

The inhabitants of Mexico Tenochtitlan, of course, kept their own accounts about the place, and then Hernando Cortés and his fellow conquerors, starting in the second decade of the sixteenth century, were swift to write letters, chronicles, and sweeping histories about it. Most of the reports by the Spaniards were composed to seek favor from the Spanish crown, and although they included eyewitness observations as well as certain information from local natives, they were nevertheless largely neglectful of the indigenous writings, which to them seemed indecipherable.

A half century later, religious who had come to New Spain, as it was then called, realized that in order to optimize their success in spreading the Gospel, they needed to know the language and customs of the indigenes among whom they lived and worked. It was no easy task, and they came to depend on a cadre of educated young men who had become knowledgeable in alphabetic writing and the Spaniards' customs and intentions for record keeping. Some exemplary histories were the result, with the Franciscans, Dominicans, and Jesuits learning the languages and collecting information from a variety of individuals and written sources as they became available. They were not alone; the natives themselves were writing their own histories of Aztec life, many with the distinct advantage of already knowing the language and having important contacts with individuals who were caring for the precious old manuscripts, of which there were still a great many even at the beginning of the seventeenth century. All were written in the vernacular, either Nahuatl or Spanish, and a few are extant and available today in printed form. They are a welcome complement to the templo mayor finds.

The various accounts could not fail to mention the great imperial headquarters of the Aztecs and all that they had accomplished in a relatively short time. In terms of political, economic, social, and religious complexities, no other place in the Americas could match what the Aztecs had achieved over the course of two or three generations of successful rulers. Indeed, one might even suggest parallels with the classical era in ancient Europe. Moreover, three of the histories credit one man, Tlacaelel the Cihuacoatl, with bringing it about. The authors of the histories were convinced of the greatness of Tlacaelel, who was in turn responsible for the magnificence of the Aztec state. But other histories do not mention the man. Did he exist?

ACKNOWLEDGMENTS

Chimalpahin came to me by way of the telephone in the late 1970s. James Lockhart, my adviser at the University of California, Los Angeles, had just returned from Mexico City and called to say that Luis Reyes García had provided him a photocopy of Günter Zimmermann's two-volume work on the writings of the Nahua annalist don Domingo de San Antón Muñón Chimalpahin Quauhtlehuanitzin. At the time, Zimmermann's transcription was the most complete available. Jim and I discussed my undertaking an intellectual history of the Nahuatl sociopolitical concepts in Chimalpahin's accounts about Chalco. Heretofore, studies on Chimalpahin had focused on precontact topics. My research was to identify continuities into the colonial era. Indeed, subsequent archival research in Amecameca, Chimalpahin's hometown in Chalco, revealed that the political organization of Amecameca, founded in 1261, was ostensibly unchanged until Mexico's reform laws in the 1850s.

His holographic works are largely in the form of annals, and what was extant in the late 1970s was located at the Bibliothèque Nationale de France, except for a few folios at the Archivo Histórico in Mexico City. Although written in the early years of the seventeenth century and frequently signed by the man himself, someone over the course of the centuries erroneously labeled the manuscripts at the Bibliothèque "Relaciones" and "Diario" when clearly they were traditional Nahuatl annals. Neither term does justice to the annals genre, and numerous scholars have essentially misrecognized Chimalpahin's historical methodology and purpose. Never realizing that each set of annals has intrinsic ethnic and temporal value, they claimed that he contradicted himself and confused dates and other facts. Zimmermann's transcription went so far as to decontextualize and reorganize chronologically all the annals, obfuscating the fact that each was a composition by generations of individuals about a different place and followed its own reckoning of events and time.

One of the most important contributions that I hoped to make to an expanding corpus of Chimalpahin scholarship was to reiterate the unique quality, variety, and abundance of sources that he had at his disposal. Fortuitously, in 1983 a cache of long-lost Nahuatl annals by Chimalpahin that had been traded for Protestant Bibles in 1827 was discovered in England. A year later the Boturini copy (1746) of Chimalpahin's Spanish-language version of Francisco López de Gómara's *Conquista de México* (1552) was brought to me by a physician in Yuma, Arizona, who had kept it in his safe deposit box for decades. And after perusing Arthur J. O. Anderson's 1993 translation of what was said to be Sahagún's *Exercicio quotidiano*, I realized that the work was in Chimalpahin's hand and style. The identification of these extraordinary Chimalpahin-authored writings is testimony to the substance and diversity of his oeuvre.

Chimalpahin is often thought to have written only about his home region of Chalco. By far the majority of his annals, though, are about the Mexica Tenochca and the majesty of their state. He was living in the Spanish capital of New Spain one hundred years after the Spanish invasions and writing about what remained of Aztec Mexico Tenochtitlan. He seems to have been undaunted by the challenge, working for years to collect an array of sources and then pridefully recording an epic history in his own language for the generations of Nahuas who would follow him.

His Nahuatl is eloquent, substantive, and consistent, and it is revealing of the formation of ancient polities, the deeds of their kings, the importance of women and family, the role of local deities, and the intricate networks crucial to the elaboration of the great states and then empire. But Chimalpahin was also a man of colonial Mexico City, an intellectual, and a Nahua Christian, and there appears to have been little, if any, conflict as he reconciled the two cultures and epochs that he shared. I never imagined that my last work on Chimalpahin would focus on the precontact era. But for Chimalpahin, Tlacaelel was surely as important as was Chalco, largely because the old warrior-politician epitomized the glory and grandeur of all that Mexico

Tenochtitlan had become, most of which continued in architectural and historical memory in his time and ours.

My thanks are many, and I am indebted to Frances Berdan, Elizabeth Boone, David Tavárez, and an anonymous reader who read the entire work and offered invaluable suggestions. Frances Karttunen shared her Nahuatl expertise when asked. In Mexico City, Christoph Rosenmüller greatly facilitated my acquisition of an image. John McManamon, S.J., translated the documents in Italian and has been a mainstay for many years. Others contributed ever so much by simply listening to my Tlacaelel stories or furnishing yet another source of information: Brad Benton; Sheila Berg; Amber Brian; Louise Burkhart; Edward Calnek; Bill Connell; Richard Conway; Lori Diel; Erika Hosselkus; Mark Lentz; Dana Liebson; Stafford Poole, C.M.; Lisa Sousa; Kevin Terraciano; Jon Truitt; and Dana Velasco Murillo. Above all, Wayne Ruwet tirelessly opened his remarkable library to me and shared his precious books. They are a marvel to behold! Alessandra Jacobi Tamulevich, of the University of Oklahoma Press, was always gracious and helpful as she shepherded this work through the publication process. Finally, my beloved family during all these years has patiently understood that the dining room table, where I always sit, was at least some of the time as much for Chimalpahin as it was for our meals. I thank all of you for your forbearance.

TLACAELEL
REMEMBERED

Gulf of Mexico

MICHOACAN

Veracruz

TEHUANTEPEC

Oaxaca

Pacific Ocean

HONDURAS

Ecatepec•

•Tetzcoco

Azcapotzalco•
Tlacopan•

Lake Texcoco

Mexico Tlatelolco•
Mexico Tenochtitlan/
Mexico City

Iztapalapa

Coyoacan•
Lake Xochimilco

•Colhuacan   Cuitlahuac
Lake Chalco

•Toluca

Xochimilco•

•Chalco

Mizquic

Tlaxcala•

Huexotzinco•

Cholula•

Cuauhtinchan•

Tepeaca•

Oaxtepec •

Lake Chalco

• Chalco Atenco/
Acxotlan Chalco

Mizquic

Tlalmanalco•

IZTACCIHUATL

Tenanco •

Amecameca •

N

POPOCATEPETL

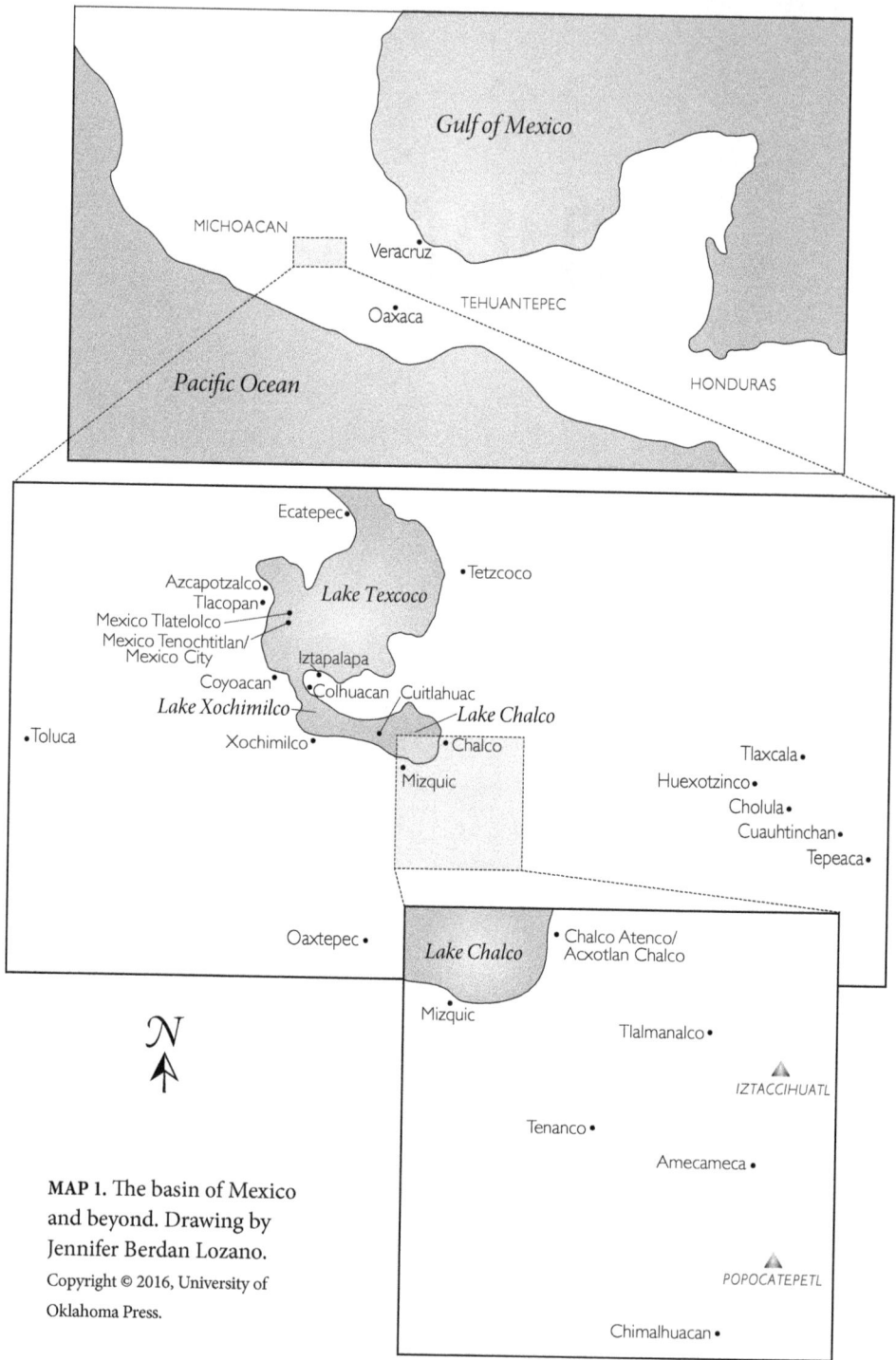

MAP 1. The basin of Mexico
and beyond. Drawing by
Jennifer Berdan Lozano.

Chimalhuacan •

THE WHO AND THE WHY OF TLACAELEL
AN INTRODUCTION

❀

The first [of the principals] was his [Moteuczoma
Ilhuicamina] royal adviser, [the] Cihuacoatl Tlacaelel[.]
Alvarado Tezozomoc

Tlacaelel was to become the greatest warrior, the bravest
and the mightiest, that the Mexica nation ever had. He
was the wisest, the most cunning man in the art and
science of war ever found in Mexico Tenochtitlan.
Durán

Tlacaelel then came as the most powerful, feared, and esteemed
man of all that the world had seen up to that time.
Chimalpahin

WHO WAS TLACAELEL?

In 1964, the anthropologist H. B. Nicholson, and later, in 1974, the historian Stephen Colston proposed that as a historical figure the omnipo-
tent Tlacaelel of Aztec fame and fortune was likely the creature of his
descendants who perhaps were seeking perquisites from the Spanish
crown.[1] These relatives had written an edifying account about him, they
believed, an elusive work that is now referred to as the "Crónica X." Even as
recently as 2000 Nicholson maintained that information about the "whole
Tlacaelel tradition" was "virtually confined to the 'Crónica X' group of

3

sources (Alvarado Tezozomoc, Durán, and Tovar)," and he urged "considerable caution" regarding their veracity.[2] Nicholson's and Colston's idea has hovered over the scholarship for a great while. The sources on which they based their theory, as best I can determine, were the Dominican fray Diego Durán's Spanish-language *Historia* and a work that has come to be called the *Crónica mexicayotl*, a Nahuatl-language account once attributed to the Mexica historian don Hernando de Alvarado Tezozomoc but now established unequivocally to have been written by the Chalca annalist don Domingo de San Antón Muñón Chimalpahin Quauhtlehuanitzin, better known today as Chimalpahin.[3]

All three men did write at length about Tlacaelel, and we have countless examples of his cunning and feats of bravery as well as his brutality and cannibalism. It is all quite fantastic, and it is entirely possible to come to think of Tlacaelel as a figment of some clever, ambitious person's imagination. But Nicholson and Colston seem not to have been familiar with everything that Chimalpahin had to say about Tlacaelel, and that is because until recently his writings have been largely inaccessible or unknown, and the Nahuatl is difficult. The corpus of Chimalpahin's work is now available in either English or Spanish translation, and as a result a wealth of information about Tlacaelel has come to light. Moreover, it seems that Chimalpahin personally knew the Tlacaelel family, who lived in Acatlan, next to his church of San Antonio Abad in Xoloco, the site of the famous first encounter of the Mexica Tenochca emperor Moteuczoma Xocoyotl and the Spanish conqueror Hernando Cortés (see map 1).

Therefore, we have three established authors writing independently and deliberately for posterity and portraying Tlacaelel as a towering figure with manifold abilities.[4] Alvarado Tezozomoc's *Crónica mexicana* relates the grand history of early Mexico Tenochtitlan, the home polity of the Aztecs, or, more correctly, of the Mexica Tenochca; his account is written in Spanish but suffused with Nahuatl terminology and phrasing. Alvarado Tezozomoc, grandson of Moteuczoma Xocoyotl (r. 1502–20) and distant relative of Tlacaelel, was born some time before 1541, and it is likely that he had contact with any number of Nahuas and Spaniards who knew firsthand of Mexica life in the capital. Tezozomoc's *Crónica mexicana* is dated 1598. Fray Diego Durán's *History of the Indies of New Spain* is also in Spanish but was written in a more vernacular style. He too believes that Tlacaelel and the Mexica kings could do no wrong. The *History* contains a trove of more than one hundred illustrations, which appear interspersed in the manuscript. Worth noting is that despite Tlacaelel's importance to Durán's history, Durán did not include an image of him, even though his likeness was said to be carved in stone at Chapoltepec along with those of the Mexica kings. Doris Heyden believed that Durán's *History* was written in 1581.[5]

Chimalpahin's Nahuatl annals were written generally between the years 1610 and 1620. His purpose, he stated, was to furnish a true history of all that had transpired so that future generations of Nahuas would know of their illustrious past. And he optimistically wrote in Nahuatl, anticipating a readership in that language.[6] Chimalpahin was also a pious Christian, a man steeped in the writings of the early church fathers, men like Saint Augustine and Saint Thomas Aquinas. Yet without hesitation he wrote the history of Tlacaelel and the Mexica, which during his time some readers might have thought to be heretical. Chimalpahin, like his predecessors, depended on a variety of sources, most of which, by all the evidence, were pictorial, although he made use of oral interviews and Latin, Nahuatl, and Spanish books and manuscripts, as Alvarado Tezozomoc and Durán surely did.

The three historians portray Tlacaelel as the individual central to the growth and glory of the Mexica state. As Chimalpahin states, "He was the commencer, the beginner, through wars [of the system] by which he made the great city of Mexico Tenochtitlan eminent and exalted and made it the head of all [other] *altepetl* [ethnic state(s), kingdom(s)] everywhere. (He was the founder of the Mexica empire)."[7] Tlacaelel eventually served as mainstay and adviser to five high kings. His story spans the years 1398 to 1650, and it is a story worth telling.

But what of the other sources about Mexica history and Tlacaelel? The Franciscan Juan de Torquemada and the Jesuit Francisco Javier Clavigero were certain that Tlacaelel did not exist. Chimalpahin's contemporary, the mestizo historian of Tetzcoco, don Fernando de Alva Ixtlilxochitl, mentioned him only once. And in the opus of fray Bernardino de Sahagún, Tlacaelel is a conspicuous omission, even though Sahagún devoted an entire book to the topic of the kings and lords of early Mexico. We know that there were a great many indigenous manuscripts extant in Mexico City in the late sixteenth and early seventeenth century, and surely they circulated in some fashion among these same Nahuas and Spaniards who were writing their histories during those years. The discrepancy between the two schools of opinion is real, and it is easy to see why Nicholson and others were puzzled by such a confusion of sources.

The name Tlacaelel doesn't quite roll off the tongue, nor is it easy to parse. From what we can tell, it is a compound of *tlacatl,* "human being," and–*el,* which relates to the liver and all its profound and perilous properties. The linguist Frances Karttunen has suggested that Tlacaelel might be translated as something equivalent to "Anguish Incarnate."[8] Certainly, he looked the part in his role as an administrator, for in the early years, when he served as the Tlacochcalcatl and was in charge of military affairs, his warrior costume was principally made up of an open-mouthed skeleton head with a stylized liver pectoral (see fig. 3).[9] Tlacaelel also served as the deity impersonator for the powerful god Cihuacoatl, and assumed different attire on the occasions when he served this function. The two positions are not to be confused, despite possible overlap in their graphic representations.

WHY WRITE ABOUT TLACAELEL?

According to Chimalpahin:

> So great and so many were the achievements and deeds of this man Tlacaeleltzin that it seems as difficult for me to reduce them to brevity as to write and tell about them. As to treating of them with some dispatch and brevity, however, because he was the beginning and foundation of this edifice, it will be necessary to extend and expand [their treatment] more than that of matters ahead [of us]. Among the great achievements of this incomparable man Tlacaeleltzin that may be told of, in my opinion the greatest of all and the one that most arouses my admiration is that this man had the spirit and daring to think of and then undertake and in the end succeed in making [himself and Itzcoatzin] lords of the Mexica people and republic, mistress and subduer of the greater and best part of all the New World, and of as much as [that nation] had been able to subdue and conquer in

three hundred and eighty-five years (for such, and even a little more, was the length of time that had elapsed since the founding of Mexico until Tlacaeleltzin [the] Cihuacoatl took over the republic); three hundred and three years under captains general, and then sixty-two under government by kings. This was indeed a very short space of time to form and conquer as great an empire as the one the Mexica had achieved when the Cihuacoatl Tlacaeleltzin converted it from a free commonwealth to the rulership of one.

It was without doubt the greatest in both size and power of any that the New World had seen or that men had achieved. Such do all the ancient Mexica authors and truthful histories affirm and attest.[10]

Chimalpahin had examined numerous sets of pictorial annals and was apparently familiar with the written and oral histories that were known and shared among Spanish and Nahua intellectuals in Mexico City at the time. Information about Tlacaelel appears in several sets of his extant alphabetic annals, and he even cross-referenced him in his contemporary annals in Mexico City.[11] As will become apparent later, there is good evidence that someone by the name of Tlacaelel from the district of Acatlan in the capital of Mexico Tenochtitlan did exist and that he and his descendants had some influence in political affairs in early Mexico. And it may well be the case that some of his descendants were trying to capitalize on his fame for their personal benefit. They would not have been alone, since we know of the Spanish-language histories by the Tetzcoca Alva Ixtlilxochitl (b. ca. 1578–1650), who wrote extensively and at least in part to secure his family estate in San Juan Teotihuacan.[12]

Another such case is that of the family of don Alonso de Castañeda, who, as early as 1546, initiated litigation in Mexico City to have the original boundaries of Cuauhtinchan, his home territory, restored. He commissioned a pictorial and alphabetic text to support his argument, and we know the manuscript today as the *Historia Tolteca-Chichimeca*.[13]

This document served his descendants for more than a century and appeared in the will of don Alonso's heir, doña María Ruiz de Castañeda, as testimony of the extent of her Cuauhtinchan estate. Did Tlacaelel's descendants craft a Crónica X for a similar outcome? There is no such evidence.

Chimalpahin's extensive documenting of the Tlacaelel family tends to further confound the issue, for he tells of the man's marriage and lists nineteen of his eighty-some children as well as the great variety of marital alliances, careers, and later deaths of his descendants in the seventeenth century. Nor do we have any evidence that Chimalpahin, Durán, and Alvarado Tezozomoc were concerned with either political or financial incentives, that is, seeking meritorious awards for writing histories essentially about what a fine place it was that Cortés had conquered.[14] Rather, each man had his own reason for writing his extraordinary account of the Mexica. Perhaps it was not Tlacaelel as superlative warrior and politician who mattered so much as the fact that he was a means to not only glamorize the past but legitimize it as well.

For a while I thought of Chimalpahin as the Roman Gaius Suetonius (b. ca. AD 69) writing *The Twelve Caesars*, with the Mexica's "Twelve *Tlatoque*," or Kings (sing. *tlatoani*), as a parallel of sorts. Suetonius had the distinct advantage of living during the reigns of four of his subjects—Tiberius, Caligula, Claudius, and Nero—and was thus able to furnish eyewitness reports of much that transpired. He also checked his facts, when possible, although he was perhaps too accepting of omens and such that were contemporaneously a part of interpreting current events. Chronology was not of primary concern; rather, he took a thematic approach to the organization of his material. For this reason, he came to be classified as more of a biographer than a historian, which takes nothing from his accomplishments.[15] Chimalpahin did not have the luxury of firsthand experiences with the Mexica kings. With all the accounts available one hundred years after the conquest, when he was writing, his was a different perspective, one based on multiple vantages. At any rate, I am more inclined now to think of him as Tacitus (ca. 56–ca. 120), seeking to know the full history and why it was more important than ever to write it all down.[16] As the historian Peter Villella and the art historian Lori Diel have recently documented, following two centuries after the conquest, subsequent generations of Nahuas and mestizos appropriated these first-generation histories and fashioned them as primordial legacies that then became codified as colonial truths.[17]

To put their writings in context, Alvarado Tezozomoc, Durán, and Chimalpahin were witnesses to the devastating epidemic diseases and the sharp population decline of the native peoples (among others) in and around the capital. Even as late as Thirteen Calli (House), 1609, smallpox was taking its toll: "Very many children of us commoners died of it, and likewise children of Spaniards and children of blacks; all died mixed together, as well as some adults who died of smallpox," as Chimalpahin describes.[18] And he furnishes vivid testimony to the realization of the permanency of the Spaniards and the long-term consequences of their presence. For just one example, he was seemingly outraged as the Spaniards pushed back the lakes, ostentatiously draining the wetlands, filling the area with dirt, and then building stores and houses right before his eyes in Xoloco: "The other land, in addition [to what has been built on], is now a lake. Who knows what will happen to it when sometime in the future some Spaniards build on it? The reason I have recorded here . . . [is] so that the Mexica and the citizens who live and are born later will see and know that it was still just like this when I set down and recorded the account of the said lake that is there now, if it is later seen at some future time that it is filled with churches, monasteries, and houses that are there where now nothing appears yet and it is full of water all around."[19] His description of the devastation, to say nothing of the futility, caused by the draining of the lakes surrounding the capital is another such report. In the year Five Tochtli (Rabbit), 1614, for example:

> The poor commoners (macehualtzitzin) were excavating a mountain there [Citlaltepec], making a hole in the side of it. . . . It was halted, and the excavation was done no more, because, it was said, a great many poor commoners from far away, a full 50,000, died at the place of excavation; people from all around were greatly afflicted. And it was said that a million [pesos] of the king's assets were spent there.[20]

Among other changes was the supplanting of the Nahuas' precious pictorial form of record keeping by Roman alphabetic writing. It was increasingly important that the oral and pictorial accounts be preserved in a form that would serve everyone. During those same years, the Jesuits arrived, bringing a new rigor to education and society, it was hoped. The Jesuits settled in Mexico City in 1572, and Chimalpahin was particularly taken with the erudition and grace of a father doctor Pedro de Morales, of the Company of Jesus, about whom, upon his death in Five Rabbit, 1614, Chimalpahin worried, "in future times another religious like him will not be seen again here in Mexico."[21] And then there was the Holy Office of the Inquisition, which meant additional constraints on intellectual development and social activity in the capital: "And here are mentioned the very reverend inquisitors who have come to preside in Mexico on the royal seat of justice called the Holy Office here in New Spain, beginning in the year [One Acatl (Reed)], 1571."[22] Finally, the Franciscans, who had been advocates for the Nahuas and who had contributed so much to their education and acculturation, were targeted by the crown for secularization. Fray Juan Bautista seems to have been the last of the religious literary *nahuatlatoque*, "Nahuatl speakers," and he flourished only in the first few years of the 1600s:

> Today, Friday, at 3 o'clock in the afternoon on the 10th of the month of June of the year [Two Reed], 1611, was when the covering of the face of the sun happened. . . . Here is a separate instructive statement taken from the book and sermon collection which the very reverend father fray Juan Bautista, a late Franciscan friar, composed, that he did in the Nahuatl language, where among other things he talks about how the sun disappears, or as they say is eaten.[23]

Chimalpahin was around for a bit longer, until 1624, when the friar who administered his little church of San Antonio Abad, fray Agustín del Espíritu Santo, died of a stomach ailment.[24] Augustinian friars immediately invaded and took over the church, resulting in city authorities padlocking the building to prevent entry. Chimalpahin was out of a job. He was the last of the Nahua annalists and historians in the capital. We know nothing of him after that time. Fortunately, most of his many manuscripts survived; they serve to corroborate as well as enhance the Tlacaelel legacy.

CONVENTIONS AND ADDITIONAL CONSIDERATIONS

The natives discussed in this work about Tlacaelel were for the most part Nahuas, the name for a great variety of indigenous peoples who shared a common language, Nahuatl, which over time came to be something of a lingua franca in that it served the Mexica empire for political and economic purposes. Although in the Nahuatl annals the term "Azteca" appears in reference to migrating peoples in the eleventh century—*i Tecpatl xihuitl, 1064 años. Ypan in yn onpa hualquizque ynchan Aztlan yn mexitin azteca chichimeca yn axcan ye motenehua tenuchca,* "One Tecpatl (Flint), year 1064, in this year the Mexitin Azteca Chichimeca, who are now called Tenochca, departed from their home in Aztlan"[25]—Chimalpahin states that their deity Huitzilopochtli changed their name to Mexica. "[Huitzilopochtli] said: Now no longer is your name Azteca: you are now Mexitin. . . . Hence they are now called Mexica." And that is how they are referred to in the annals and chronicles.[26] However, in the English-language historical literature, "Aztec" found favor again upon the publication of William Hickling Prescott's *History of the Conquest of Mexico* in 1843.[27] Heyden, in her English translation of Durán's *History*, substituted "Aztec" for the "mexicano" recorded by fray Diego. For consistency and to avoid confusion, in the quotations from Durán's *History* that I have included in this work I have replaced "Aztec" with "Mexica," adhering to Nahuatl usage. In addition, there were two altepetl of Mexica, that of the Mexica Tenochca and that of the Mexica Tlatelolca. Unless otherwise stated, "Aztec" is most commonly associated in this work with the Mexica Tenochca of Mexico Tenochtitlan, where their collective identity endured and was encouraged even by religious well into the seventeenth century.[28] Also, since Alvarado Tezozomoc's and Durán's chronicles frequently contain similar information, most of the quotations by Tlacaelel are from Durán's *History*, since it is already in English translation.

The Nahuatl term *altepetl* best describes the fundamental indigenous sociopolitical corporation of the disparate groups of peoples who came to inhabit central Mexico. (Inanimate Nahuatl nouns do not require the English or Spanish plural *s*; hence altepetl can be singular or plural.) Chimalpahin uses the term constantly to identify three different levels of complexity of altepetl organization. First, as subentities, were the *tlayacatl*, "district(s)," altepetl, of which there were usually four, each of which had its own tlatoani. Tlayacatl most typically comprised *calpolli*, or *tlaxilacalli*, the smallest units, which commonly numbered four to six. Second, each group or set of tlayacatl then made up a larger altepetl, again with its own ruler and subordinates, which then could be confederated into an essentially overarching larger altepetl. There was no primary tlatoani. Rather, the altepetl were ranked within the confederation. The best-documented example of altepetl organization in central Mexico is Chalco, about which Chimalpahin furnished an abundance of information, although there was considerable variation of levels of complexity among and within the many altepetl.[29]

Mexico Tenochtitlan came to be referred to as a *huey*, "great," "large," altepetl, which typically designated the Mexica Tenochca empire. "Huey" was also used to describe the tlatoque, often called emperors, who ruled during those same years.[30] But we lack explicit terminology to identify all the subdistricts, or constituencies. The accounts relate that nearly from the time the Mexica first settled there, Tenochtitlan was divided into four (probably ranked) districts: Teopan (the southeastern quadrant), Atzaqualco (the northeastern quadrant), Cuepopan (the northwestern quadrant), and Moyotlan (the southwestern quadrant) of the island altepetl.[31] All were surely tlayacatl, although we have only one such reference:

> *Yn omoteneuhque don Andrés Motelchiuhtzin yhuan don Pablo Xochiquentzin ca ymomextin oncan chaneque catca yn ipan ycce tlayacatl motenehua Teopan, yn axcan ye S[an] Pablo.*[32]

> The aforementioned don Andrés Motelchiuhtzin and don Pedro Xochiquentzin were both from there, the first tlayacatl, called Teopan, which now is [called] San Pablo.

It is worth noting that San Juan Moyotlan is ordinarily thought to be the highest ranked of the four divisions, which in the later years of Mexica history may have been fact.[33] In this instance, though—and it may well be the case in other altepetl—Teopan was the first to be settled by the Mexica upon their arrival on the island and was thus ranked accordingly.

In other sets of annals, Chimalpahin refers more generally to the migrating and earliest settler groups in Mexico Tenochtitlan as tlayacatl:

> *yn ayemo nican tenochtitlan yn oquic innenemillizpan ynic huallatiaque yn oquic hualmotlatlallitiaque ynic yecoque yn ixquichti yn izqui tlayacatl yn huehuetque yn azteca mexitin teoculhuaque chicomoztoca*

> before they were here in Tenochtitlan, while they were coming in the time of their wandering, as with frequent stops all the tlayacatl of the ancient Azteca Mexitin Teoculhuaque Chicomoztoca leaders arrived.[34]

in izqui tlayacatl in mexica huehuetque. cece ymichpochhuan quima-
caque yn intlahtocauh ynic mopilhuatiz moxinachoz ynic onyezqui
pipiltin tlahtoque yn tenochtitlan

all the ancient Mexica of all the tlayacatl each gave a daughter to their
ruler so that he would have children, his seed would spread and thus
there would be noblemen and rulers in Tenochtitlan.[35]

As the Mexica state conquered different altepetl in and beyond central
Mexico, the subjected polities retained their names and the inhabitants
maintained their identity and loyalty to their home region. Thus, the Chalca,
Xochimilca, Tepaneca, and other subjugated altepetl recognized the suzer-
ainty of the Mexica, paid tribute, furnished the labor, supplies, and women,
and fought the battles for their conquerors. Moreover, for the Nahuas, the
English-language term *conquest* did not mean the termination of the existence
of an altepetl, in spite of the loss of sovereignty and dignity of the victims.
Nevertheless, the Nahuatl transitive verb *pehua*, "to conquer someone," and
the intransitive verbs *polihui*, "to disappear," "be destroyed," "be defeated,"
and *yauh*, "to go [cease to exist]," were standard terminology to describe the
conquest and subjugation of altepetl and tend to suggest an utter end. On the
contrary, the polity continued to operate much as it had before, though subject to the Mexica and no longer autonomous.[36] Crucial to the longevity of the
altepetl was its time-honored *tlatocatlacamecayotl*, "royal lineage," and the
tlatocayotl, "rulership," which traced to the founding of the altepetl centuries
before. An altepetl could be destroyed, but it survived as long as the lineage
and rulership were still intact.[37] For example, as Chimalpahin reported, even
though their rulerships were restored twenty years after being conquered by
the Mexica, the Chalca remained their subjects:

yece ca ça yuhqui yn ompa tetlahtocamacehualhuan mochiuhque
Mexico Tenochtitlan, ompa ça tetetlahtocatetlapacholhuan, ça temac
yn catca[38]

But [the Chalca tlatoque] were only as though they were like royal
or governed subjects of Mexico Tenochtitlan. They were still in their
(the Mexica's) hands.

In addition, the altepetl were prideful and resilient, and on more than one occasion the chronicles report that the Mexica were taking up arms against previously "conquered" altepetl. In many ways, the Mexica Tenochca conquerors were themselves responsible for the tenacious micropatriotism of their subject altepetl, since they did not require drastic transformation of either the social or the political structure of the polities. Indeed, as the historian James Lockhart states, "Each altepetl imagined itself a radically different people."[39]

Alvarado Tezozomoc and Durán organized their histories chronologically, although they seldom included dates. Both works start in the early precontact period, when different groups of native peoples were setting out on their migrations toward central Mexico, and continue from the formation of the Mexico Tenochtitlan altepetl to the arrival of the Spaniards, with Durán taking his account through the conquest of the capital. Also, both men made use of pictorial and alphabetic Nahuatl sources, which typically would have followed the Nahua calendar. It is not clear why actual dates are of so little importance in their histories. On the other hand, annals, by definition, mark the passing of the years assiduously. Chimalpahin's Nahuatl annals trace back to before the beginning of biblical time and then continue with information about Abraham, Adam, Eve, and Noah and the flood. He describes the calendar cycle, beginning in the year One Rabbit and concluding in the year Thirteen House.

> *Yzcatqui yn iccentetl xiuhtlapohualyahualli, mochipa yehuatl yc quipehualtiaya yn i Ce Tochtli xihuitl, auh yehuatl yc quitlamiltiaya yn Matlactliomey Calli xihuitl*[40]

Here is the first cycle of the year-count, which always begins in the year One Rabbit and concludes with the year Thirteen House.

Tochtli, Acatl, Tecpatl, and Calli follow one another in a cycle that repeats over the eons, although Chimalpahin credits the first Four House as the date of the birth of Christ. Switching to Spanish, he records, "*iiii Calli xihuitl, 1. Aqui comiença en que año nació el Señor.*"[41] "Four House year 1. Here begins the year in which Our Lord was born." Nahua life and time in the Americas starts in One Rabbit, the Christian calendar year 50, when he writes that the ancient Chichimeca arrived, nude, by canoe at an island called Teocolhuacan Aztlan. The passengers spoke only one language.[42] As with all annals, there are gaps in the series, but depending on the contents of his sources, he rigorously included the Mesoamerican and Christian dates for each annals entry. While living in Mexico City, as the years passed Chimalpahin became more precise in his marking of time. He included the day and month and even the time of day when noting events during the colonial era: "*Axcan Sabado ynic, 6. mani Metztli Septiembre de 1614 años yhcuac teotlac ypan chicuacen tzillini.*" "Today, Saturday the 6th of the month of September of the year 1614, in the afternoon at 6 bells [o'clock]." There were so many entries for 1614 that the Mesoamerican calendar date, "1614. Five Rabbit Year," was recorded only at the beginning of the annals for that year and was not repeated as the days and months progressed.[43]

Chimalpahin's interest in recording the histories of ancient times was divided between his great love for his homeland, Chalco, (*tichalca*, "we Chalca"), and for Mexico City (*timexica*, "we Mexica"), where he lived most of his adult life.[44] He made a point of bringing together as much information as possible about his home, Tzaqualtitlan Tenanco, in Amecameca, Chalco, and recording the most complete history possible, from the town's founding through the time he was writing in the seventeenth century. It may well be more than a coincidence that Chalco figures so prominently in the lives of Tlacaelel and his descendants.

I have often thought that Chimalpahin patterned his account of the history of Chalco after the Spanish and Nahuatl histories by Alvarado Tezozomoc that he had in his possession. For example, both treatises begin with eloquent, idealized depictions of their home altepetl:

the altepetl of Mexico Tenochtitlan, the place of renown, the sign, the site of the rock tuna cactus, in the midst of the waters; the place where the eagle rests, where the eagle screeches, where the eagle stretches, where the eagle eats; where the serpent hisses, where the fish fly, where the blue and yellow waters mingle[45]

here in the kingdom of Chalchiuhmomozco Amaquemecan Chalco, the famous and exemplary place, the place of [the god] Totolin, at the edge of the forest, at the edge of the snows, called Poyauhtlan, in the flower patio, in the misty patio, where the white quail dwells, where the snake coils, where the jaguars live, Tamoanchan, the place of flowers[46]

His account about Chalco is in the form of a chronology, although it is based on oral testimony, pictorial records, and alphabetic documents.[47]

Nahuatl annals themselves are occasionally cause for concern with regard to their accuracy, since they were generated by individuals in different altepetl at different times. By definition episodic and focused on key events in the lives of particular individuals and polities, as well as celestial and environmental phenomena, the annals may contain contradictions and conflicting dates. Chimalpahin had collections of annals and genealogies from a wide range of altepetl, including Azcapotzalco, Chalco, Colhuacan, Tetzcoco, and Tlatelolco, to name a few, and he did what he could to corroborate the information by speaking with knowledgeable individuals and checking his sources, one against the other. He also named his contacts and identified the altepetl, when he knew them. Chimalpahin, like Alvarado Tezozomoc and Durán, sought accuracy as he wrote his accounts.

Auh ynin huehuetlahtocanemiliztli in huehuetlahtocatenonotzal-izamoxtlahtolli nican ye mihtoz ye motenehuaz in ye mopohuaz, ca amo çan çaçanilli ca amo çan tlapicpictli amo çan tlahtlaquetzalli ynic tlatecpantli, ca mochi neltiliztli ca mochi omochiuh[48]

Here this ancient life history account, this ancient history book relation, that was painted about the rulerly life of the ancients, will be told and revealed and related, because this ordinance is not a simple fabrication, or story, or invention but the complete truth about all that transpired.

One cannot help but think of the Greek historian Herodotus (ca. 484 BC–ca. 420 BC), who is frequently referred to as the "Father of History" because he was reportedly the first to collect a variety of materials, test their reliability, and then organize them into a reasonable historical narrative. According to Donald Lateiner, "Herodotus reports his purpose as commemoration and recognition rather than rectification, stresses human achievements and the causes of the wars rather than an indefinite variety of undifferentiated divine and earthly stories."[49] But Herodotus is also called the "Father of Lies," since he was too often credulous of the stories that he heard.[50] Is it possible that Chimalpahin, Alvarado Tezozomoc, and Durán were deceived about Tlacaelel as they sought to document all that was known about the history of Mexico Tenochtitlan? It is a beguilingly facile notion that ignores historical context, not to mention authorial authority.

Serving to telescope the occasional fictive distance in time and place between Mesoamerican and early U.S. history, the historian Jill Lepore, in *The Story of America*, challenges our lore about American icons, men who have come to be enshrined as nearly infallible, by examining their histories, which, it turns out, are mostly grand stories.[51] For example, Noah Webster and his *American Dictionary*, which became literary doctrine, was for decades ridiculed and rejected by his contemporaries. And our nearly always starving but beloved poet Edgar Allan Poe wrote brilliant, horrifying tales and poems but was mostly contemptuous of his readers. And how can one know the habitually celebrated first American president, George Washington, who was apparently purposefully unknowable? Even the U.S. Constitution, written with great deliberation and high purpose, with its magnanimous "We the People" promise, had essential shortcomings. Yet all have weathered the years uncritically to become canon in American belief; their flaws and shortcomings were airbrushed away without real loss. Tlacaelel and the great and even the lesser kings he created and served were no different to their storytellers and to posterity.

Some secondary scholarship has tended, however tentatively, toward acceptance of Tlacaelel as an important Mexica political figure. Early on, the nineteenth-century historian Carlos María de Bustamante can probably be considered a secondary source for his recognition of the role of "*su ministro Zihuacóatl*" at the Mexica royal court.[52] Later, in 1964, the anthropologist Hasso von Winning, possibly bowdlerizing somewhat, credited Tlacaelel as being responsible for the "reorganization of the government, the initiation of public works, and the reorientation of religious thought."[53] Later, fellow anthropologist J. Rounds conceived of Tlacaelel as a "stand-in" of sorts for the tlatoque. He filled in during interregnums of rulership, although according to Chimalpahin there were seldom breaks in the continuity of the regimes (see fig. 13). Rounds postulated that Tlacaelel optimized his position in the government, forsaking the kingship, in order to ensure that his descendants would succeed him in perpetuity, doubtless living posthumously through them.[54] The Mexican historian Miguel León-Portilla, too, has been a stalwart advocate in support of Tlacaelel's vital role as second in command of Mexica affairs, asserting that "Tlacaelel's advice was so extensive and of such transcendence" that he can be credited with most of what the Mexica Tenochca accomplished.[55] Other authors, such as the art historian Cecelia Klein, have recognized Tlacaelel but have focused on his role as the Cihuacoatl, the administrator, as well as impersonator, of the Mexica god of the same name.[56] Going to the extreme, R. C. Padden, in a popularized edition, referred to the man as a "brilliant psychopath" who "assumed control of Mexica destiny, which he was to hold for the next sixty-eight years." He added that "it was Tlacaelel and his peers who promoted human sacrifice as a political instrument."[57] Padden's use of Chimalpahin as a primary source is sorely limited. More recently the tendency has been to support Nicholson's reservations regarding Tlacaelel as a historical person.

TLACAELEL'S STORY

After a rigorous examination of the sources in chapter 1, the succeeding chapters tell of the life, deeds, and successors of Tlacaelel. They follow the chronology so diligently assembled by Durán and Alvarado Tezozomoc, with actual dates furnished by Chimalpahin's annals. Although written in alphabetic script, it is an altepetl history rich in foundational genealogies derived from the ancient pictorial manuscripts.[58]

> *in tliltica tlapaltica ycuiliuhtoc machiyotoc amapan ayc polihuiz ayc ylcahuiz, mochipa pieloz*[59]

[This account] which has been painted and written on paper in black and red will never perish or be forgotten; it will be kept for all time.

Both Alvarado Tezozomoc and Durán include the eloquent and decisive discourse articulated by Tlacaelel, furnishing a sense of firsthand reportage.[60] From the arc of his life, one observes Tlacaelel's birth and then his maturation from an impulsive young man (yet one concerned about

providing for his family) to an able warrior and administrator to a self-in-
dulgent potentate. Chalco figures importantly from time to time, largely
because Chimalpahin concerned himself with emphasizing the importance
of his home altepetl whenever he could but also because Tlacaelel and the
Mexica had strong social and economic ties there. The inclusion of the
Chalco information furnishes a unique perspective on interaltepetl relations over an extended period.

Of course, we always want more, especially from the annals, which can
seem cryptic and incomplete. Where, for example, did Tlacaelel live? A man
with his authority surely had his own *tecpan*, "palace," and presumably it was
located close to that of the tlatoani, since they were in almost constant contact, it seems. Did Tlacaelel perhaps stay in or near the Casa de las Águilas, as
it has come to be called, where the Mexica nobility held their ceremonies? Or
did he return home to Acatlan at the end of the day, presumably transported
by canoe through Tenochtitlan's waterways?

We do know something of his attire, his spiritual piety, his family, and
his devotion to his brother Moteuczoma Ilhuicamina. He was an extraordi-
narily wealthy man, although there is no information about how his fortune
materialized. Perhaps the exceptional opulence of the capital might serve as
a one-way reflection of his personal holdings. It can be said that as he aged he
became nearly obsessed with warfare, human sacrifice, and cannibalism, all
of which might be explained as a manifestation of his devotion to Huitzilopochtli. It should be noted, though, that the sources, especially the annals,
seldom specify the reasons for going to war. Perhaps it went without saying
that warfare, conquest, and booty; temple building; and human sacrifice and
cannibalism were, one and all, Mexica Tenochca religious orthodoxy.[61]

Any number of scholars believe that religion was the incentive for all Mexica political, economic, and social undertakings, and it is true that from the
earliest years the deity Huitzilopochtli figured importantly in their fortune.[62]

ca nel quimoteotia çan icel, ca amono quinmoteotia yn inteohuan y
azteca yn chicomoztoca ca centlamantin[63]

For this reason [the Mexica] worshipped only [Huitzilopochtli] and
did not worship the deities of the [other] Azteca Chicomoztoca,
which were different.

Moreover, the chronicles tend to implicitly, and occasionally explicitly, say as much, although the annals are less direct. Therefore, this history of Tlacaelel follows the sources, which largely emphasize political and economic imperatives, rather than religious ones. This is not to deny the ubiquity of the Mexica's gods, or their omnipotence, for that matter, but rather presumes their absolutism.

⚜

Almost from his birth in Ten Rabbit, 1398, until his death in Eight Reed, 1487, Tlacaelel was the Mexica Tenochca's guiding force. He was the son, brother, nephew, and great-uncle of kings, and there was hardly a time when he did not figure importantly in their lives. Tlacaelel was born in the Mexica's late formative years, when the altepetl was coming into its own and the royal lineage, based on marriage alliances with prestigious yet formidable adversaries, conferred an increasingly exalted pedigree.

Processual military conquests ensured bountiful revenues that afforded an increasingly luxurious lifestyle in an ostentatious city.[64] Royal favorites, who received honorable titles and offices and ample rewards, came to form a reliable bureaucracy of administrators and military leaders. As time passed, social containment was achieved through rigid regulations that influenced everything from architecture to courtly deportment. Yet, there were abundant festivities in the capital, too, with flowers, parades, music, dance, and feasting. And Tlacaelel planned and executed all of it for decades in his protean role as "second king," valiant warrior, officious urban administrator, traditional polygamist, dutiful father, pious deity impersonator, and Mexica Tenochca zealot. Mexico Tenochtitlan was seemingly all the better for it, flourishing while making ready for generations of Cihuacoatls to come.

CHAPTER 1

THE MAN, THE OFFICE, AND THE DEITY
THE SOURCES

❀

They came once again to pay their respects to Moteuczoma
and Tlacaelel.

Alvarado Tezozomoc

The president of the kingdom, Tlacaelel, was distinguished
by the title of the Cihuacoatl. Cihuacoatl means
president and chief judge.

Chimalpahin

The goddess Cihuacoatl was made of stone. She had a huge,
open mouth and ferocious teeth.

Durán

THE MAN

To realize the historic Tlacaelel is something of a challenge. Most important, certainly, is coming to know the man versus the deity. His name, Tlacaelel, identifies the man, although, as noted, there is a suggestion of mythmaking or apotheosis in the sources when one considers all that he reportedly accomplished during his lifetime. Moreover, at least one author claimed that Tlacaelel lived to the improbable age of 120, when it is more likely that he died at 90.[1] That he was mortal—to the extent that we can validate the existence of any precontact human figure—is evidenced by his birth record; his affiliation with the Mexica royal dynasty over the course of five rulerships; his close relationship with his half brother, King Moteuczoma Ilhuicamina

21

(r. 1440–69), and his interest in the king's heirs and his own wives and children; his profound dedication to developing and celebrating the majesty of Mexico Tenochtitlan; his desire for lucre; his piety; his avarice; his cruelties; his cannibalism; and the generations of heirs who continued his legacy.

THE MAN AND THE OFFICE

Tlacaelel bore the cognomen of "Cihuacoatl" (Female Serpent), a title of office that came to signify the most prestigious political position in the realm and was second in standing only to that of the king.[2] Chimalpahin repeatedly refers to Tlacaelel the Cihuacoatl as the "President of the Supreme Council," "chief judge," "great president," and "king and emperor like his brother." He added that Tlacaelel "gloried in being called [the] Cihuacoatl, and it remained consecrated as the highest title and rank in the world after that of emperor."[3] Fray Bernardino de Sahagún described the Cihuacoatl as the "ruler's vicar," and Alvarado Tezozomoc wrote that he was a "second king."[4] Although the title reportedly appears elsewhere, by Tlacaelel's time it was a position tailored for him based on his audacity, influence, and accomplishments. With Tlacaelel as the Cihuacoatl, the office ostentatiously became fundamental to the optimal operation of the Mexica state. Even Sahagún lists the Cihuacoatl first among titled lords (*teuctlatoque*) serving the king.[5]

Tlacaelel took the title during the early years of the rule of his half brother Moteuczoma, when the king became emperor and Tlacaelel "had himself named perpetual Cihuacoatl": solely he and his descendants subsequently enjoyed the esteem and benefits of the office of the Cihuacoatl.[6] Their legacy endured well into the seventeenth century. It was even earlier, however, under his uncle King Itzcoatl (r. 1427–40), that Tlacaelel began to acquire his office and titles. His first title was the Atempanecatl, bestowed for his ingenuity and prowess after he almost singlehandedly made his way behind the enemy lines of the Tepaneca of Azcapotzalco and brought down Maxtlaton (r. 1410–26), their king.[7] The Mexica had been subordinate to the Tepaneca, and, making matters worse, under the aegis of Maxtlaton the Tepaneca and Tlacopaneca had killed King Chimalpopoca (r. 1415–26), the third dynastic ruler of Mexico Tenochtitlan.[8] Tlacaelel distinguished himself by being sly and brave. Afterward, he had much to do with the reorganization of the

Tepaneca altepetl, shifting its headquarters to Tlacopan. This conquest was a turning point in Mexica history, leading to the confederation of the large, influential altepetl of Tetzcoco, to the east, a tertiary Tlacopan in the west, and Tlatelolco-Tenochtitlan in the center, along with the inexorable imperial pretensions of their kings. Soon thereafter, Tlacaelel also became the Tlacochcalcatl (Person at the Armory) of Mexico Tenochtitlan, the man in charge of the weaponry and certain military affairs for the Mexica. The office was granted after Tlacaelel and the Mexica returned from a successful campaign of conquest against Coyoacan. His brother, Moteuczoma Ilhuicamina, became the Tlacateccatl (People-Lord).[9]

These two titles in particular, the Tlacateccatl and the Tlacochcalcatl, distinguished the leaders in military affairs, and most if not all Mexica tlatoque held one office or the other before assuming the throne. Sahagún noted, "Is not one a nobleman? Is not one a warrior? Is not one a military Tlacatecutli, one a Tlacochtecutli? . . . who provide drink, who give offerings to the sun."[10] In view of his royal affiliation and battlefield experience, it was fitting that Tlacaelel would hold the Tlacochcalcatl office. It is assumed that he relinquished the position when he became the Cihuacoatl.[11] And it was not untypical for military titles to pass from father to son, as was the case in later years. For example, Çaca the elder the Tlacateccatl, son of Huitzilihuitl the younger and brother of Moteuczoma Ilhuicamina, was the Tlacateccatl while his brother ruled. His son, Tzontemoc, served as the Tlacateccatl during the reigns of Axayacatl and Ahuitzotl.[12]

Another badge of honor came when Tlacaelel and the Mexica successfully conquered the long independent and resistant altepetl of Chalco in 1465. At that time Tlacaelel the Cihuacoatl also took the title of the Tlailotlacteuctli, the prestigious office of the kings of the Tenanca Chalca, Chimalpahin's own people, while likely allocating goods, women, workers, and sacrificial victims for himself from this distinguished polity.[13] For many years, the Mexica and Chalca had maintained a reciprocal and autonomous existence, but it began to erode when Tenochtitlan initiated demands for timber and stone from Chalco. Yet, as discussed in chapter 3, Tlacaelel's primary wife and his daughters-in-law were Chalca. So his co-optation of a postconquest kingly title from there could only have added insult to injury. It should be noted, however, that the Tenanca Chalca rulers carried on as Tlailotlac lords well into the sixteenth century, in spite of the affront. Their office and status were confirmed by the viceroy, don Antonio de Mendoza (r. 1535–50), in the 1540s.[14] The specific duties of the Tlailotlacteuctli are not stated.

Men with titles and offices served on the Mexica king's advisory council as judges, and eventually Tlacaelel the Cihuacoatl would chair this august body and occupy the position for decades. There was reportedly a Council of Four, of which the Cihuacoatl, the Tlacochcalcatl, and the Tlacateccatl were among the charter members along with the tlatoque from Tetzcoco and Tlacopan.[15] The council could be expanded depending on the circumstances. Sahagún speaks of the deliberations of the council and the weighty responsibilities of titled judges. He states that as "great captains" they wore long labrets, leather earplugs, and headbands with two eagle-feather tassels to bind their hair.[16] The *Codex Mendoza* documents with painted images selected titled personages, displaying respective title glyphs, cloaks, and headdresses. Military officers are shown wearing quetzal feather headdresses, an item also worn by Tlacaelel when he led troops into battle.[17] It is here that we have a notion of the clothing of the Atempanecatl and the Tlacochcalcatl

FIG. 1. The Atempanecatl, Codex Mendoza, fol. 65r. Bodleian Libraries, Oxford University, MS Arch. Selden A1.

FIG. 2. The Tlacochcalcatl, Codex Mendoza, fol. 65r. Bodleian Libraries, Oxford University, MS Arch. Selden A1.

(Tlacaelel's first two offices), both represented as men in profile with the former displaying a title glyph with a lip, or "edge," that is surrounded by water on three sides. There is also a gloss in alphabetic characters, "atenpan-ecatl tecutli." The figure is without a headdress but wears a loincloth and a rust-colored cloak with a dark-red patterned border. He is barefoot (fig. 1).[18] The Atempanecatl is described by Sahagún as a noble or general and one of the executioners who put to death individuals judged guilty of onerous crimes by the royal tribunal.[19] In one representation the Tlacochcalcatl's title glyph depicts a palace with darts on the roof, and he wears a beautiful quetzal-feather headdress, a loincloth, and a burgundy-colored cloak with a white conch shell design. The cloak has a double border of a different color and design. And he too is barefoot (fig. 2).

But elsewhere, in a more elaborate painting, the Tlacochcalcatl is identified by the gloss "valiente tlacochcalcatl," his quetzal warrior insignia with a shield and spear, and a stunning uniform and headdress that is highly suggestive of an association with Tlacaelel. The headpiece is a skull with a gaping maw topped with plumes of quetzal feathers. The warrior suit is white with red stripes on the forearms and lower legs, and from a red and gold stripe across the chest dangles a pectoral of a liver. The liver, from the Nahuatl el-, is an essential element of Tlacaelel's name.[20] The liver image, suggestive of both the man Tlacaelel and the deity Cihuacoatl—who is often depicted with a skull for a head and an open mouth and said to be ravenous for the human hearts that her human counterpart produced

FIG. 3. The Valiente Tlacochcalcatl, Codex Mendoza, fol. 67r. Bodleian Libraries, Oxford University, MS Arch. Selden A1.

by the thousands—is in truth related to Tzitzimitl images and appears in various pictorial codices. It is perhaps coincidental that the liver image was a part of the Tlacochcalcatl warrior suit that in all probability was also worn by Tlacaelel (fig. 3).[21]

THE DEITY

The deity Cihuacoatl was called the sister of Huitzilopochtli, the great god of Mexico.[22]

In addition to the man and the office he held, a third aspect of Tlacaelel the Cihuacoatl relates to the deity Cihuacoatl. Sahagún's Tlatelolca informants were silent about the man, although there is an occasional reference to the office, notwithstanding that an entire book in the *Florentine Codex* is devoted to the topic of Nahua kings and lords.[23] Rather, the all-important Cihuacoatl in the codex is the deity described as one of the "highest of the goddesses."[24] It was Cihuacoatl who gave humans the digging-stick and the tumpline, which is to say work and hardship.[25] Believed to be a prognosticator of war, she brought great misery and suffering, and for that reason there were many offerings and sacrifices on her feast day.[26] She was clad in white and covered with chalk, "like a court lady," while wearing obsidian earplugs (figs. 4 and 5).[27] Her appearance is described elsewhere in greater detail:

THE ARRAY OF CIHUACOATL
Her facial paint; the lips are painted with rubber; [her face]
    is half red, half black.
Her headdress of eagle feathers.
Her gold ear plugs.
On her is her evening primrose shift.
Her undershift has her fringes.
Her white skirt.
Her small bells.
Her sandals.
Her shield is covered with eagle feathers.
Her batten.[28]

Cioacoatl.

Capitulo sexto,   to ibidem.

FIG. 4. Ciuacoatl, Florentine Codex, c. 10v. Florence, Biblioteca Medicea Laurenziana, MS Med. Palat. 218.

FIG. 5. Cihuacoatl, Códice Durán, fol. 278v. Biblioteca Nacional de España, MS 26-11.

Perhaps most important, it was Cihuacoatl that Nahua midwives invoked during pregnancy and parturition. The goddess was an important agent in preserving the well-being of the mother, whether she was blessed with a healthy infant or suffered the agony of having her fetus dismembered in utero, but was also conjured if the mother died.[29]

Moreover, Sahagún included a song about Cihuacoatl that emphasized her political and military attributes, surely deriving from her role as patron of Colhuacan, although eagle plumes, deer, and a war woman also appear in the lyrics:

The eagle
The eagle Quilaztli
With blood of serpents
Is her face circled
With feathers adorned
Eagle-plumed she comes
To sweep up the path
Chalmecan cypress
Colhuacanian

Fir tree of our sustenance
Corncob of the godly field
On rattle stick upraised
The spines
The thorns fill up my hand
The spines fill up my hand
Like corn of the godly field
Like rattle stick upraised

The broom fills up my hand
Like corn of godly field
On rattle stick upraised

Thirteen Eagle is our mother
Chalmecan lady
His shaft of cactus is his glory
May he sate me
He
My lord of cloud-snake land
Our mother
War woman
Our mother
War woman
Deer of Colhuacan
In plumage arranged

The sun proclaims the war
Let men be dragged away
It will forever end
Deer of Colhuacan
In plumage arrayed
Eagle plumes are no mask
For he rises unmasked[30]

Possibly foretelling the arrival of the Spaniards and Mexica doom, during the reign of Moteuczoma Xocoyotl fray Bernardino de Sahagún states that Cihuacoatl "[the demon] went about weeping, at night. Everyone heard it wailing and saying: My beloved sons, now I am about to leave you."[31] It is Durán, though, who has the most to say about Cihuacoatl.[32] According to his sources, she was the principal deity in Xochimilco (and Colhuacan), although most major altepetl had temples in her honor. In Mexico Tenochtitlan, there was a large room at the top of her temple, "Tlillan," which was painted black, perhaps to emulate a cave, with images of all of the "gods of the land" lining the walls inside.[33] No one was allowed to enter the room, other than the priests

FIG. 6. Fire sacrifice in honor of Cihuacoatl performed before a maiden representing the goddess. Códice Durán, fol. 280r. Biblioteca Nacional de España, MS 26-11.

who occupied an antechamber and whose charge it was to guard the deities. The priests were covered with a black substance and were always available to keep a sacred fire burning in her honor. Her visage, made of stone, had a gaping mouth and huge teeth. Her hair was long and disheveled. Durán states too that she was outfitted in women's attire, all white (see fig. 5).

Cihuacoatl's feast day was Huey Tecuilhuitl, the eighteenth day of July, following Durán's calendar, and the eighth festivity of the Mexica liturgical year. A female slave was purchased and dressed as Cihuacoatl and feted during the celebration before her death. Called Xilonen, she was kept tipsy, presumably an anodyne in anticipation of her fate.[34] Four captives were slain as well, and all five had their hearts extracted and their blood given as an offering, with some of it sprinkled on the stone idol. Fire sacrifice was incorporated into the gruesome ritual (fig. 6).

The community, outfitted in their finest attire and wearing jewels and feathers and carrying bouquets of flowers, celebrated with a festival lasting ten days. There were banquets with all manner of delectables, including chocolate, pinole, and pulque, all furnished by subject altepetl trying to outdo one another, the Chalca always being the first to provide what was required. In addition, a captive was sacrificed every eight days to nourish Cihuacoatl. Durán asserted that Cihuacoatl was so preeminent that as the "sister" of Huitzilopochtli her temple was adjacent to his and serviced as lavishly.[35] Fray Diego, though, reported that in his time the ruins of her temple were thought to be haunted because of all the idols that had once inhabited the place. The natives continued to call the site Tlillan, while local boys thought of it as the "House of the Devil."[36]

According to Ferdinand Anders, Maarten Jansen, and Luis Reyes García, the importance of Cihuacoatl in Mexica life and religious ritual can hardly be overstated. They have found Cihuacoatl to be the centerpiece of the New Fire ceremony as it was celebrated by the Mexica and as the deity and calendar cycle were depicted in the *Códice Borbónico*. Moreover, they have renamed the codex *El libro del Ciuacoatl*.[37] Cihuacoatl's image appears at least six times in the book, with her signature skeletal maw, ornate shield of eagle feathers, and machete, as they describe it, held aloft in her right hand (fig. 7). The machete, or batten, reportedly is suggestive of weaving and her role as patron of women. She has long, dark, curly hair common to the images of malevolent creatures; a quetzal headdress distinct from that of the Tlacochcalcatl and others in that it has a row of hearts and a crest of banners (and as seen in the Tzitzimitl figures mentioned earlier); and long skirt that appears to combine features of leather back-aprons ending in shells with beautiful feather over-lays. This image, or aspects thereof, depicts accoutrements familiar to several other deity representations. Initially, she is paired with Moteuczoma Xoco-yotl, and her image is glossed "papa mayor," indicating her preeminence. Sub-sequent figures are avatars of her various religious functions. Most notable is Cihuacoatl standing on a *tzompantli*, "a skull-embellished platform," in front of a temple, ostensibly presiding over at least fourteen other deity repre-sentatives processing in a courtyard in her presence. Doubtless the temple is Tlillan and the gods the constituency housed therein as described by Durán. H. B. Nicholson, with Elizabeth Hill Boone in agreement, believes that the Codex Borbonicus likely originated in Colhuacan, where Cihuacoatl was the primary deity along with a strong emphasis on the New Fire ceremony.[38]

FIG. 7. Ciuacoatl. *El libro del Ciuacoatl . . . Códice Borbónico*, 36. Akademische Druck- u. Verlagsanstalt.

Two scholars in particular have generated important studies of this remarkable deity. One of them, Cecelia Klein, has amply treated the qualities of the cult of Cihuacoatl, her imagery, her idiosyncrasies, and her symbolism. This was a deity of complex and fluid morphology and name, whose origins, in different guises, Klein traces back to early altepetl formation in the basin of Mexico. Cihuacoatl's attributes are not untypically associated with warfare and travail. By the time Cihuacoatl became a centerpiece of Mexica devotion, she epitomized eternal militaristic subordination, with an implicit promise of redemption by means of perpetual sacrifice. Klein elaborates on the god's relationship to Tlacaelel, who, upon assuming the political office of the Cihuacoatl, simultaneously took on the role of deity impersonator; he dressed the part as signifier and participated in her sacred rituals. Then, Pete Sigal has a masterful exegesis of Cihuacoatl and related issues of masculinity, femininity, sexuality, and spirituality and how such qualities were perceived by native authors and subsequently portrayed in their historical accounts. Sigal, treating the pictorial representations, Nahuatl philology, and Nahua beliefs and practices in context, situates Cihuacoatl in her sacred pantheon.[39]

All the self-fulfilling excesses of ecstasy and despair were conveyed in her attributes, such as consummate *patrona* during childbirth, awesome warrior combating both good and evil, and perpetual cannibalizer, cleaning up to keep things right. Thus, the cross-dressing deity impersonator Tlacaelel was death and life incarnate, literally. As a nobleman and valiant warrior Tlacaelel had led the Mexica in battles of conquest against lush and fertile Colhuacan, Xochimilco, Cuitlahuac, and other major altepetl south of Mexico Tenochtitlan. He appropriated their god and their bountiful resources and brought it all home for himself and his fellow Mexica.[40] The numinous goddess Cihuacoatl, juxtaposed with Huitzilopochtli, was a perfect counterpoise for the secular dyad of the female impersonator Cihuacoatl and each great king that he served.[41]

THE SOURCES

Does the hummingbird find everything?[42]

Above all, Alvarado Tezozomoc, Chimalpahin, and Durán are the richest and most reliable sources of information about Tlacaelel the Cihuacoatl and the deity Cihuacoatl. Yet, Tlacaelel was unknown or ignored by many other authors. The following is a survey of what is extant of the information about him and his descendants.

ALVARADO TEZOZOMOC

As noted, the historians Chimalpahin and Alvarado Tezozomoc enthused and wrote abundantly about Tlacaelel the Cihuacoatl and Mexica exceptionalism. Although both men were Nahuas, they wrote different sorts of histories for different audiences. Alvarado Tezozomoc was the grandson of the last huey tlatoani, Moteuczoma Xocoyotl. His grandmother was Tlapalizquixotzin, *cihuatlatoani*, "queen," of Ecatepec, who married Moteuczoma Xocoyotl. Their daughter, doña Francisca de Moteuczoma, married her first cousin, don Diego de Alvarado Huanitzin, who also became a ruler of Ecatepec (r. 1520–38) and then was installed by Viceroy don Antonio de Mendoza as the first governor of Mexico Tenochtitlan (r. 1538–41). Alvarado Tezozomoc could not have wished for a finer pedigree, and his extended family came to include the Franciscan Juan de Tovar and Antonio Valeriano, the erudite Nahua administrator. There is no record of his birth date, but his father died in 1541, which indicates that Alvarado Tezozomoc was at the least close to forty years Chimalpahin's senior. This allowed him the very real advantage of growing up among witnesses of the Spanish invasion, the battles, and the reconstruction of the city.[43]

The Moteuczomas were known to be based in Atzaqualco, the Nahua quarter in the northeastern part of Mexico City, although it has not been established that Alvarado Tezozomoc lived there.[44] Certainly, he was recognized and celebrated for his famous family, even impersonating his grandfather on at least one festive occasion as he was carried about the city on a covered litter accompanied by dancers and then taken before the viceroy's palace.[45] And we know as well that he was in contact with family members who passed on to him manuscripts containing the family's royal genealogies and altepetl history, doubtless the source of much of the material for his own work.

ça nocel y nihuehuetlacahualli y nihuehuenenonotzalle . . . yn iuhqui matticatca yn iyollotzin yn inhuehuenenonotzaltzin yn tlacatlahtoque

Don diego de alvarado huanitzin niccauhtzin. Don Pedro tlacahue-
pantzin notlatzin. Don diego de S. Fran.co tehuetzquititzin. yhuan oc
cequintin tlaçopipiltin yn oniquincaquilli yn huel mellahuac quimatia
yn huehuenenonotzaliztli. yn nican niccuic yn intlatoltzin.

I myself am the ancient ones' survivor, I who possess the accounts of
the ancient ones . . . as they understood their ancient ones' accounts.
I listened to the rulers don Diego de Alvarado Huanitzin, my parent, don Pedro Tlacahuepan, my uncle, don Diego de San Francisco
Tehuetzquititzin, and other highborn noblemen who indeed rightly
understood the ancient ones' accounts. Here I took their statements.[46]

Alvarado Tezozomoc was obviously fluent in Nahuatl, although only a
few folios of his writings in his language are extant.[47] Rather, he compiled a
massive history about Nahua life in Spanish, a work he completed sometime
around 1598. His *Crónica mexicana* contains information about the earliest
dynastic years of the Mexica and concludes with the arrival of the Spaniards. A second volume, presumably also in Spanish, about the conquest and
its aftermath, has been lost, but solid proof of its existence is revealed by
Chimalpahin, who by the evidence had all of Tezozomoc's manuscripts in
his possession and made use of them for his annals and other writings.[48]
Alvarado Tezozomoc's *Crónica* is a grand, heroic story brought to life with
the endless speeches and conversations of Mexica gods and kings and their
cohorts. In some ways, it is more theater than chronicle, for it includes col-
orful and dramatic settings, as when Tlacaelel the Atempanecatl volunteers
to confront the Tepaneca ruler to avenge the death of the Mexica king Chimalpopoca:

Señor y rrey mío, ¿para qué soy en está bida? ¿Para quándo me guardo
de hazer serbiçio a mi rrey y patria? Yo quiero tomar la demanda de ser
mensajero y si allá muriere, a la fin e de morir, con consentimy[ento]
de estos n[uest]ros hermanos y deudos y parientes. Y les encargo a mi
muger y hijos.[49]

My lord and king, what is my purpose in this life? Why would I
spare myself doing service for my king and homeland? I would like

to assume the responsibility of being messenger, and if I were to die there, then there I shall die, with the consent of these our siblings, relations, and relatives. And I entrust my wife and children to them.

Alvarado Tezozomoc's Spanish is poignant, and elsewhere in this work I have deliberately kept it as he wrote it since a translation to English cannot begin to do justice to his message.

CHIMALPAHIN

The great majority of Chimalpahin's works are in the form of Nahuatl annals, although there is a small portion in Spanish, and there is an entire Nahuatl text of daily spiritual devotions by Sahagún that he copied and rewrote in his own manner.[50] Chimalpahin also made a copy of Francisco López de Gómara's *Conquista de México* (1552) and interpolated numerous additions and changes in this Spanish-language history. Writing primarily between the years 1615 and 1630, his aim was to record the course of Mexica history.

> So that you may know it, I, don Domingo de San Antón Muñón Chimalpahin Quauhtlehuanitzin, sought out all this ancient lore from whoever still knows it in our time, now during our lives. And so that it will not disappear or be forgotten, today once again I am verifying it. I am redoing it, putting it all in a book. . . . Here people's children [nobles] who live in the present time, and those who live afterward who did not know about the ancient story and account of the altepetl, will see and know it in the ancient altepetl history, the book of life.[51]

His oeuvre numbers some fifteen hundred pages.

It is doubtful that Chimalpahin moved in the same social circle as Alvarado Tezozomoc and their fellow intellectuals. He was a commoner from Amecameca, Chalco, although the family had once been members of the nobility. Born in 1579 and baptized Domingo Francisco, he probably received some primary schooling from the Dominicans who oversaw the Amecameca *doctrina*. At the age of fourteen, he moved to Mexico City to live and work in Xoloco at the church of San Antonio Abad. He stayed there for more than twenty years. The tlaxilacalli of Xoloco is located at the junction of the Iztapalapa causeway leading from the south to the southeastern shore of the island capital, famously the site of the initial encounter of Moteuczoma and Hernando Cortés, which was a spectacle to behold.

Chimalpahin worked as a *fiscal*, assisting his priest, fray Agustín del Espíritu Santo. Fray Agustín was the sole member of his order in New Spain, but that did not keep him from being actively involved with the Nahua community that surrounded the church. I suspect that the priest was also a *nahuatlato*, although Chimalpahin never says as much. When fray Agustín said mass for the first time at San Antón, the Jesuit Juan de Tovar, known widely as the "Cicerón de mexicano [Nahuatl]," served as his sponsor.[52]

It was while he was working at San Antón that Chimalpahin began to collect his sources and write his annals. He was also a member of the congregation of San Joseph Chapel at the San Francisco church, the hub of Nahua Catholicism in the sixteenth century. San Francisco had an important library of manuscripts and books, which Chimalpahin may have made use of. In addition to Alvarado Tezozomoc's materials he had dozens of pictorial manuscripts at hand, and he brought together as many as he could to write a history of early Mexico that spanned the years from Eleven House, 73, when the land came to be populated, to 1631, his last recorded entry. Chimalpahin also wrote a complete history of his hometown, Amecameca. It includes information about when it was first formed, in Six Flint, 1160, and continues well through the sixteenth century. The altepetl's history demonstrates remarkable continuity of the royal rulerships that governed both Amecameca and the confederated altepetl of Chalco.[53]

Essentially an autodidact, Chimalpahin read widely, from the ecclesiastical treatises of the early church fathers, Saint Augustine and Saint Thomas Aquinas, for example, in addition to the Old Testament. He was also knowledgeable about classical literature, citing Sophocles, Plato, and Ovid, among other great intellectuals of the ancient Western world. In addition, he had access to the books and manuscripts that were available in the capital. He knew of the prominent Franciscans of his time and before—Alonso de Molina, Bernardino de Sahagún, and Juan de Torquemada—and made references to them in his annals. He may have known of the Dominican Diego

Durán, although he refers to him as Hernando, a mistake that occurred elsewhere in those years.[54] A devout Christian, his piety is manifested in his annals from time to time.[55] Even so, he saw no contradiction in writing about Tlacaelel, when anyone else would have considered the subject matter unorthodox.

ALVA IXTLILXOCHITL AND CRISTÓBAL DEL CASTILLO

Chimalpahin and Alvarado Tezozomoc's mestizo counterpart, don Fernando de Alva Ixtlilxochitl (ca. 1578–1650), barely discusses Tlacaelel in his extensive and impressive history of the Tetzcoca, although he treats the Mexica rulers.[56] He does, however, mention Tlacaelel's role as the Cihuacoatl, or "sacerdote mayor," and notes the death of the great priest.[57] Alva Ixtlilxochitl's interest, always, was in his home altepetl, Tetzcoco, and his recounting of events—often to the exclusion of everything else—consistently reflects that bias. Cristóbal del Castillo (fl. 1600), whose ethnicity is uncertain, was a contemporary of Chimalpahin, Alvarado Tezozomoc, and Alva Ixtlilxochitl.[58] He too wrote a history of the Mexica and another about the conquest, although only fragments of the Nahuatl text survive. There is no reference to Tlacaelel or the Cihuacoatl in what exists of his accounts.

CORTÉS, DÍAZ DEL CASTILLO, AND LÓPEZ DE GÓMARA

Hernando Cortés (ca. 1482–1547), on the other hand, in the course of his letter-writing campaign to Holy Roman Emperor Charles V, early on recognized the importance of the office of the Cihuacoatl and put its occupant, Tlacotzin, Tlacaelel's grandson, in charge of rebuilding and repopulating Acatlan, the southeastern quarter of Mexico City. Cortés and his interpreter, Malintzin, had many interactions with the Cihuacoatl, and the conqueror eventually installed Tlacotzin as the first full-fledged Mexica king of colonial Tenochtitlan.[59] Bernal Díaz del Castillo (1496–1584), a member of Cortés's company who wrote his own chronicle of the Spanish conquest, referred to "a priest and a chief" and various "captains" who served as intermediaries between Cortés and the successors of Moteuczoma Xocoyotl (r. 1502–20) but does not identify the Cihuacoatl by name.[60] Later, when the Spaniards were on their way to Honduras, rapporteur Díaz wrote that

Tlacotzin the Cihuacoatl was responsible for the hanging of Quauhtemoc, the last of the great Mexica emperors. Díaz's attribution of Tlacotzin as the man responsible for the death of his king is in stark contrast to all other Nahua-related historical reports.[61] Francisco López de Gómara (1511–64), Cortés's priest and secretary, also makes scant mention of the Tlacaelels or their office in his tome about the Spaniards and their early conquests in the Americas (1552). It is only in the Nahua Chimalpahin's rewriting (ca. 1620) of Gómara's conquest history that we learn of the prestige and role of the Cihuacoatl at the time of Spanish contact with the Mexica. Chimalpahin's focus was a son of Tlacaelel, Totomotzin, who was a member of the royal entourage of Moteuczoma when the emperor met Cortés in Xoloco, and then on the tragic demise in Honduras of Mexica king Tlacotzin, the old Cihuacoatl's grandson.[62]

THE FRANCISCANS: SAHAGÚN, MENDIETA, AND TORQUEMADA

The early Franciscans wrote their own histories of native life, the best known of which is the twelve-volume opus compiled by fray Bernardino de Sahagún (ca. 1499–1590). By his own account, Sahagún depended on a cohort of native informants from Tlatelolco, where he was posted for several years. As noted, the Tlatelolca recorded nothing of Tlacaelel. The omission suggests they may have tended to minimize anything that would put their sister altepetl, Tenochtitlan, in a favorable light. The deity Cihuacoatl, however, appears in several books, an indication of her importance among the Nahuas.[63] Fray Gerónimo de Mendieta (1528–1604), active in and around the capital, writes in his own grand account about the Mexica ruling hierarchy and native life but makes little mention of Tlacaelel or the deity Cihuacoatl, other than a ritual association with tobacco.[64] Fray Juan de Torquemada (ca. 1557–1624), in contrast, goes on at great length to categorically deny the existence of Tlacaelel as a historical figure. Torquemada states that he never found information about the man in any of his sources. Nevertheless, he includes information about Tlacaelel's heirs (without making the association with Tlacaelel), specifically his son Tlilpotonqui the Cihuacoatl under Moteuczoma and his grandson Tlacotzin the Cihuacoatl under Quauhtemoc. Confounding the issue and blurring

the distinction of the office, the deity, and a structure, Torquemada records
that a Cihuacoatl was a temple built by King Itzcoatl after the defeat of the
Cuitlahuaca (1433).[65] It is possible that the Mexica under Tlacaelel initiated
construction of a temple dedicated to Cihuacoatl as a token trophy after
successfully completing their campaign of conquest against the altepetl
south of Mexico Tenochtitlan.

THE DOMINICANS

Las Casas

Surely one of the first of the mendicants to discuss the Cihuacoatl, fray
Bartolomé de las Casas (1474-1566), in Spain writing his *Apologética historia sumaria* in the late 1550s, described the office of the Mexica's sec-
ond-in-command:

> *De los jueces, el supremo, después del rey, en el señorio mexicano, era*
> *el presidente o juez mayor, cuyo nombre, por el oficio era* cihuacóatl.
> *Este oficio ninguno lo podia proveer sino solo el rey de México.*[66]

He elaborates on the sweep of the Cihuacoatl's duties and authority and his
relationship with the Mexica tlatoani. Noteworthy are the terms used to
describe the office, supreme judge, president, and so forth, which are among
those identical in Chimalpahin.[67] There is no mention of Tlacaelel by name
or the deity.

Durán

By far the richest Spanish-language source about Tlacaelel by sixteenth-century religious is that of the Dominican fray Diego Durán (ca. 1537–88),
who wrote long, plentifully detailed and illustrated histories about Nahua
life and religion.[68] It is here that Tlacaelel receives full treatment, and one
cannot help but puzzle over the contradiction between Torquemada's vehe-
ment denial of Tlacaelel's existence and Durán's partiality for the man.
Their sources were surely some of the same individuals and manuscripts
available in the capital, although Durán stated that he depended largely on
a particular Nahuatl-language text that he corroborated with information
from oral accounts and other sources: "All of this seemed so incredible to
me that if the *Historia* [Duran's Nahuatl source] had not forced me to put it

down, and if I had not found confirmation of it in other written and painted manuscripts, I would not dare to write these things for fear of being held as a man who invents fables."[69] Durán is generous in his descriptions of Tlacaelel and his vital role as a political engineer over the course of several generations of Mexica rulerships. There is likewise ample information about Tlacaelel's activities as a deity impersonator, and he devotes an entire chapter to the god Cihuacoatl and her ritual celebration.

Durán's histories, along with the writings by Chimalpahin and Alvarado Tezozomoc, are the primary sources of information for this study about Tlacaelel and Mexica life in central Mexico over the course of nearly two centuries. Of these three principal sources, Alvarado Tezozomoc's *Crónica*, which is laced with Nahuatl terminology and high, formal Spanish suggestive of the Nahuatl vocative, can be considered intermediary, almost transitional, following fray Diego Durán's more vernacular Spanish-language *History* by some twenty years, which Chimalpahin then followed several years later with his very traditional Nahuatl annals. The style and languages of the three collections of manuscripts are the inverse of what is expected at the end of the sixteenth century and the beginning of the seventeenth.

Not to be overlooked are the illustrations furnished by fray Diego in his *History* and other treatises about the Nahuas. They total some 118 ink and paint drawings that are invaluable regarding all that is revealed about indigenous life in central Mexico. The paintings are inserted in the double columns on both the recto and verso folios of his manuscript and are intended to illustrate the contents of each respective chapter. The illustrations have been reproduced, often poorly, and much desired is a color facsimile of what is believed to be the original, or at the least the earliest known version, of Durán's work, which is housed at the Biblioteca Nacional, Madrid.[70] It is here that we see the true color and style as he intended, furnishing a handsome visual complement to his narrative. The illustrations are not labeled, but studies by the art historians Donald Robertson, Elizabeth Boone, and Christopher Couch have gone a long way toward bringing to light Durán's purpose for the paintings and how they came to be a part of his history.[71] Tlacaelel, or rather his office as the Cihuacoatl, can be positively identified in only one of these illustrations. It

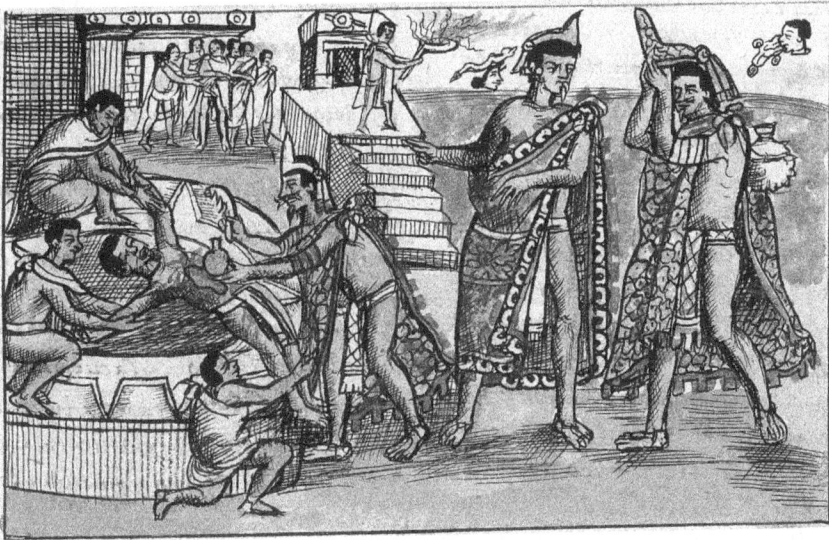

FIG. 8. Tlacaelel the Cihuacoatl and King Axayacatl (or Moteuczoma Ilhuicamina) preparing to sacrifice captives. Códice Durán, fol. 70r. Biblioteca Nacional de España, MS 26-11.

FIG. 9. A crowned, robed, and enthroned Tlacaelel the Cihuacoatl in the company of fellow tlatoque, Códice de Huichapan, pl. 26. Instituto Nacional de Antropología e Historia, Mexico.

FIG. 10. Death of Tlacaelel (reportedly). Códice Durán, fol. 140v.
Biblioteca Nacional de España, MS 26-11.

is curious that Durán, considering the importance he gives to Tlacaelel in
his invaluable coeval role with each of five rulers, never actually included
the man in any of the portrait-like images of the sitting kings. To date,
in what is extant of the surviving corpus of pictorial representations of
Mexica tlatoque, Tlacaelel is not to be found.

Noteworthy, though, is that Durán does portray Tlacaelel the Cihuacoatl wearing a *xiuhhuitzolli*, "crown," as he surely did, being "second
king." He is even garbed in a Tenochca-style ruler's cloak, fashioned after
the type worn by Itzcoatl, Axayacatl, and other rulers. However, there is
none of the iconography relating to Tlacaelel that later became associated
with the man and his office. Confirmation of Durán's assertion that Tlacaelel wore a royal xiuhhuitzolli is found in his painting that portrays a
crowned individual who was certainly Tlacaelel, this time with an actual
Cihuacoatl title glyph, and King Axayacatl as they prepared to take their
turn sacrificing war captives (fig. 8).[72] Pictorially reiterating his high status,
in the Otomi Codex Huichapan the authors not only depict Tlacaelel the
Cihuacoatl wearing a xiuhhuitzolli and a ruler-styled cloak, but he also
sits upon a throne when in the company of fellow tlatoque (fig. 9).[73] Finally,
again by Durán, there is a painting supposedly of Tlacaelel after his death,
as his body is being prepared for his funeral (fig. 10). It is evidently a misattribution.[74] All of the activities in the paintings are discussed in detail in
the narrative in fray Diego's *History*.

ENRICO MARTÍNEZ

Contemporaneously, Enrico Martínez (b. ca. 1550), also known as Heinrich Martin, interpreter for the Inquisition, printer, engineer, and eventually Royal Cosmographer of Mexico City, also knew of Tlacaelel and credited him as a valiant warrior and a person "a quien se debe casi toda la Gloria del Imperio Mexicano" in his Spanish-language *Reportorio* of 1606.[75] Martínez was well known in the capital, and as the owner of a printing press he was likely familiar with many of the manuscripts circulating in the city. Certainly, Chimalpahin knew of Martínez's *Reportorio* and incorporated sections of it into his annals, after translating them into Nahuatl. It is improbable that Chimalpahin's annals served as Martínez's source, since Chimalpahin was in the early stages of his research and writing, but it is not impossible.[76]

THE JESUITS

Tovar and Acosta

Juan de Tovar (ca. 1546–ca. 1626), Durán's Jesuit counterpart and relative, also conveys favorably the exploits of the warrior, leader, and coadjutor Tlacaelel but makes no mention of the office of the Cihuacoatl or, for that matter, the deity.[77] It is known that he made use of Durán's histories after his own had been lost. Tovar, too, complemented some of his alphabetic history with handsome paintings of native rulers, important deities, and other aspects of Nahua life. But there are no readily apparent images of Tlacaelel the Cihuacoatl.

A second Jesuit, José de Acosta (1539–1600), wrote a sweeping history of the Indies that contains a praiseworthy but by now standard version of Tlacaelel as assistant to the Mexica kings, and little else. Acosta relied on Tovar's *Relación* as his primary source of information about Mexico, which of course depended on Durán's *History*.[78]

Another Jesuit

Two centuries later, Jesuit Francisco Clavigero (1731–87) had at his fingertips what was extant and available of the early histories and came to his own conclusions about Tlacaelel: he did not exist. Clavigero believed that King Huitzilihuitl (r. 1227–99) gave *two* names to his son and successor, Moteuczoma:

"Tlacaellel, o sea hombre de gran corazón y el de Ilhuicamina, es decir, flechador del cielo."[79] He acknowledged that he was in disagreement with his two distinguished Jesuit predecessors, Acosta and Tovar, who believed that Tlacaelel and Moteuczoma were distinct individuals, but added that they were incorrect.[80]

THE CRÓNICA X

Because this book depends so much on Chimalpahin, Alvarado Tezozomoc, and Durán as sources of information about Tlacaelel the Cihuacoatl, mention is warranted regarding the ongoing disputation about the "Crónica X." Alfredo Chavero, the first among many to puzzle over and publish the similarities among the different texts, observed in 1876 that they were "en realidad una sola." Then Adolph Bandelier and Joaquín García Icazbalceta published their own observations regarding the matter.[81] Later, in the 1940s, Robert Barlow reinvigorated the discussion with his comparison of Durán, Tovar, and Alvarado Tezozomoc's Spanish-language histories and was the first to postulate a common Nahua source for the text and the images and to coin the label "Crónica X." Identifying specific passages that duplicated—although seldom perfectly—information about events and individuals, Barlow was confident that the three men had depended on one indigenous chronicle, now lost. Alfonso Caso, Ignacio Bernal, and Edmundo O'Gorman, among others, weighed in.[82] Chimalpahin as a source was seldom part of the debate, perhaps because of his Nahua annals' format and surely because they were written in Nahuatl. One tantalizing leitmotiv is the intense and generally positive focus on Tlacaelel by Alvarado Tezozomoc and Durán, both of whom accorded him the essential role in the formation and later glory of Mexico Tenochtitlan.

Most recently, in 2007 Sylvie Peperstraete produced a six-hundred-page French-language study of the Crónica X, addressing the same concerns. She ostensibly focuses on Durán and Alvarado Tezozomoc and treats chronology, differences, propagandizing, Tlacaelel, and so forth. However, she believes the Crónica X is paramount as the master text, with the Durán and Alvarado Tezozomoc chronicles essentially derivative. Regarding how this came to be, she writes that "the presence of speeches and dialogues reported in a detailed way and of elements too complex to draw suggests a written adaptation of an oral tradition recited by a specialist in front of a codex rather than a simple explanation of the scenes represented; it is all the more probable as often noted, in the reconstruction, characteristic of an oral account."[83] There is little discussion of the great and rich quantity of additional and unique information found in both Durán and Alvarado Tezozomoc, although she is convinced that the latter's *Crónica mexicana* is "nearer to his principal source than the Dominican [for he] uses terms in Nahuatl, [and] one can prefer them to the generalities or approximations that Durán proposes in Spanish."[84]

Peperstraete states that Chimalpahin too made use of the Crónica X as well as the Nahuatl "Crónica mexicayotl," which she mistakenly attributes to Alvarado Tezozomoc. She notes that Chimalpahin does include information about Tlacaelel but feels that his sources fail to portray the Cihuacoatl as anyone extraordinary.[85] My research on Chimalpahin's interest in Tlacaelel has yielded conclusions that are quite the contrary to those of Peperstraete. Of all the ongoing research about a Crónica X, surely the most lucid, practical, and succinct approach to the topic is by Rafael Tena, who advocates a scholarly and critical analysis of the original manuscripts, consideration of the context in which they were produced, and less of the singular all-or-none approach to evaluating the histories by Alvarado Tezozomoc, Durán, and Tovar and their relationship to a hypothetical document.[86]

Moreover, all the energy and time invested in researching the existence of a vanished template have tended to delegitimize the contributions of Alvarado Tezozomoc, Durán, and Tovar. In some ways, interest in their grand histories stalled: it was as though without the original (the Crónica X) their intrinsic value was in question. Now, with all of Chimalpahin's known works published and available in either English or Spanish, their contents should help to substantiate and valorize each indigenous history for what it is. Peperstraete claims, though, that Chimalpahin's sources were uniquely Chalca, and for his history of his own Amecameca, they were.[87] But by far the majority of his annals were dedicated to Mexica history, and those sources were copious. It is in these many manuscripts that Tlacaelel figures so prominently. With Chimalpahin writing some thirty to forty years after Durán and Tovar and close to a generation after Alvarado Tezozomoc, it is remarkable that so many of his source manuscripts were extant. Most were of pictorial images that he corroborated with oral explanations from knowledgeable elders. Chimalpahin names the author or painter of the work, when possible, and furnishes the provenience, which ranged from Azcapotzalco, Colhuacan, and Cuepopan (of San Juan Tenochtitlan) to Huexotla, Tetzcoco, and Tlatelolco, to name a few.

> ynin tlahtolli vmpa tlaquixtilli yn tlatilolco ytech tlapaltlacuilloli huel neltiliztli

This account was taken from a colored picture-writing in Tlatelolco. It is indeed the truth.[88]

> o yhuin inyn quihtohua yn aquin catca ytoca Martin Tochtli Mexicatl

So said he whose name was Martín Tochtli, a Mexica.[89]

> ynin tlahtolli ytech tlaquixtilli yn bintula quimocahuilitiuh Don Alonso ximenez culhuacan chane

This account was taken from a painting that don Alonso Jiménez, a resident of Colhuacan, left.[90]

Chimalpahin also had access to Latin-, Spanish-, and Nahuatl-language alphabetic manuscripts and books. And most famously, he used some of Alvarado Tezozomoc's Nahuatl writings, giving him full credit by leaving the account in the first person:

> auh yn axcan ypan xihuitl de 1609. años ye no nehuatl Don hernando de aluarado teçoçomoc. nixhuiuh yn tlacatl catca huey tlatohuani Moteucçomatzin xocoyotl.

But now this is the year 1609. I, don Hernando de Alvarado Tezozomoc, am also a grandson of the late lord, the great ruler Moteuczomatzin Xocoyotl.[91]

In other words, Chimalpahin had dozens of Mexica sources, many of which complemented one another, though some were contradictory. He checked and rechecked his documents and often selected those of greatest antiquity, as if venerability ensured reliability. And he masterfully cross-referenced his information, encouraging his reader with such reminders as, "as will be seen below" or "as mentioned above," which abound.[92] However, it was in his annals contemporary with his stay in Mexico City and his reference to Tlacaelel, where he states, "for above appear all the different things he did during the reigns of each of the said late rulers of Tenochtitlan," that I first began to realize what Tlacaelel meant to Chimalpahin's understanding of the greatness of Mexica history.[93] In his large corpus of annals, it is difficult to find even one set that is without some mention of the Cihuacoatl. Chimalpahin also labored to find the truth as he researched and wrote.

Nevertheless, all Chimalpahin's original Nahua sources have long since disappeared, which by no means diminishes the worth of his contributions. Knowing the history of the sharing of sources and manuscripts, whether published or not, that had gone on among Nahuas as well as Europeans for centuries and referring specifically to the dilemma about the Crónica X, Ignacio Bernal cautioned years ago that we would be wise to pay attention to Edmundo O'Gorman, who admonished his colleagues against "the excessive quest for originality in information."[94]

❁

For all his celebrity, there seem to be few, if any, colonial-era images of Tlacaelel. Durán states that in the precontact period Tlacaelel had his portrait carved in stone along with the Mexica rulers at Chapoltepec, but almost all of those sculptures have disappeared (fig. 11).[95] Fortunately, fray Diego dedicated one of the earlier-mentioned paintings to [Tlacaelel] the Cihuacoatl, which serves to corroborate his importance to Mexica history (see fig. 8) . Miguel León-Portilla has devoted considerable effort to bringing information about Tlacaelel to light and concludes that he "must be recognized as one of those authentic, successful reformers that appear only rarely on the world's stage."[96] He supports his assertion with information from familiar sources along with the Codices Cozcatzin and Azcatitlan.[97] Cecelia Klein has achieved the greatest result, though, in identifying the symbolism relating to the deity Cihuacoatl and Tlacaelel in the Codex Magliabechiano, the Codex Mendoza, and the Codex Borbonicus (and see fig. 7), among other pictorial works, as well as particular stone sculptures in Mexico City's Museo de

FIG. 11. Moteuczoma Ilhuicamina and the sculpting of his likeness at
Chapoltepec. Códice Durán, fol. 91v. Biblioteca Nacional de España,
MS 26-11.

Antropología.[98] Needless to say, none is flattering or even seemingly related
to the historical portrait of Tlacaelel as an imperious leader going about
Mexico Tenochtitlan in a cloak that "fell long; the upper half was white, and
it was black below."[99]

It warrants mention that Chimalpahin seldom if ever commented on the
deity and cult aspect of Cihuacoatl and her impersonator, Tlacaelel—perhaps
a purposeful oversight. But both Chimalpahin and Alvarado Tezozomoc
depended largely on pictorial manuscripts and oral histories as their primary sources, which, after perusing Klein's graphic depictions, challenges
one to ponder what Chimalpahin and Alvarado Tezozomoc were seeing and
hearing to make them believe and record for posterity that Tlacaelel was
unequivocally the cause and end all of Mexica magnificence.

CHAPTER 2

THE BEGINNINGS OF THE MEXICA HISTORIES, AND THE EARLY YEARS

✿

The beginnings of Mexica history in our three primary sources about Tla-caelel are something of a hodgepodge. Alvarado Tezozomoc is the most direct; he gives only a cursory treatment of the deities, Chicomoztoc, and the legendary journey from Aztlan to Mexico Tenochtitlan before launch-ing almost immediately into his version of the Mexica's dynastic history. Durán, on the other hand, furnishes the context for his Mexica history by establishing his subjects as members of the ten lost tribes of Israel, using Old Testament sources to support his claim. He mentions Chicomoztoc but believes that the seven groups that departed from there were seven tribes of Jews. He says little about their peregrinations and focuses instead on events that transpired once the migrating groups reached the basin of Mexico.

Chimalpahin's chronology on the same topic can be reconstructed, though it is uncertain which of his many texts was written first.[1] He ranges from discussing Adam, Eve, and Noah to the arrival of the first peoples (*huehuetque Chichimeca*) in Aztlan, which occurred, he says, in One Rab-bit, 50, when they disembarked somewhere in the north in Yancuic Mexico (New Mexico). Moreover, he is adamant that the first natives were not Jews, since they had already been in America for twenty-four years when Emperor Vespasian destroyed Jerusalem in Eleven House, 73.[2] His annals then con-tinue in meticulous detail with the departures from the Seven Caves and the Mexica's various migrations over the years, with their trials and tribulations as they made their way south to central Mexico. But Chimalpahin credits everything that made the Mexica special over the long term to Tlacaelel: "He was the beginning and origin of this monarchy. For if it had not been for him, nothing would have been done; this Mexica Monarchy would not have been an empire."[3]

Despite the disparate sources and their challenges, it has been possible to construct a narrative that covers a significant portion of Tlacaelel's life. Family relationships were important and, for him, lasting, but they were largely only one aspect of what became an extraordinary career of leadership and service to five Mexica high kings.

A golden age for the Mexica of course followed. But a golden age is always relative and often comes to be at the expense of others. Certainly, that was the situation in Mexico Tenochtitlan. Battles and booty increasingly made for a cosmopolitan and showy capital, whose governance, while celebrated, was marked by an entrenched royal dynasty, fostered and perpetuated by Tlacaelel. Wars of conquest seemed to increase exponentially, and enemies were targeted and treated savagely. All the while, temple building continued apace, and the worship of Huitzilopochtli was both cause and effect of empire. Providentially, Tlacaelel saw to everything.[4]

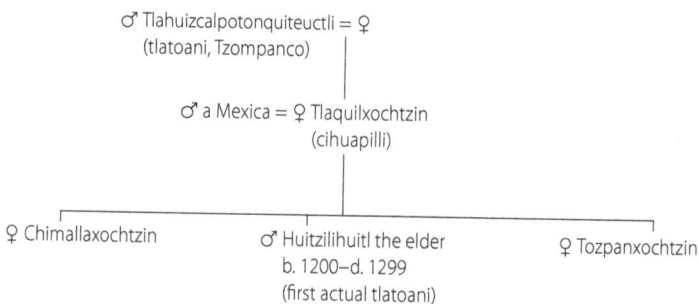

FIG. 12. The Mexica Tenochca royal lineage (first dynasty), according to Chimalpahin.

♂ Coxcoxtli = ♀
1281–1307
(Colhuacan)

♂ Opochtli Iztahuatzin = ♀ Atotoztli
(Chichimeca Mexica (tlatocacihuapilli)
macehualli)

♂ Acamapichtli the younger = ♀ Ilancueitl
1367–1387 (tlatocacihuapilli, Coatl Ichan)
(first and founding tlatoani)

= ♀

♀ (slave, vegetable seller =
Azcapotzalco)

♀ Huitzilxochitzin = ♂ Itzcoatl   ♂ Huitzilihuitl the younger = ♀
(cihuapilli,   1427–1440   1391–1415
Tiliuhcan   ("bastard," fourth   (second tlatoani)
Tlacopan)   tlatoani)

♂ Chimalpopoca   ♂ Tlacaelel = ♀   ♂ Moteuczoma
1415–1426   (Cihuacoatl)   Ilhuicamina
(third tlatoani)   1440–1469
                                      (fifth tlatoani)

♀ Atotoztli = ♂ Tezozomoc the elder
(daughter of   (tlatocapilli)
Moteuczoma
Ilhuicamina)

♂ Axayacatl = ♀   ♂ Tizoc   ♂ Ahuitzotl = ♀ Tecapantzin   ♂ Tezcatl teuctli
1469–1481   1481–1486   1486–1502   (Tlatelolco)
(sixth tlatoani)   (seventh   (eighth
                   tlatoani)   tlatoani)

♂ Cuitlahuac   ♂ Moteuczoma   ♂ Quauhtemoc   ♂ don Juan Velásquez
1520   Xocoyotl   1521–1524   Tlacotzin the Cihuacoatl
(tenth tlatoani) 1502–1520   (eleventh tlatoani) 1524–1526
                  (ninth tlatoani)   (twelfth tlatoani, first
                                                        colonial tlatoani)

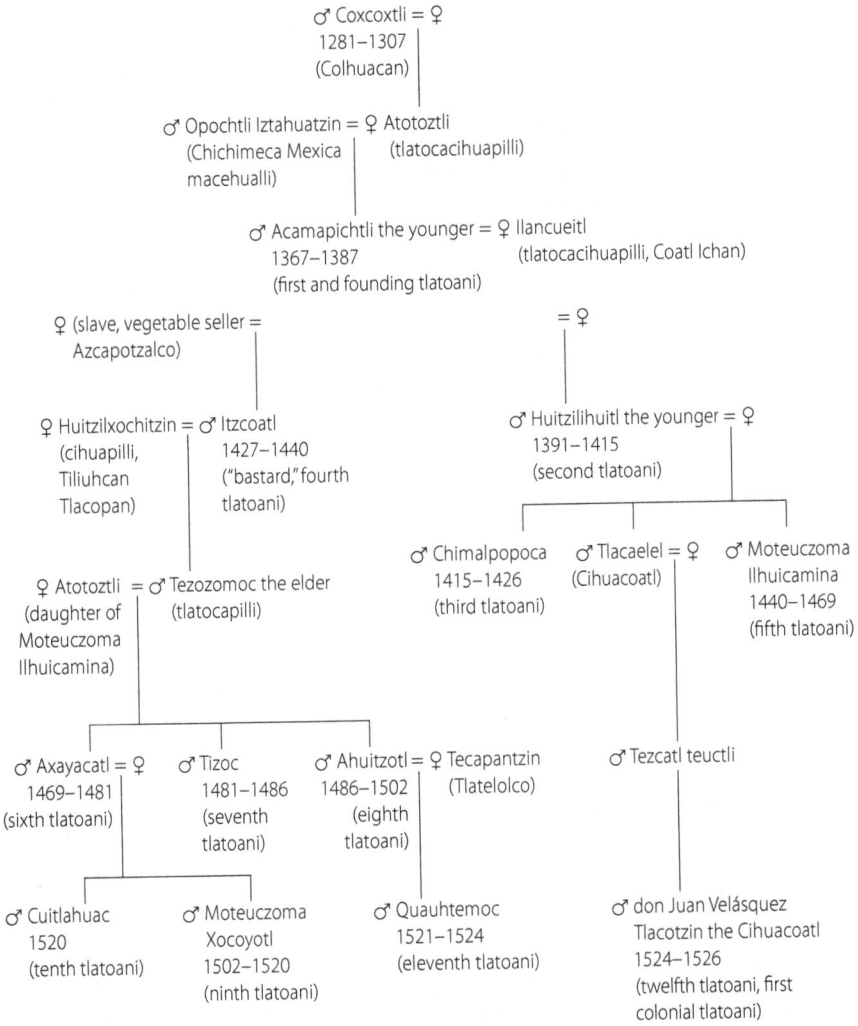

FIG. 13. The Mexica Tenochca royal lineage (second dynasty), according to Chimalpahin.

I, Tlacaelel, wish to give more courage to those of a strong
heart and embolden those who are weak.[5]

Durán

With rashness and audacity Tlacaelel went to wage war.[6]

Chimalpahin

Tlacaelel and his soldiers performed such bold and
courageous feats that no man dared face them but fled
before them as though they were wildcats.[7]

Durán

Since the beginning Tlacaelel was very courageous in
the battles and conquests, as was later realized . . . in
the power and wealth of the five high tlatoque who
ruled Mexico Tenochtitlan, . . . they were great rulers,
universally feared. And it was the valiant warrior
Tlacaeleltzin who initiated the aggrandizing and
exalting of their rulership, as is seen in the annals.[8]

Chimalpahin

It is fitting, then, to begin this history of the Mexica with Tlacaelel's
birth, which occurred in Ten Rabbit, 1398, in the morning, just as the sun
was rising. His parents were Huitzilihuitl the younger, second tlatoani of
Mexico Tenochtitlan, and Cacamacihuatzin, a *cihuapilli*, "noblewoman,"
of Teocalhueyacan.[9] Later that day, as the sun was setting, his half brother
Moteuczoma Ilhuicamina was born.[10] The two boys shared the same father:
Moteuczoma Ilhuicamina's mother, Miyahuaxiuhtzin, was a noblewoman
from Quauhnahuac (Cuernavaca). It is likely that Miyahuaxiuhtzin was
Huitzilihuitl's primary wife, since it was her son who carried on the royal
dynasty. Though the king had many children, Tlacaelel and Moteuczoma
remained close all their lives, whether as warriors or as rulers.

We know nothing of their childhood, other than that the Mexica, who
had arrived in Mexico Tenochtitlan in Two House, 1325, were subjects of the
Tepaneca. "And really they were on [other] people's land when they settled
in the sedges and reeds. For it was land of the Tepaneca, the Azcapotzalca,

and the Acolhua. They were within those people's boundaries, and within the boundaries of the Colhuaque. And therefore they were in great misery."[11] It had taken the Mexica 251 years to complete the journey from Quinehua-yan Chicomoztoc, and once arrived on the island they stopped first at a place they called Temazcaltitlan, which Chimalpahin describes as "where there [now] is the church of [our] Lord San Pablo [in Teopan]" (see map 2). Shortly thereafter, they found the stone cactus, on top of which an eagle stood eating a viper, with birds' feet, bones, and feathers scattered about. The cactus was located where the cathedral is now, Chimalpahin added (surely in Atzaqualco).[12] And although they settled into the four quarters that came to constitute their altepetl—Moyotlan, Teopan, Atzaqualco, and Cuepopan—the Mexica's existence was tenuous.[13] Later, there was a Council of Four to advise the king, and it is possible that each of the royal advisers was, at least initially, a representative of the respective fourfold organization of the capital. Shortly after establishing themselves on the island, in One House, 1337, a faction of Mexica split off and formed a separate altepetl, Tlatelolco, to the north. There was genuine animosity between the Mexica of the two polities—"Very perverse were those who then thus settled [there]. The Tlatelolca were evil, very bad-tempered. Their grandsons are now like that, they live like evil ones"—and it led to constant friction, warfare, humiliation, and, eventually, retaliation.[14]

The Mexica Tenochca's existence was largely hardscrabble, as they harvested all manner of creatures from the lakes for their subsistence and market.[15] The early temple they built for their god Huitzilopochtli can at best be described as modest in appearance: "None of the stones was very large; they were all very small. Likewise the wood: none was thick; all the wood was very thin. . . . Thus they made a foundation for the altepetl and Huitzilopochtli's house, his temple."[16]

TENOCHTZIN AND HUITZILIHUITL THE ELDER

Tenochtzin, the Mexica leader and the man who brought them to Tenochtitlan (*yn teyacan Tenochtitlan*), died in One Reed, 1363.[17] He was a leader but never a tlatoani, and with their altepetl established the Mexica believed that they were ready for a full-fledged king. Colhuacan was the most prestigious altepetl in central Mexico during those years, and the Mexica had had dealings there since their first king, Huitzilihuitl the elder (r. 1227–99), had been ambushed and captured at Chapoltepec, taken to Colhuacan, and slaughtered there by King Coxcoxtli (r. 1281–1307) (fig. 12). The annals, though, vary regarding the dates of Huitzilihuitl the elder's rule. The son of a Mexica and Tlaquilxochtzin, a noblewoman and the daughter of Tlatoani Tlahuizcalpotonqui of Tzompanco, Huitzilihuitl the elder was born in Seven Flint, 1200, in Tiçayocan. He was installed as *huel achto yntlatocacauh*, "their very first tlatoani," in either Six Rabbit, 1238, or One Flint, 1272.[18] Huitzilihuitl the elder had children, and his daughter, along with her father, was taken, stripped nude, and killed by Coxcoxtli, who commented at the time, "It is well. . . . Now we have destroyed Huitzilihuitl, no longer will there be his offspring."[19] With no survivors eligible to succeed him, the lineage was therefore terminated.[20]

Apparently, the Mexica were moving into what was already a crowded landscape. The annals add that they were attacked and defeated because they were "attending to the obtaining of land."[21] At Chapoltepec they were initially besieged by the Azcapotzalca, Tepaneca, and Xaltocameca, who were operating in league with the Chalca, Colhuaque, Cuitlahuaca, and the Xochimilca.[22] Chimalpahin reported, "They were brought to ruin from four directions when [their enemies] defeated them."[23] Not altogether unprepared to fight, the Mexica had acquired the atlatl in Seven Rabbit, 1226, or Five Flint, 1276, and bows and arrows were also among their weaponry.[24] In Six Reed, 1251, or Five Rabbit, 1302, more probably, they signed on as mercenaries for Colhuacan and captured eighty Xochimilca, whose ears they cut off.[25] Before they went to battle, though, the Mexica asked that the Colhuaque give them paper and obsidian, perhaps additional evidence of their lack of resources.[26] After their attack on the Xochimilca, the Mexica built another temple for themselves, used their fire drill (finally), and were given a heart for their altar. The heart, from the Colhuaque, was made of excrement and whip-poor-will feathers, yet another form of degradation for the Mexica.[27] They were allowed to stay in the area but encouraged to settle in the more rugged, desolate area of Tiçaapan, where, undaunted, it seems, they began to intermarry with their overlords.[28]

ACAMAPICHTLI THE YOUNGER

Some Mexica stayed on in Colhuacan, though, and one of their warriors, Opochtli Iztahuatzin, married King Coxcoxtli's daughter, Atotoztli, a *tlatocacihuapilli*, "rulerly noblewoman."[29] Opochtli Iztahuatzin is described variously as *in çan ce mexicatl chichimecatl macehualtzintli* and *çan huel mexicatl tequihua* "only a Mexica Chichimeca commoner"; "only a Mexica seasoned warrior," yet his humble status did not diminish his prospects in marriage and producing an heir.[30]

The Colhuaque had been seemingly among the first to establish their altepetl in the basin of Mexico. Durán states that Colhuacan "always possessed great fame as the place of the leading people of the land. . . . It became the capital and subjugated many provinces, notably the people of the *chinampa*, "aquatic gardens," who then became their neighbors and allies."[31] The annals add that Xochimilco was the first altepetl they subjugated.[32] In Five House, 717, the Colhuaque installed Tepiltzin Nauhyotzin as their first tlatoani. In Three House, 845, a Yohuallatonac became the third ruler, and eleven years later, on One Flint, 856, they established a tripartite rule in Colhuacan, which may have served as a precedent for later years, when a triumvirate prevailed among the Mexica, Tetzcoca, and Tlacopaneca. In both instances, the threefold rule was based on regional hegemony.

> *yn tlahtohuani Culhuacan yn itoca Yohuallatonac yehuatl çan ye*
> *tlahtocatauhcan mochiuh, y noncan Culhuacan quiyacatiticacatca yn*
> *itlahtohuayan. Auh ytloc quinhuallali yn ocomentin tlahtoque: yn icce*
> *yehuatl yn tlahtoani Tullam tlaopochcopa hualmotlalli y ye tlahto-*
> *hua, auh yn icomentin tlahtoque yn itloc quihuallalli tlamayecancopa*
> *yehuatl yn tlahtohuani Otumpa y ye teuctlahtohua. Quicepanitohuaya*
> *ymeyxtin yn tleyn quitzontequia yaoyotl noço ytla huehuey tequitl;*
> *ayac mopanahuiaya ynic tlapachohuaya, ynic mihtohua yexcan tlah-*
> *tolloyan mochiuh yn teucyotica tlahtocayotica.*[33]

The king of Colhuacan, whose name was Yohuallatonac, was the principal ruler, and from Colhuacan he presided over his realm. At his side he placed two rulers: the first, who was the ruler of Tollan, he placed at his left as his lord ruler; and the second, who was the ruler of Otompan, he placed at his right, as his lord ruler. Among the three [of them] they discussed what they were to decide in regard to war or whatever [other] important matter; none had more authority [than the other two] in government, and that is why it is said that there was a tripartite sovereignty.

The Mexica, however, would subsequently also have a similar tripartite sharing of government function among the highest lords, who were titled as tlatoque, seen first during the rule of Chimalpopoca, then during Huitzili-huitl the younger's reign with Itzcoatl and Cuatlecoatzin, and finally during the rulership of Itzcoatl, Tlacaelel, and Moteuczoma Ilhuicamina.[34]

The Mexica Tenochca were cognizant of their kinsmen in Colhuacan and that Opochtli Iztahuatzin and Atotoztli had a son named Acamapichtli the younger, the namesake of a former Colhuacan tlatoani. Moreover, they believed that Acamapichtli the younger was an ideal candidate to initiate a new Mexica dynasty that would bring the renowned Colhuacan legacy to their rulership. They therefore petitioned Teuctlamacazqui Nauhyotl, the current Colhuacan tlatoani, to grant them the privilege to take the young man to Tenochtitlan. And it is here that the account becomes complicated, for Acamapichtli was not in Colhuacan but in another altepetl altogether, Acolhuacan Coatl Ichan, where its king, Acolmiztli, along with his sister Ilancueitl, had raised and educated the boy. Ilancueitl was in truth Queen Ilancueitl, wife of the late King Acamapichtli the elder of Colhuacan, who had left her husband because of his jealousy, it was stated, since she was sterile.[35] She had brought the boy and his wet nurse with her and kept them in Coatl Ichan.[36] The Mexica were granted their request. They then asked that his aunt, Ilancueitl, be allowed to accompany Acampichtli to Tenochtitlan as his wife. In speaking with Tlatoani Teuhctlamacazqui Nauhyotl, the Mexica said:

> We who are your grandfathers, your fathers, we Mexica Chichimeca have come [before you], O lord our grandson, O ruler, [not to] make you forgetful and confused, [but] to humbly ask you for your altepetl, Tenochtitlan. We come to take the offspring of Opochtli Iztahuatzin who was your vassal; the child, the babe, our necklace, our precious quetzal feather, whose name is Itzpapalotl the third (Acamapichtli). And you will grant him [to us]: for he is truly our Mexica child and

we know in our hearts that he is the grandson of the Colhuaque, the very hair, the very fingernail, of Colhuaque lords and nobles. And we say this: Let him guard your altepetl among the sedges and reeds, Mexico Tenochtitlan; and this: Let the noblewoman Ilancueitl come to be our daughter.[37]

In Five Reed, 1367, Acamapichtli the younger and Ilancueitl were "placed on the reed mat and seat [of authority]," establishing their rulership in Mexico Tenochtitlan, surely enhanced by their esteemed affiliation with Colhuacan. The Mexica told their new king:

My grandson, tlatoanie, you are most welcome. We have put you into your home among the sedges and reeds. And your grandfathers and uncles the Mexica Chichimeca are poor. And you are to guard the *tlamacazqui*, "offering priest," the portent Huitzilopochtli. And also, you know in your heart that we are not on our own land [but] within others' boundaries, within others' walls. And you will become tired and suffer for you will work and serve [on our behalf], for here [we live on the sufferance of others on] Azcapotzalca islands.[38]

Acamapichtli had no child with Ilancueitl, and for that reason high-ranking men from many polities sent their daughters to him, initiating a process of perpetual political and marital miscegenation.[39] Of course, numerous children were born of these unions, and it was said that Ilancueitl lay in bed with each child, feigning her maternity.[40]

According to Durán, Acamapichtli the younger ruled for some forty years, although Chimalpahin's annals state that it was twenty-one years, which is more likely considering the succession and reigns of subsequent Mexica tlatoque (see fig. 13).[41] Fray Diego also wrote that during Acamapichtli's tenure Mexico Tenochtitlan was tranquil and prosperous, although it continued to be subject to the onerous, seemingly impossible, tribute requirements imposed by the Tepaneca in Azcapotzalco: "together with the usual tribute of fish, frogs, and food plants, they must now add fully grown willow and bald cypress trees. . . . [The Mexica] were to construct a raft on the water, sown with all the fruits of the earth, such as maize, chiles, beans, squash, and amaranth." With the support of their god Huitzilopochtli, the Mexica

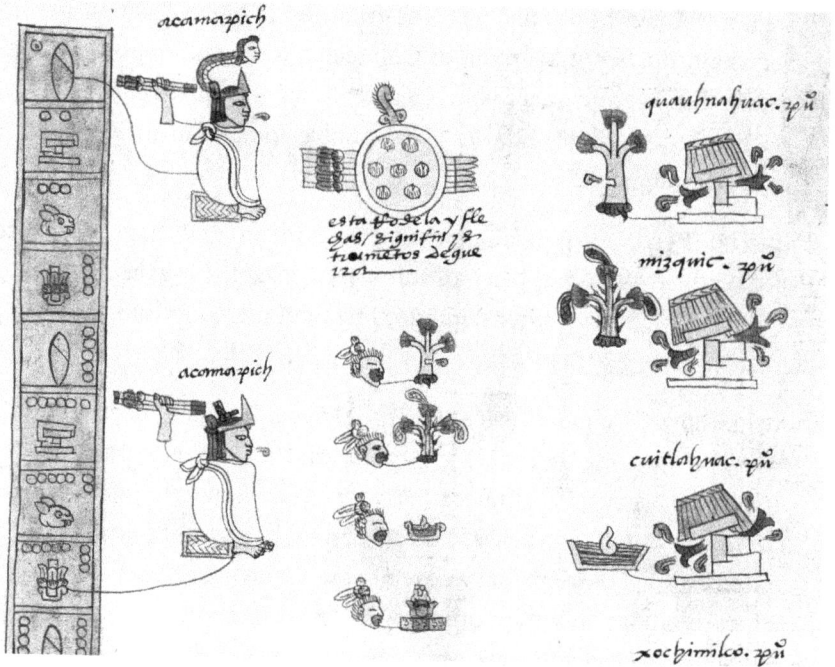

FIG. 14. Acamapichtli the younger the Cihuacoatl. Codex Mendoza, fol. 2v. Bodleian Libraries, Oxford University, MS Arch Selden A1.

complied immediately, to the amazement of King Tezozomoc of Azcapo-tzalco, who then compounded their burden.

> On the raft garden sprouted maize must be growing, together with other seeds and ripe plants and greens, but in the midst of those plants there must be a female duck sitting upon her eggs and a heron hatching her eggs. And at the moment the raft with the tribute arrives in Azcapotzalco [the chicks of the duck and the heron] must come out of their eggs. If this is not done you will perish.[42]

Acamapichtli's Mexica met the challenge, and Durán adds that they continued to do so for fifty years, although other sources state that the tribute requirements were soon modified significantly upon the request of King Tezozomoc's daughter.[43] Moreover, the annals state that all the while, even as a "fledgling Acamapichtli made war on Chimalhuacan and Cuixtoteuctli," its tlatoani. Later, in Two House, 1377, he followed up with attacks against

Mizquic and Xochimilco, and again against Chimalhuacan, which fell a second time.[44] The Mexica then fought the Xilotepeca in Four Reed, 1379, which indicates that Mexico Tenochtitlan was by no means free from turmoil.[45] Suggestive of Acamapichtli's formidable prowess in war, the *Codex Mendoza* portrays Acamapichtli with not only his personal name glyph but also a Cihuacoatl glyph. For the Mexica, the office obviously traced back years before Tlacaelel made it his signature title (fig. 14).

Acamapichtli the younger died in Twelve Reed, 1387, and because of the Mexica's still impoverished state, the funeral ceremonies were unpretentious. Chimalpahin had in his possession a genealogy that contained the names of many of the king's descendants.[46] Two sons in particular were noted, for they came to succeed Acamapichtli and contribute significantly to the development of the Tenochca altepetl.

Itzcoatl (r. 1427–40), in one set of annals, was said to be Acamapichtli the younger's only child. He was actually born of a slave, a seller of vegetables from Azcapotzalco, and although he was said to be a "bastard," Itzcoatl established a royal lineage of such acclaim that it led eventually to the birth of don Pedro Tesifón de la Cueva de Moteuczoma, who became a knight of the Order of Santiago and was living in Spain in 1621, according to Chimalpahin, who knew of him at the time.[47] Itzcoatl distinguished himself as a warrior and later was installed as the fourth dynastic ruler of Mexico Tenochtitlan. He of course had many children, but of the most remarkable, Tezozomoc the elder—a *tlatocapilli*, "royal nobleman"—stands out for his statesmanship as well as for being the father of three Mexica emperors.[48] Above all, King Itzcoatl was a crucial figure in the history of Tlacaelel and the rise of the Mexica state. More will be said of him later.

HUITZILIHUITL THE YOUNGER

Preceding Itzcoatl on the throne, however, was Huitzilihuitl the younger, who was said to be the second son of Acamapichtli the younger.[49] This child was the product of Acamapichtli's relationship with a woman named Tezatlan Miyauhtzin, daughter of the *principal*, "high-ranking individual," Acacitli, who was among those who sent their daughters to the king. Acacitli was said to be one of the first Mexica Chichimeca to arrive in Mexico Tenochtitlan.[50]

Huitzilihuitl the younger was installed on the Tenochca throne in Three Reed, 1391, following a three-year hiatus of rulership. Quatlecoatzin became the Tlacateccatl but was killed soon afterward (1399) in battle against Chalco.[51] Huitzilihuitl held sway for twenty-five years, and reportedly it was he who started the wars, even going to fight against Colhuacan, the home polity of his father, although there is plenty of evidence to indicate that the Mexica had taken to the battlefield earlier.[52]

In the meantime, even though the Mexica were beginning to expand their territory by means of warfare and plural marriage, they were still subject to the Tepaneca, who constituted a vast, seemingly confederated polity divided into what appear to be three, possibly four, altepetl, Azcapotzalco, Coyoacan, Tlacopan, and probably Colhuacan, each with its own ruler. Azcapotzalco was the headquarters of Tepaneca political authority during Huitzilihuitl's sovereignty.[53] The king was the earlier-mentioned Tezozomoctli (r. 1367–1426), and the Mexica complained, "somos ya basallos de estos tepanecas azcapuçalcas," whose tlatoani "sufrió con mucha paçiençia esta serbidumbre, pobreza, este laje laguna" Believing that they might be able to alleviate their encumbrance, the Mexica resolved to go to Azcapotzalco and to ask Tezozomoctli for his daughter, who would become the wife of their still unmarried King Huitzilihuitl.[54] Tezozomoc was amenable to the idea and gave the Mexica his daughter, Ayauhcihuatzin, who obviously became Huitzilihuitl the younger's primary wife, since their son Chimalpopoca was the king's eldest son and succeeded him as the third dynastic ruler of Mexico Tenochtitlan. The Mexica, of course, already had ties to Azcapotzalco: Chimalpopoca's uncle, Itzcoatl, was the son of a vegetable seller from there.[55]

CHIMALPOPOCA

Chimalpopoca's birth was celebrated in both Mexico Tenochtitlan and Azcapotzalco, and it would seem that King Tezozomoc was a doting grandfather. When Ayauhcihuatl brought her son to visit him, knowing his pleasure, she also asked him to lessen the Mexica's tribute assignment. The king first had to consult his advisers, who reluctantly agreed, and the required amount was forthwith reduced.[56] Durán states that Ayauhcihuatl died when Chimalpopoca was quite young and that his father died a year later.

The Mexica, wanting their altepetl to flourish, were all the while suffering continued privation. Huitzilihuitl the younger had died in One Reed, 1415, and considering it politically expedient, the Mexica installed Chimalpopoca at the age of ten on the throne that same year, seeking to mollify their Tepaneca overlords. As was becoming customary, though, Huitzilihuitl had many other children. Among the most eminent were two other sons who were growing up during Chimalpopoca's reign, Tlacaelel and Moteuczoma Ilhuicamina, the latter becoming the fifth Tenochca king.[57]

Durán furnished considerable information about the rule of Chimalpopoca, which started well enough.

> They placed the child upon the royal seat and, after having crowned him with the diadem and anointed him with divine ointment, they then gave him the royal insignias: in his left hand they placed a shield and in the right hand a sword with [obsidian] blades in it. They dressed him with the garb and weapons of the god they wished him to represent. All of this was a sign that he had sworn to defend the city and die for his people.[58]

Surely because of his youth, his uncle Itzcoatzin was with him (*ytlan*) as the Tlacateccatl, and a Teuhtlehuac became the Tlacochcalcatl. Both were military titles and offices.[59] They all took office in One Reed, 1415, on the day count Three Serpent, July 21, and the fifth day of the ancient month of Huey Tecuilhuitl.[60] During Chimalpopoca's reign, the Mexica reportedly conquered the altepetl of Xochimilco (again) and Cuitlahuac.[61] They also waged war against Colhuacan, following the practice of Chimalpopoca's father, Huitzilihuitl the younger.

The Mexica were determined in other ways too, and seeking to capitalize on the favored status of their ruler, they began to make demands of Azcapotzalco. First, they asked for access to fresh, clean water, which, since the Tepaneca had no use for it, was granted. Next, because they had little in the way of natural resources on the island, they demanded building materials to construct a proper aqueduct.[62] But with this request they had gone too far, and they incited not only King Tezozomoc but the rulers of Coyoacan and Tlacopan, who decided to wage war against the impudent Mexica. Tezozomoc pleaded for mercy for his grandson. Realizing the inevitable, the old tlatoani died in Twelve Rabbit, 1426, and in spite of being his nephew, Chimalpopoca was killed as he slept with his son by his uncle, Maxtlaton, and Acolnahuacatl, the rulers of Coyoacan and Tlacopan, respectively, and a man named Tlacacuitla.[63] Unprepared for such a tragedy, the Mexica grieved while proceeding with funeral ceremonies, to which they invited nobles from empathetic altepetl, who attended and then returned for the inaugural festivities for the next Mexica king. Chimalpahin adds that Chimalpopoca ruled for twelve years and left numerous children, some of whom assumed rulerships in different polities while others married advantageously.[64]

ITZCOATL

Following traditional practice, the Mexica consulted one another regarding Chimalpopoca's successor. The annals state that Xihuitl Temoc, Chimalpopoca's son, was the first to succeed him but that he died after being in office for only sixty days.[65] It should be remembered too that Chimalpopoca was in his early twenties, and although it was said that he had several children it is doubtful that his son had reached his majority. The Mexica instead selected the above-mentioned Itzcoatl, Huitzilihuitl the younger's half brother, who was installed on the throne in Thirteen Reed, 1427. Chimalpahin noted, "on the day count Thirteen Water, June 22." It is during Itzcoatl's rule that Tlacaelel comes to the forefront of Mexica history.[66] The annals add that at the time of his accession, Moteuczoma Ilhuicamina became the Tequihua and the Tlacateccatl, while Tlacaelel served as the Atempanecatl and the Cihuacoatl, the three men taking charge of the rulership (*yz ymeyntin quecahuiticate yn tlahtocayotl*), although elsewhere it is stated that Tlacaelel had not yet been granted the title of the Cihuacoatl.[67] They likewise donned crowns, "*copilli*," likely the "miter-shaped cap" also known as a *xiuhhuitzolli*.[68]

But at the same time, things were worsening in Azcapotzalco. Maxtlaton, who had ruled Coyoacan for seventeen years and had traveled to Azcapotzalco ostensibly for the purpose of attending his father's funeral, instead immediately had himself declared tlatoani.[69] He then put his son Tecolotzin on the throne in Coyoacan, while different men assumed the rulerships in Tlacopan and Colhuacan.[70] Maxtlaton became nearly maniacal in his demands; he impeded the Mexica's access to food and other supplies by closing all roads and waterways.[71] On more than one occasion, Mexica women, unaware of the restriction on their travel to market, were robbed and raped by Tepaneca guards as they made their way to Coyoacan.[72] Friendly altepetl accommodated the Mexica by allowing them to make use of their stores of goods. Then all interchange between Azcapotzalco and Tenochtitlan was prohibited.[73] Although Durán believed that the Mexica had little experience in warfare, they nevertheless began to prepare themselves for the possibility of conflict. Apparently there was comfort in knowing that Tlacaelel was among them: "Tlacaelel was to become the greatest warrior, the bravest and mightiest, that the [Mexica] nation ever had. He was the wisest, the most cunning, man in the arts and science of war ever found in Mexico Tenochtitlan."[74] It should be remembered, though, that the animosity and battles between the Mexica and the Tepaneca were not unique. Rather, several altepetl were at war, some emerging as confederations and conquest states.[75]

Still, fray Diego states that the Mexica were terrified of the ineluctable prospect of war against the Tepaneca. The annals add that even before then, "the aforesaid ruler Chimalpopoca, the ruler Tlacateotzin [of Tlatelolco], and Itzcoatzin wept bitterly when it was known and they told them that now the Mexica were to perish, that now they were under siege."[76] Rather than suffer such a fate, the Mexica determined to travel to Azcapotzalco and formally subject themselves to the Tepaneca. They convinced the priests who attended their god Huitzilopochtli to prepare to relocate the image there—the ultimate subjugation and demoralization—as they made ready to move in among their enemies. Even King Itzcoatl was apparently willing to go along with the plan—that is, until his nephew Tlacaelel spoke up: "What is this, O Mexica? What are you doing? You have lost your wits. . . . Are you such cowards that you feel you must take shelter in Azcapotzalco?"[77] He implored the king to reconsider, to think of Mexica honor. Itzcoatl then reportedly asked for a volunteer to travel to meet with fractious Maxtlaton and negotiate a peaceful accord between the two altepetl. With no one willing to participate, Tlacaelel stepped forward, and with a display of bravura, knowing well that he might die, promised to deliver Itzcoatl's message.[78] The king responded with gratitude:

If you undertake this task, I promise to reward you with generous gifts and to make you one of the leading men in my kingdom. And if you die in this mission your children will receive these favors. You will be remembered eternally for this brave act because you will die for your country and be the honor of [the Mexica] people.[79]

Employing great cunning, Tlacaelel managed to get behind enemy lines not once but twice, which impressed the Tepaneca ruler, who assured him safe passage at one point. Durán, whose account of these events is richest, does not identify the Azcapotzalco king. The annals, though, are clear that Tlacaelel was dealing with the brutal and ruthless Maxtlaton. But nothing could be done to avert a war, and Tlacaelel warned the king of his fate by giving him the symbolic pitch, feathers, shield, and arrows, following Mexica conventions of war. As Tlacaelel departed Azcapotzalco, he stopped to taunt the guards, who had no idea how he had managed to get past them.[80] Alvarado Tezozomoc furnishes the response upon Tlacaelel's return: "Señores mexicanos, qué es la causa que bosotros no queréis [que] bamos en poder y suxeçión y dominio de los tepanecas en Azcapulçalco?"[81] War against the Tepaneca was now inevitable. Alvarado Tezozomoc confirms that Tlacaelel already held the title "Atenpanecatl" and identified him as such thereafter but never furnished an explanation of the title's significance.[82] It is described elsewhere as "an executioner," but it is not clear if the office related to the practice of human sacrifice.

The Mexica commoners, still not appeased, asked Itzcoatl what would become of them if the Mexica were not victorious against Azcapotzalco. Itzcoatl and his nobles responded, "We shall place ourselves in your hands so that our flesh will become your nourishment." If the Mexica lords were successful, the commoners in turn were to respect and serve them in any capacity needed.[83] But the Mexica prepared for war as best they could and met their foes at Xoconochnopaltitlan. The Tepaneca were in full battle regalia, "carrying shields with insignia richly done in gold, silver, jewels, and feathers, and with splendidly adorned emblems upon their backs," according to Durán. Tlacaelel, as commander of the Mexica's forces, with fearless disregard planned his battle strategy to maximize Mexica effectiveness. Tlatoani Itzcoatl was also in the field and sounded the drum, which unleashed the fury of the Mexica. Tlacaelel led the attack and forced their enemies' retreat to Azcapotzalco, where they laid siege to the city, sparing no one. Tlacaelel drove his warriors hard until the Tepaneca were utterly defeated. "This was done with no pity but with the greatest cruelty in the world. Not a house was left standing, not a man, woman, or child was left alive."[84] As Chimalpahin noted, "Tlacaelel remained master of the field."[85]

The Mexica benefited enormously from the newly acquired land, subjects, and booty. From the Tepaneca who had fled and thus survived, they were promised land and service, including stone, lime, wood, and a variety of foodstuffs. Regarding the land, the most valuable went to the king, his brothers, and his nephews. Tlacaelel received ten pieces scattered across the realm, for he was credited with the conquest. The other nobles received two parcels each, and the most valiant of the commoners were also given plots of land. Calpolli as well received land, which was to be dedicated to the provisioning of their deities.[86] It was a division of the spoils that was soon institutionalized to the obvious benefit of Tlacaelel and the tlatoque. Durán states that thereafter there was to be no ruler in Azcapotzalco and that allegiance was to be to the Mexica Tenochca tlatoani.[87]

Maxtlaton, or the sitting king of Coyoacan, was not to be undone and sent a man to spy and see if the Mexica were ready to attack.[88] With no such sign, he switched tactics and consulted with his nephew, Tlacateotl, the tlatoani of Tlatelolco, and together they hosted a banquet, inviting guests from across central Mexico as well as from Huexotzinco and Michoacan. Tlacateotl had negotiated the Tlatelolca's tribute requirement with Maxtlaton and, receiving a favorable outcome, joined sides with the Tepaneca. Nevertheless, he was dead within the year, killed by his new cohort.[89] The two rulers had even invited the Tenochca and gifted everyone with exquisite quetzal feathers and maguey skirts and shifts.[90] Durán adds that Tlacaelel attended the feast but would not permit Itzcoatl to go. Exuding both caution and Mexica pride, Tlacaelel told his king:

> Lord, we do not want you to go to these festivities, partly because it is not proper that you condescend to a minor chieftain—it would lower the dignity of your majesty and that of the kingdom of Tenochtitlan, and partly because we do not know why this feast is being celebrated.

In fact, we would not go without weapons of defense, in case they decide to attack us treacherously.[91]

Tlacaelel and his men brought quantities of gifts, following protocol, and they were served delicious food while being entertained with song and dance. But instead of being given flowers at the end of the festivities, as was expected, fray Diego states that in spite of the Mexica's disdain for their hosts, they were forced to wear the women's clothing that had been given to them, the intention being their humiliation. But the actual significance is ambiguous here, since Tlacaelel not long thereafter began to wear with aplomb the female attire of Cihuacoatl, the deity that he was to represent, and it became his signature dress once he formally assumed his legendary political title and office of the Cihuacoatl.

The Mexica, though, were not to be bested by the Tepaneca and retaliated with no end of subversive activities to debase and intimidate their foes.[92] It was all a prelude to another war. Fully aware of the Tepaneca's animosity, Itzcoatl discreetly planned to avenge the death of his nephew, Chimalpopoca. Despite the stigma of his birth, Itzcoatl had proved himself a stalwart statesman, and he had the support of the Tetzcoca in the person of his nephew, Nezahualcoyotl, whose late father, King Ixtlilxochitl (r. 1410–18), had been married to Itzcoatl's sister.[93] Ixtlilxochitl had been killed by the Chalca and the Tepaneca, and his son Nezahualcoyotl, hidden nearby in a tree, had witnessed his death.[94]

Magnanimously, Durán repeatedly claimed that the Mexica themselves never initiated a war: "It is admirable that in all the wars in this land [the Mexica] never provoked anyone; they were always provoked and incited to fight by others."[95] But the Mexica already had military titles, such as the Tlacateccatl and the Tlacochcalcatl, which signified a martial mentality and operation already in place. Doubtless it was their gradual but increasing battlefield encounters with other altepetl that had been cause for Tepaneca militancy since the Mexica had first entered their territory.

In Coyoacan, the Tepaneca, arguably naturally aggressive, were on the alert as well as fearful of the possibility that they too might lose their land and sovereignty. Their tlatoani, Maxtlaton, who obviously fled Azcapotzalco after its defeat and returned to Coyoacan, made overtures to other major altepetl to urge them to join the Coyoaque and the Colhuaque to fight the Mexica.[96] To his surprise, several refused to participate. Nevertheless, representatives from the many polities decided to meet in Chalco to deliberate, with each expressing an opinion and then listening to the decision of its two rulers, Cuateotl (or Quateotl) and Toteociteuctli. The principal Amecameca king, Cuateotl, though, wise and eloquent in his address, reminded the delegation that many of them were relatives of the Mexica who had a powerful deity and that war and subjugation would be costly, difficult, and improbable. He added, "He who has a toothache must take out his own tooth. . . . And so, Tepaneca, my opinion is that you should wage your own war by yourselves, and each one here do what is most convenient for him. Take your problem in your own hands, provoke the Mexica, there you will have your war; we do not wish to be involved." Refusing to participate in the Tepaneca's warmongering, the king of Amecameca, Chalco, spoke for all the nobles assembled before him.[97] The mighty league of altepetl under Tepaneca sway had been compromised and would subsequently—largely through conquest—be brought into the Mexica orbit of influence and success.

Amecameca and Chalco figure prominently in this history of Tlacaelel, in part because it was Chimalpahin's home and in part because Chalco enjoyed wide influence as an autonomous, wealthy, and powerful polity. Chimalpahin, unsurprisingly, compiled a complete history of Amecameca and nearly as much for Chalco, and he gives long lists of all the kings for each polity, traced from their founding to the time he was writing in the seventeenth century.[98] However, it appears that Durán's source confused the kings of Amecameca, Acxotlan Chalco, and Tlalmanalco. Acxotlan, seemingly the first altepetl to be established in the territory of Chalco, later came to be a part of Tlalmanalco and thus the dominant polity in the four-part altepetl federation, although Chimalpahin was always reluctant to admit that his own Amecameca was second to Tlalmanalco. In Acxotlan, Toteociteuctli was serving as tlatoani from 1407 until 1446, and a noblewoman from his court, "itecpanchan," married Tlacaelel's son. He very likely did serve as host of the gathering in Amecameca.[99] And as far back as 1341–56, a Quateotzin the Tlatquicteuctli ruled Itzcahuacan Tlacochcalco, the second-ranking Tlalmanalco altepetl in Chalco. Twenty-five years later a Quateotzin Miccacalcatl (r. 1381–84) was tlatoani of both Itzcahuacan and

Opochhuacan Tlacochcalco (Tlalmanalco). Finally, in 1413, Quateotzin the younger the Tlatquicteuctli assumed the rulership of Itzcahuacan, and it was this king who surely served as spokesman for the large group of nobles congregated in Amecameca. It was his speech that did so much to enhance the standing not only of the people of Amecameca but also of the Mexica. It is illustrative of a healthy respect on the part of the Mexica for the Chalca but likewise confounds their horrific treatment of them some forty years later.[100] Chimalpahin dutifully included a ranked list of all the nobles who came to Amecameca for the deliberations. They assembled at the home of Ayo-quanteuctli.[101] It is assumed that most of the rulers traveled in quite splendid entourages by canoe through the lakes' channels to be able to participate at the various meetings as well as the military encounters.[102]

With the help of Nezahualcoyotl of Tetzcoco and other allies, the Me-xica had pursued the Coyoaque, even capturing their *nahualli*, "sorcerer." Maxtlaton wept upon learning of the loss (*niman ye choca yn Maxtlaton*). Following up with additional Mexica victories in the field, the annals state that Maxtlaton wept again and then fled to Tlachco, where he mysteriously disappeared along with some of his soothsayers (*teyolloquanime*).[105] In a final act of submission, the Coyoaque said, "We will cultivate your fields and

Always vigilant, Tlacaelel personally investigated the surrounding reeds and rushes in the nearby lake's marshes to monitor the Coyoaque's preparations for war. In doing so, he encountered and recruited three rogue Colhuaque warriors to serve as his aides in battle. Coyoacan fell quickly, and certain Mexica wanted revenge for having been forced to wear women's clothing. But some clemency was granted to survivors this time. Durán adds that Tlacaelel and his Colhuaque aides, knowing well the Mexica reward system, devised a method to count their captives: they cut a lock of hair from each one and thus were able to demonstrate that they had taken twice the number of prisoners, compared with the other warriors.[103] Maxtlaton, infu-riated at the loss of Coyoacan, marshaled his remaining soldiers and sought revenge at Azcapotzalco, his own Tepaneca, killing the king and men of the court. Doubtless, Itzcoatl had left what remained of the ruling hierarchy of Azcapotzalco intact to ensure efficient government and allegiance. The murders brought an end to the Azcapotzalco's traditional tlatocayotl, and the altepetl never regained its preeminence in Tenochca history.[104]

we will build your houses," and they delivered maguey skirts, huipiles, and loincloths, along with precious stones (*chalchiuitl*) and a little gold, to begin to satisfy their tribute obligations. The year was Four Reed, 1431.[106]

By now, Tlacaelel, according to Durán, was thought by the Mexica to be "almost like the Redeemer of Tenochtitlan as Joseph was [to the Pharaoh of Egypt]," and Itzcoatl wanted to reward him. After taking the royal share of Coyoacan's bounty for the court, Tlacaelel was given eleven pieces of land, and the nobles received one, two, or three shares, depending on their contributions on the battlefield.[107] Tlacaelel, though, believed that the bravest warriors deserved additional recognition and asked King Itzcoatl to consider granting them official titles. By this gesture, social mobility was ensured while creating and expanding a true and patriotic Mexica upper class. The king was eager to comply, and the voluble Tlacaelel announced the good news: "Friends and brothers, your lord and sovereign King Itzcoatl, my close relative and yours, greets you and wishes to honor you according to your merits. He wishes to give you preeminence, award you titles, as well as distribute among you lands that will support you and your families; for this is your right."[108]

Twenty-one ranked titles were granted, and, according to Durán, with each title came a given quantity of tribute and service. Four men, with the respective offices of the Tlacochcalcatl, the Tlacateccatl, the Ezhuahuacatl, and the Tlilancalqui, became members of the king's royal council and served as advisers and judges. Tlacaelel became the Tlacochcalcatl, and his brother, Moteuczoma Ilhuicamina, was granted the second-in-rank office of the Tlacateccatl.[109] Itzcoatl also ordered that the officers' portraits be carved in stone (at Chapoltepec, presumably), and the scribes were to record their accomplishments in their books.

The three Colhuaque aides who had served Tlacaelel so ably in the battle for Coyoacan spoke up. They had been denied their share when the land and tribute were allocated, and Tlacaelel agreed, asking Itzcoatl for titles for the three men as well as for two Mexica warriors who had accompanied them. "In return for their services," he said, "they deserve titles so that they can be known as noblemen."[110] A total of twenty-six titles were conferred. Alvarado Tezozomoc adds, "and so then by his order Tlacaelel first began [to be] principal."[111] Locking in their privileges (including his own) was an extraordinary strategy to recruit warriors and foster their loyalty, institutionalize as well as delineate the royal bureaucracy, and of course exalt Itzcoatl's rulership. The fusion of militarism and government had Tlacaelel's signature.

The Mexica, according to Durán, had already settled back into familiar routines, aiming to maintain affable relations with their neighbors. Women went to the markets, as was their custom, and trade continued as usual. But the Xochimilca were angry about the destruction of Coyoacan and worried that the same would happen to them. Two rulers met with the nobles of their altepetl, and all agreed that they would never "sweep the houses or water the gardens of the [Mexica], or be mistreated or serve them water to wash their hands."[112] They began to prepare for war. They decided to meet and have a banquet, buying fish and fowl from Mexica market women. But as they began to eat, to their horror their food turned into human body parts, everything from head and hands to hearts and intestines. It was surely an omen of death and destruction for the Xochimilca. Yet they were not deterred.

The Mexica, reportedly unaware of any animosity on the part of the Xochimilca, decided that work needed to be done on a temple for Huitzilopochtli, and envoys were sent to Xochimilco to request large stones and white pine wood. Not being subjects of the Mexica, the Xochimilca were outraged that anyone would presume that they might comply. The Mexica messengers returned to Mexico Tenochtitlan empty-handed, and their king, Itzcoatl, retaliated by boycotting all travel and trade with Xochimilco. However, some time later a convoy of Mexica traders bearing cotton was attacked while returning with their cargo from Quauhnahuac. The Xochimilca robbed and beat the Mexica merchants. Itzcoatl took his revenge by denuding Xochimilco milpas and brutalizing anyone who tried to prevent the Mexica from doing so. Then Itzcoatl and Tlacaelel made one final attempt to sue for peace, but their ministers were turned back, unable to deliver their message to the ruler of Xochimilco.[113]

With no alternative, then, Tlacaelel gathered his most formidable warriors in Teyacac, rallied them with praise, and took them to the field at Ocolco. The Mexica knew that the Xochimilca greatly outnumbered them, for theirs was an altepetl of vast resources and territory. Durán recorded that the Xochimilca were strikingly beautiful as they went into battle: "The gold, jewels, precious stones, and plumes they carried on their weapons, insignia, and shields were so splendid that they shone in the sun as they reflected its rays. What a spectacle it was! Weapons of many colors: green, blue, red, yellow, black, multicolored."[114]

Exhilarated, Tlacaelel prevailed, performing "marvelous feats" while destroying the barricades constructed by the Xochimilca to protect their homes. "The Mexica's darts and arrows were so numerous that they darkened the sun." He spurred his men on: "Hail, my valiant [Mexica], victory is ours. Do not tire yourselves overmuch. Let them die little by little and let perish those who unjustly wished to destroy us."[115] With their defensive obstacles gone, the Xochimilca rulers surrendered, asking the Mexica to think of the elderly and the children, who should be spared. They promised delivery of the coveted stones and white pine, their servitude, and their domain. Normally, the Mexica would have plundered the altepetl, the treasure a part of their reward. But Tlacaelel had something else in mind, and he refused his men, sending them back to Mexico Tenochtitlan without compensation, much to their dismay. Rather than destroy an altepetl that would only have to be rebuilt and repopulated, he refrained and ordered that the Xochimilca build a sturdy causeway of stone and earth "three *brazas* wide" all the way to Mexico Tenochtitlan.[116] It would cross the lake and furnish an invaluable means of travel between and beyond the two polities. With their conquest of Xochimilco, the Mexica had made formidable headway into the chinampa-lake district, essentially the breadbasket of the Mexica heartland. The year was Three Rabbit, 1430.[117]

Upon the completion of the causeway, the Mexica finally went to collect their due. They were feted with food, feathers, flowers, mantas, and jewelry, in addition to song and dance. Regarding the Xochimilca's land, after the royal share and Tlacaelel's, each lord and warrior was granted two plots of land, four hundred varas each, with common soldiers who had distinguished themselves also receiving a portion. The Xochimilca were devastated by their loss, and as a conciliatory gesture Itzcoatl invited the king of Xochimilco to join his royal council and dine at his table.[118] Xochimilco, along with Colhuacan, had been among the first and most commanding of the founding altepetl in central Mexico. The Mexica, as lackeys of the Colhuaque, had fought Xochimilco more than a century earlier. But now Xochimilco was to become a vital part of Mexica imperial sprawl.

Still always the aggrieved, according to Durán, the Mexica were then antagonized by the Cuitlahuaca, who were also agitating for war. Itzcoatl got wind of it, and to be certain he and Tlacaelel sent messengers to invite Xochitl Olinqui, the ruler of Cuitlahuac, to come to a feast. The tlatoani was to bring the nobles of his court and all the young maiden women, who were to dance before the Mexica and entertain everyone. Livid at the presumptuousness of the Mexica, Xochitl Olinqui sent messengers to convey his response: "rresolutamente no quiere obedeçer uuestro mandamiento." Durán explained, adding that the king said, "I respect the virgins of my city too highly, even those of the lowest rank, to send them at his command as the playthings of his god. . . . Neither on this occasion nor on any other shall I obey him." He sent the messengers back to Mexico Tenochtitlan, without either food or gifts for Itzcoatl and Tlacaelel, requisites of diplomatic protocol. Itzcoatl ordered his envoys to return, giving Xochitl Olinqui another chance, but they were rebuffed. Thus, another war was to be launched, and Itzcoatl mollified his subjects, saying, "They will fall like birds into a net."[119]

The Cuitlahuaca, being islanders, believed that they would have the advantage, since the Mexica typically fought their battles on land. The Mexica worried only that Chalco, a neighbor and a part of the chinampa agricultural district, might be drawn in to support Cuitlahuac, which would be a problem for them. Chalco was a large, confederated altepetl with abundant resources, an ample population, and a reputation of military strength. As recently as Eleven Rabbit, 1438, Nezahualcoyotl, ruler of Tetzcoco, had gone to Chalco to ask the tlatoque for assistance against the Tepaneca, and Moteuczoma Ilhuicamina the Tlacateccatl even went there in Thirteen Flint, 1440, for aid, because, it was said, Mexico Tenochtitlan was in great danger and at risk of disappearing.[120] But after receiving assurances from Chalco that they knew nothing of any plan on the part of the Cuitlahuaca, Itzcoatl, to further humiliate his foe, ordered Tlacaelel to form an army of boys and young men to demonstrate that Mexica novices alone could conquer Cuitlahuac. The boys trained and were outfitted with "quilted cotton armor, lances, arrows, swords, and shields." A thousand canoes delivered them with backup warriors to the island.

The Cuitlahuaca met them on foot at the shore and in their festooned canoes. They were in full battle array, perhaps one last public display of the grandeur of their altepetl:

The men were richly dressed and armed with fine weapons, and the rowers were also handsomely attired with feathers and great shields. The warriors were well armed and their weapons were covered with white, red, yellow, blue, green, black, and multicolored plumes. On their heads and backs were elaborate feather ornaments. From their necks hung many ornaments of gold inlaid with jewels. On their arms were wristbands of shining gold, on their ankles gold bands like short gold stockings. All these things covered them from head to foot and it was as if they were meant to give a final touch to the splendor of the weapons.[121]

The Mexica boys were brave and omnipresent in battle, and the luckless Cuitlahuaca, as they were losing, resorted to supplicating the god of the water and of the creatures that surrounded their island, but to no avail. Canoes, bodies, and weapons floated in the lake waters. Xochitl Olinqui, realizing that all was lost, approached Tlacaelel, "knowing that he was a merciful man," and surrendered.[122] The Mexica were triumphant again, and the warriors stripped the bodies, weapons, and canoes, taking the treasure for themselves. Tlacaelel was then feted at the Cuitlahuac palace, and he sent his men home, where they told Itzcoatl of their good news. There was little in the way of land in Cuitlahuac to benefit the Mexica, but tribute and service would be theirs, and Cuitlahuaca maidens would finally come to Mexico Tenochtitlan to dance before the gods. The rulers of all the conquered altepetl subsequently came to Mexico Tenochtitlan to acknowledge and render obedience to Itzcoatl and to Tlacaelel, and all "remained members of Mexico's council forever until Captain don Hernando Cortés came."[123]

Itzcoatl was ill at the time, but he rejoiced upon receiving word of another victory. His condition worsened, however, and although he was soon moribund, he had unfinished business. First, he summoned his nephew Nezahualcoyotl from Tetzcoco and told him to refrain from making war on the Mexica. The annals state that in Four Reed, 1431, the Mexica had fought the Tetzcoca for only half a day before Nezahualcoyotl surrendered.[124] Durán credits Itzcoatl with forming the triumvirate at this time, which placed Nezahualcoyotl as the second-in-rank king and the ruler of Tlacopan as the tertiary ruler. "Only those three kings ruled the land from that time on, but the ruler of Tenochtitlan over all the others, like an emperor of the New World."[125] The tripartite model replicated that of the Colhuaque seven centuries earlier. Second, Itzcoatl asked that a magnificent temple in honor of Huitzilopochtli be built by his successor, capitalizing on the material and human resources that had been won and brought into Mexica dominions during his rule. Third and finally, he asked that his likeness be carved in stone, again most likely alongside the other royal sculptures at Chapoltepec. Itzcoatl died in Thirteen Flint, 1440. His funeral ceremony lasted eighty days, with the traditional solemnities, feasting, and gifting.[126]

Chimalpahin had glowing commendation for Itzcoatl:

> In war he conquered those of Azcapotzalco, Tlacopan, Atlacuihuayan, Coyoacan, Xochimilco, Cuitlahuac, Mizquic, Tetzcoco, and Quauhnahuac. . . . This Itzcoatl was the last king who governed Mexico Tenochtitlan and its first emperor. He was so excellent a man that there is not sufficient language for his praises, and so his name has been and will be perpetually celebrated in this city. . . . But though these accomplishments are much to be praised, what is the most important of all his works and what is most worthy of perpetual praise is his having exalted for a long time his lineage to such a high degree of glory through his nephew, the great captain Tlacaelel, son of his brother Huitzilihuitl.[127]

Regarding Tlacaelel and his military success, Chimalpahin exclaims: "Tlacaelel then came as the most powerful, feared, and esteemed man of all that the world had seen up to that time, having subdued and conquered the greater part of it with little army or force of arms in the same length of time, it seems that [any] other leader could cover in many a day of marching. . . . This was the origin of the emperors."[128]

❀

Durán believed that the Mexica were always the victims of unwanted aggression on the part of other polities. Yet the annals, though sketchy, tell of a people long familiar with warfare and other sorts of brutalities. As they traveled from place to place before settling at Mexico Tenochtitlan, their deity Huitzilopochtli, who had been with the Mexica since they departed

Chicomoztoc, not only furnished guidance and support but also set the standard for fiendish atrocities, such as matricide, decapitation, and cannibalism. Already traveling with bows, arrows, spears, atlatl, net carrying-bags, and shields, they were prepared to defend themselves when necessary.[129]

Mexica activities in and around estimable Colhuacan are probably the best known, and early on, when they were forced to live at mountainous, snake-infested Tiçaapan, they adapted and ate the snakes. Then, after currying the favor of the king of Colhuacan, they killed and cannibalized his daughter, to the man's horror.[130] By Three Reed, 1323, they were already sacrificing people, supposedly to use the hearts to supply an earthen mound, in all likelihood a makeshift temple.[131] A flower war with Chalco followed, with the Chalca being defeated, and "all the Mexica were killed" along with the Itztapallapaneca.[132] Now, in spite of fray Diego's tender denials, there is every indication that the Mexica were conditioned for warfare and that the timing was optimal, with the Tepaneca no longer a menace, for Tlacaelel and Moteuczoma Ilhuicamina to set about augmenting the estate of Mexico Tenochtitlan and creating a grander life for their people. Unfortunately, Chimalpahin's beloved Chalco would be among the victims of Mexica imperial prowess and progress.

CHAPTER 3

THE QUINTESSENTIAL ALTEPETL AND A GOLDEN AGE

❀

There were such vast quantities of all these things that
    came to the city of Mexico that not a day passed
    without the arrival of people from other regions who
    brought large amounts of everything, from foodstuffs
    to luxury items, for the king and the lords.

Durán

Moteuczoma Ilhuicamina was ruling with his older brother
    Tlacaelel the Cihuacoatl. Together they decided matters
    of war and who was condemned to die.

Chimalpahin

The great captain Tlacaeleltzin to his greater advantage
    had himself named perpetual Cihuacoatl of Mexico . . .
    that is, president of the supreme council of the Mexica
    Empire, and chief judge, and also king or emperor like
    his brother, though not with the [same] high title or
    lordship as that of his brother Huehue Moteuczoma.

Chimalpahin

[Moteuczoma Ilhuicamina to Tlacaelel]: "Brother Tlacaelel, I
    am well pleased with these images! They [the sculptures]
    will remain as a perpetual memorial to our greatness, in
    the way we remember Quetzalcoatl and Topiltzin."

Durán

MOTEUCZOMA ILHUICAMINA: PEACE AND WAR

Tlacaelel's brother, Moteuczoma Ilhuicamina Chalchiuhtlatonac Quetzaltecolotl the Tlacateccatl, was installed as the fifth tlatoani of Mexico Tenochtitlan in Thirteen Flint, 1440. He is more commonly known as Moteuczoma Ilhuicamina or Huehue Moteuczoma (Moteuczoma the elder). Durán states that it was policy to select the kings of Mexico Tenochtitlan from the Council of Four but added that it was of course necessary that one belong to the official royal lineage. In this instance, Moteuczoma Ilhuicamina was the son of Huitzilihuitl the younger and the nephew of Itzcoatl, the second and fourth tlatoque, respectively. His pedigree could not be better. Upon assuming the throne, Moteuczoma relinquished his office and title of the Tlacateccatl, and a different person was appointed in his stead.[1] The many rulers who had so recently been in Mexico Tenochtitlan for the funeral of Itzcoatl returned to the capital, this time for a royal inauguration and a more festive occasion, although not without bringing their obligatory splendid presents for the new king. He could expect "rich cloth, weapons, insignia, shields, fine feathers, and jewels, as well as other riches," which served to flatter the ruler while displaying the wealth and magnanimity of the gifter.[2]

The renowned Nezahualcoyotl Acolmiztli Yoyontzin, tlatoani of Tetzcoco (r. 1431–72), was among the celebrants, and, after consulting his Tetzcoca nobles and advising them never to do anything to antagonize the Mexica, he requested an audience with Moteuczoma Ilhuicamina. Tetzcoca histories consistently exalt Nezahualcoyotl, and he has long been admired for his royal court with its libraries and gardens as well as his accomplishments as a statesman, poet, and engineer.[3] Mexica histories, on the other hand, suggest that Nezahualcoyotl was indeed important but more as a subordinate and ally. Accordingly, Tetzcoco and its kings are always at the ready, but exactly why it mattered is obscure.

At their meeting, after delivering the most precious of gifts, Nezahualcoyotl reportedly flattered the king with edifying praise: "You well know, great prince, that all your subjects, nobles as well as the common people, are under your shade for you have been planted here like a great cedar tree under which men wish to rest in order to take pleasure in the freshness of your friendship and love."[4] Nezahualcoyotl then asked that a permanent peace accord be established between the two altepetl: "I . . . beseech you, implore you, for clemency. Preserve us in peace and concord; at no time allow your people to attack us. . . . Therefore, I beg of you to receive my people as children and servants, but without war, without a quarrel."[5]

In Nahua central Mexico, Nezahualcoyotl was second in authority only to Moteuczoma Ilhuicamina, as Tetzcoco was a rich and formidable polity in its own right. Nezahualcoyotl wanted no battles, no ruin of his altepetl. Moteuczoma was said to be very pleased with the proposition. After all, the two kings were contemporaries, although Nezahualcoyotl ruled for a longer period.[6] Both dynasties derived from the same founding mother, and over the generations the familial ties were reinforced for social and political advantage by interdynastic marriages.[7] Even the Tlacaelels maintained marital alliances with the Tetzcoca royal house (fig. 15).[8] Moteuczoma Ilhuicamina brought Nezahualcoyotl's proposal for a harmonious accord to his council. Tlacaelel, always vainglorious and serving as the spokesperson for the council, was adamantly opposed to the notion of peace and instead insisted on clandestine mock battles with the Tetzcoca in their home territory—complete with full military array in the field—to be followed by mock

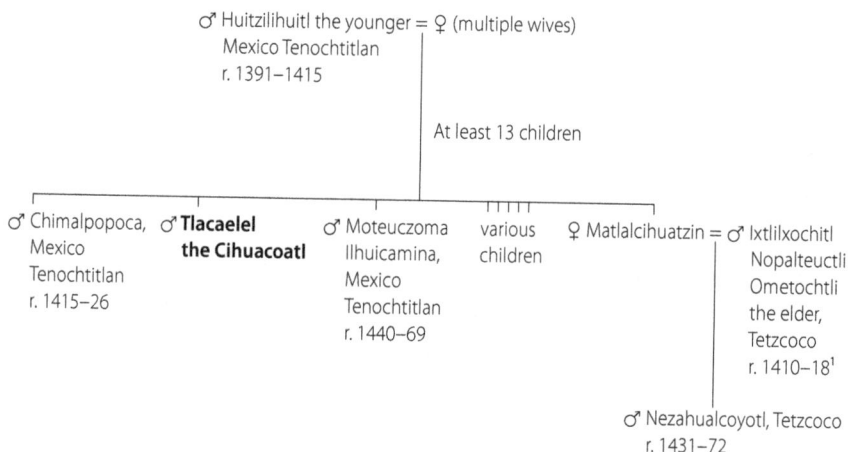

FIG. 15. Early Mexica Tenochca and Tetzcoca family ties.
Copyright © 2016, University of Oklahoma Press.

Boldface indicates which of Tlacaelel the elder's descendants became the Cihuacoatl.
1. CC 1:45; DC 2:75.

defeat and ritual submission. The climax was to be Nezahualcoyotl's torching of his own temple. Tlacaelel was concerned, he said, that other polities would consider the Mexica weak or, worse, that they too would come forward with similar propositions, which would be unthinkable and impracticable since there would be no fighting, death, and destruction, denying the Mexica further opportunities to add to their bounty of land, subjects, and magnificent treasure. Worth noting are Tlacaelel's political and economic motives and no mention of any religious prerogatives at this time.

Durán adds that although Nezahualcoyotl was unhappy, the Mexica and Tetzcoca were able to carry out the mock battles and conquest with no one the wiser. The Tetzcoca did indeed have to fully engage in the simulated conflict, and Nezahualcoyotl promised that his people would wear "the yoke of servitude forever."[9] According to fray Diego, Nezahualcoyotl's compliance "simply shows the love he had for the [Mexica]."[10] But the portrayal of Nezahualcoyotl, tlatoani of Tetzcoco, as a feckless king was more likely the creature of Mexica authorship, especially since Sahagún claimed that together with Itzcoatl, he "conquered the Tepaneca, and they conquered people everywhere."[11] Nevertheless, it seems that Tlacaelel had the last word: "Lord, we are thankful for what you have done to preserve peace between us and your province. But perhaps in the future your subjects will be offended and will not want to accept what has taken place. They may regret that their strength and valor were not tested, and when we ask favors of you they may say they are not our vassals and do not wish to serve us. I warn you of this now."[12]

To make matters worse, the Tetzcoca were required to relinquish land, and Moteuczoma, Tlacaelel, and other nobles, as was customary, were quick to collect their due.[13] Although bloodless, this first war for Moteuczoma and Tlacaelel augured what lay ahead: even a diplomatic appeal for peace could bring on war. Nezahualcoyotl, though, tried to stay true and neutral when the opportunity arose, a few years later, to take revenge on the Tenochca by siding with the Tlatelolca: "I stand on both sides. If all are to be endangered because of the lord of the Mexica Tenochca, I shall go in favor of the lord of Tlatelolco. But if all are endangered because of the lord of Tlatelolco, I shall go in favor of the lord of the Mexica Tenochca."[14] But more likely Nezahualcoyotl no longer had a choice, and later, when King Axayacatzin declared war on Moquihuix, ruler of Tlatelolco, in Seven House, 1473, the triumvirate prevailed. "Then the Tenochca and the lord of Tlacopan, the ruler Chimalpopoca, and the ruler of Tetzcoco, Nezahualcoyotl, set forth."[15]

The Nahuatl annals are silent regarding the valiant and noble Nezahualcoyotl swallowing his pride and acquiescing to the fictitious war, both to curry the favor of Moteuczoma Ilhuicamina, and, likely more important, to bolster the pretensions of Tlacaelel the Cihuacoatl. Rather, they state that earlier, under Itzcoatl, the Mexica and Tetzcoca had fought but only for half a day because Nezahualcoyotl surrendered.[16] On another occasion, though, the annals state that Nezahualcoyotl could indeed be aggressive, as when he led Tetzcoca forces in battle and conquered Tollantzinco in Ten Rabbit, 1450.[17] And when the rulers of the conquered altepetl of Tlacopan, Coyoacan, Xochimilco, and Cuitlahuac "came to Mexico to render obedience and acknowledge King Itzcoatl and Tlacaeleltzin as their masters," Nezahualcoyotl "wished no wars: he himself came to Mexico to render obedience in the name of his city to his kinsman Itzcoatzin and to his uncle Tlacaeleltzin (his mother's brother)."[18] Nezahualcoyotl was the first among many who visited Mexico Tenochtitlan as Itzcoatl lay dying, and it was at this time that Itzcoatl officially declared that the king of Tetzcoco would thereafter be second in rank to the tlatoani of Mexico Tenochtitlan, with the ruler of Tlacopan third, thereby institutionalizing the triumvirate.[19] In all probability, Moteuczoma Ilhuicamina and Tlacaelel were using the esteemed Nezahualcoyotl as a test case and then exemplary model as they strategized Mexica alliances and warfare in order to add to their realm.

TAKING CHALCO

Durán states that after the staged submission of Nezahualcoyotl and Tetzcoco, the Mexica experienced twelve to thirteen years of tranquility. He attributes the peaceful period to the fact that their subjects were paying their tribute and working more or less to the satisfaction of the Mexica rulers.[20] The annals, though, show ongoing warfare, with "Oztoman destroyed" in Two Rabbit, 1442.[21] The next year Moteuczoma Ilhuicamina took his campaign to Tlalmanalco Itztompatepec in Chalco and "laid waste to the land," and three years later Tlahco, Chapulicxitlan, and Teticpac were conquered.[22]

But in Six Rabbit, 1446, *yn tzintic huey yaoyotl Chalco*, "the great war began in Chalco." For twenty years, it was said, Chalco and Mexico Tenochtitlan had been isolated from each other. Chalco was closed, no Mexica could travel there, and likewise no Chalca could go to Mexico Tenochtitlan.[23] In Amecameca, the Mexica began to conquer the fringe altepetl, laying waste to Panohuayan first (in Three Flint, 1456) and slowly working their way to Itztlacoçauhcan, the principal altepetl, which finally fell in Eleven Flint, 1464. The Mexica ascended to the top of Mount Amaqueme and symbolically shot their arrows into the temples of the Itztlacoçauhque and Tzaqualtitlan Tenanca.[24]

The Chalca had suffered catastrophic loss even earlier, however, for there had been an invasion of grasshoppers (*chapoltin*) in Six Rabbit, 1446, that consumed all the maize and caused a famine, an event Chimalpahin steadfastly corroborates: "*ynin nelli*," "This is the truth."[25] The annals add that the Chalca also rebelled at that time. Then there was a terrible hailstorm and freeze that destroyed the crops, beginning in Ten Rabbit, 1450. For five years there was nothing to harvest, and in Amecameca, Chimalpahin reports that boys and girls were dying everywhere. Everyone's skin was "wrinkled like an old person's because of their hunger," and coyotes and *zopilotes* were eating the dead. The survivors sold themselves as slaves.[26] Three years into the famine, war between Chalco and Mexico Tenochtitlan began "definitively." Two years later, in Two Reed, 1455, plentiful rain and good harvests finally came. Nevertheless, a *cocoliztli*, "sickness," continued, and Chalco was conquered for the first time.[27] To make matters worse, there was an infestation of great numbers of rats.[28]

Obviously, the Chalca were not the only ones suffering deprivation. Durán reported on the effects of the famine in Mexico Tenochtitlan, and it is one of the few instances when he furnished a date. He stated that the year was One Rabbit, 1454, and that for two years there was a drought so severe that the Mexica and many others were starving.[29] Those who could left the capital and relocated to places where there was food and no suffering, some never to return. Some people sold themselves into slavery, for altepetl with plenty had no reservations about selling their stores of comestibles to purchase people for their personal use. Moteuczoma Ilhuicamina and Tlacaelel consulted with each other and did what they could to provide for those in the capital. They requisitioned grain from altepetl such as Chalco, Tetzcoco, and Xochimilco—note that Durán has Chalco paying tribute even though it would not be conquered for many years. But here and elsewhere, fray Diego's chronology and sequencing are off. At the beginning of the famine, the granaries in the capital were full, and Tlacaelel urged the king to process the grain and feed their people. Canoes filled with maize dough and gruel, for example, were to come to Mexico Tenochtitlan each day. With the maize dough, large tamales, the "size of a man's head," were to be distributed to the poor, and children were to be given large bowls of gruel. Unfortunately, the Cihuacoatl's goodwill gesture was brought up short when the grain ran out after a year. With no food for his people, Moteuczoma Ilhuicamina ordered that each man be given a cloak and loincloth and each woman a blouse and skirt. The Mexica thanked their king, wept, and said that they would sell their children as slaves so that at least they would survive.[30] Even so, King Moteuczoma Ilhuicamina made certain to share what there was of the tribute with his grandchildren, the future emperors, Axayacatl, Tizoc, and Ahuitzotl. Axayacatl's older sister, Chalchiuhnenetzin, the wife-to-be of Moquihuix, king of Tlatelolco, the said cause for the war and destruction between the two Mexica dynasties, also received her share from her munificent grandfather.[31]

However, life in some ways continued in the capital, as King Nezahualcoyotl directed the construction of an aqueduct from Chapoltepec to Mexico Tenochtitlan at Moteuczoma Ilhuicamina's behest in One Rabbit, 1454. The next year at Huixachtecatl the Mexica celebrated the tying of their years (*ypan in toxiuh molpilli*) for the sixth time.

Possibly because things were going relatively well for the Mexica and possibly because his uncle Itzcoatl had requested it before he died, Moteuczoma Ilhuicamina resolved to begin the renovation of the temple for Huitzilopochtli. Durán describes Moteuczoma as "like the great King Solomon who, having made peace in all the land, beloved by all the monarchs of the earth and aided by them, built the temple of Jerusalem."[32] He spoke with Tlacaelel and his council, and all supported his proposal. Moteuczoma intended to send messengers to the tlatoque in subject altepetl to requisition the building materials. But Tlacaelel objected, stating that it was wrong to send the envoys, who were nobles, because there were more places to contact than there were nobles, which reveals much about the political substance of Mexica dominions in the 1440s. Instead, Tlacaelel told Moteuczoma that all the rulers should be instructed to come before him so they would hear firsthand what was expected of them. The annals are rich in the dialogue between the two men, which culminated in Moteuczoma acquiescing: *"Ca ye qualli, Cihuacohuatzintle; ca ye oticmitalhui ma yuh mochihua, ca onitlatlaco yn oniquito, yn çan ompa quimilhuitihui." Auh ynin: "ca cenca qualli yn oticmitalhui; auh ca nel titlahtouani ca ticihuacohuatl."* (That's fine, O Cihuacoatl. Let it happen as you have just said. I was mistaken in what I said. Just let them go to summon them. What you have stated is well said. Indeed, you are the true tlatoani and Cihuacoatl).[33] Accordingly, Nezahualcoyotl of Tetzcoco, Acolnahuacatl Tzacualcatl of Tlacopan, Itztlolinqui the elder of Coyoacan, Xilomantzin of Colhuacan, Tepanquizqui of Tepetenchi Xochimilco, Quequecholtzin of Tecpan Xochimilco, Tzompanteuctli of Cuitlahuac, Xochitl Olinqui, also of Cuitlahuac, and Quetzaltototzin of Mizquic traveled to Tenochtitlan and took their official seats before Moteuczoma Ilhuicamina and Tlacaelel.[34] On hearing the king's request and apprised that they would be contributing to a grand edifice to glorify Huitzilopochtli, all the tlatoque agreed to supply what was asked of them and immediately set about to quarry the stones and process the lime and lumber.

But Moteuczoma Ilhuicamina wanted more: he wanted to draw the Chalca into his political sphere, and along with Tlacaelel he decided not to make demands but instead send messengers to Acxotlan, Chalco, to meet with the kings Cuateotzin the younger the Tlatquic and Toteociteuctli the Teohuateuctli, as well as five tlatoque in Amecameca. The emissaries would humbly explain the need for Chalco stone, which was necessary to fashion the exquisite sculptures and images for the great temple.[35] The kings of Chalco, an autonomous altepetl that was not subordinate to the Mexica, were annoyed and wondered exactly which of their polities was to furnish the materials. They stalled, stating that it would be necessary to bring everyone together to discuss the matter. They urged the messengers to return another time for their answer. Moteuczoma Ilhuicamina worried that the Chalca's delaying tactic might lead to conflict and interfere with their acquisition of the coveted stone. Tlacaelel, however, was of a different mind:

O powerful king, what is this you are saying? Is it possible that you are from a different generation than the rest of the Mexica? Is it possible that these words have issued forth from your generous heart? Why should our ambassadors not return? Perchance the Chalca hold us in such little esteem that they will mock us, jeer at us? The envoys must go, O powerful king, they must return to hear the decision, the will of the Chalca. And I beg of you, do not contradict me![36]

The Chalca, of course, would have none of it. Their rulers had met and determined that they were "free people" and not obligated to furnish the Mexica with any of the things they demanded. On hearing Chalco's response, Moteuczoma Ilhuicamina again consulted with Tlacaelel:

What is your opinion, Lord Tlacaelel, what should be done? What measures should be taken so the Chalca do not continue to laugh at us? . . . Consider carefully the advice you give me because, although I am the king, I shall abide by the wisest opinion. It is as if you and I were walking and you, as my guide, walk ahead, for in everything I shall follow you.[37]

Heartened by his brother's confidence in him, Tlacaelel answered, "For this favor, I kiss your royal hands and feet," and then he pronounced that war against Chalco was now inevitable. His concern was not so much that the Mexica would be denied their supplies for the temple but rather that they should suffer such insolence on the part of the Chalca. He urged the king to immediately send two spies to Chalco to see if preparations for battle were under way. They were.[38]

WHITHER CHALCO?

Chalco as a known political entity dates to at least Nine Flint, 1176, when the Acxoteca migrated from Tula. Acxotlan, as far as can be determined, was located close to Lake Chalco and seems to have served as fountainhead for the development of the altepetl of Chalco. Chimalpahin's own Amecameca was said to have been established in the vicinity in Three House, 1261.[39] Most peoples (the Totolimpaneca Chichimeca) who came to settle permanently in the area had migrated from Chicomoztoc, with the probable exception of the Tlacochcalca (of Tlamanalco, Chalco).[40] Tlatoque were installed on newly fashioned thrones, and temples were built to worship the images of the gods that had been brought along. Naturally, settling a new territory was not without its problems, for part of Amecameca was already inhabited, and those peoples had to be driven off.[41] Then, as newcomers entered an area and wanted to remain, there was a test of will, or skill, as when arrows were shot by rival groups at each other on Mount Amaqueme, the tall hill in the heart of the altepetl of Itztlacoçauhcan, the head altepetl of Amecameca.[42] More commonly, though, the daughter of the leader of a migrating group (*ynhueltiuh,* "their older sister") was offered as sexual carrot to a leader in an established altepetl, and a child born of that relationship became the ruler of a different polity made up of the new arrivals.[43] Each group coming to settle had its own name, leaders with wives, communal identity, and deity, and several of these entities came to constitute the esteemed confederated altepetl of Chalco.

Among the first newcomers to the northern Chalco area were the Nonohualca, Teotlixca, and Tlacochcalca, who were not Chichimeca but called Tecpantlaca because of their devotion to their deity, Tlatlauhqui Tezcatlipoca. They conceived of their god as a huey tlatoani, or great king, and therefore paid tribute to no one and never suffered hunger because, it was claimed, the rains always watered their land to the exclusion of that of everyone else. They were greatly feared as they settled in among other groups in the Acxotlan region.[44]

It was a vast territory, with fertile alluvial plains along the base of Mount Popocatepetl, abundant forests, and lake resources, which included the chinampas. The extent of Chalco is uncertain, but it was bounded approximately to the east by the mountain range and stretched west in the Tenanco Tepopolla region, perhaps extending along the lake toward Xochimilco. Acxotlan and the polities of Tlamanalco marked Chalco's northern zone near Lake Chalco, and to the south it extended as far as the hilly regions of Tepetlixpan and Chimalhuacan. The annals relate that great Chalca warriors distinguished themselves as they fought to gain more land and additional resources. A Cacamatzin the elder the Teohuateuctli of Teohuacan Tlailotlacan (in Amecameca) in Five Reed, 1367, had led all the Chalca in battle against the Mexica, Itztapallapaneca, and Tepaneca and gained significant ground, only to be killed by the Tepaneca afterward. The *huey yaotiyacauh*, "valiant warrior" Cacamatzin, fell with his gold insignia and shield bearing gold circles on it.[45] Even earlier, in One Flint, 1324, the Acxoteca and Tlacochcalca had engaged in a flower war (*xochiyaoyotl*), which was then followed by another in the same year between the Chalca and the Mexica, with reportedly disastrous consequences: "Chalco was defeated; all the Mexica were killed, as well as the Itztapallapaneca."[46] Then, in Six Reed, 1407, there were serious disputes between King Huitzilihuitl the younger and the rulers of Amecameca about their maize granaries. The Mexica forced some of the Chalca rulers to flee and killed others.[47]

The Chalca, of course, had on occasion been in league with the Tepaneca, so there appears to have always been some tension with the Mexica. Moreover, the Chalca had been long established in central Mexico before the Mexica entered the region in the fourteenth century. Shedding light on Chalca authority at the time, the annals relate an interesting episode in the year One Flint, 1428, when Moteuczoma Ilhuicamina and three other Mexica were taken as prisoners in Tetzcoco and put in jail in Acxotlan, Chalco, for the accusation of spreading malicious gossip. The two rulers of Chalco at the time were Toteotzin Teuctli the Tequachcauhtli of Acxotlan and his counterpart Aoquantzin the elder the Chichimecateuctli of Itztlacoçauhcan, Amecameca. Things were going well, it would appear. Itzcoatl, who had assumed the throne the year before, was tlatoani of Mexico Tenochtitlan, and Moteuczoma Ilhuicamina held office as the Tlacateccatl. The prisoners were transferred to Huexotzinco, where the Chalca had political and social ties, to be put to death. The Huexotzinco rulers, however, refused to harm the young noblemen and reportedly recused themselves because of their kinship affiliations with the Mexica. The prisoners were subsequently returned to Acxotlan, and tlatoque from twenty-five altepetl, among them Colhuacan, Xochimilco, and Azcapotzalco, some of them traveling from as far as Tlaxcala, came to Chalco to deliberate the fate of the captives. However, shortly before dawn and unbeknownst to the tlatoque meeting in Axcotlan, someone—probably anticipating that harm would come to Chalco—told the guards to release the prisoners, which they did. The guards were told, "Let nothing [evil] befall you; for some day the

Mexica Tenochca lord will be our mother and father, wherever he may go."

But Moteuczoma Ilhuicamina asked, "Why are we to go? We came in order to die."

The guards were adamant: "Not only must you go; nothing [evil] must befall the altepetl of Chalco."

The Mexica, watchful everywhere for sorcerers, fled to the edge of the forest, stopped for a drink of water from a *tuna* cactus vessel, hid for a while, and then found passage in the canoe of a fisherman with whom they conversed in his Acolhuaca language. The Chalca were in hot pursuit and took revenge not only on the fisherman, but on the two guards who had released the Mexica men. The guards were executed in the presence of twenty-five kings who had been summoned to Chalco. Moteuczoma Ilhuicamina and his associates soon arrived home at the palace and told Itzcoatl of all they had endured during the eighty days they spent in the custody of the tlatoque of Acxotlan.[48] There is no mention of prompt retaliation on the part of Itzcoatl for Chalca aggressions against his Mexica nobles. Doubtless, Moteuczoma Ilhuicamina and Tlacaelel never forgot the audacity of the Chalca, and, once in power, did everything possible to bring down their foes.

It was in the next year, Two House, 1429, that the Tepaneca king Maxtlaton convoked a similar gathering of tlatoque in Amecameca to garner support for his war against the Mexica. Aoquantzin the elder the Chichimecateuctli, the local ruler, had had a change of heart by that time regarding the Mexica, and Maxtlaton was refused.[49] During these years Chalco's sway was such that twenty-five altepetl claimed allegiance. Ranging from Azcapotzalco, Colhuacan, and Xochimilco to Quauhnahuac, Cholula, Huexotzinco, and Tlaxcala, their tlatoque all enjoyed rulership (tlatocayotl) affiliations with Chalco.

> ynic mihtohua motenehua ynan ytta quichihuaya yn chalco tlahto-
> cayotl y nepapan altepehuaque ynic moch oncan quihualcuia chalco yn
> intlahtocayo oncan hualmoteuctlaliaya y tlahtlahtoque nohuiyampa
> auh yn ihquac yn ayatle yaoyotl quichihuaya y mexicatl y Tenuchcatl
> çan oc catqui yn ayhtic

Hence it is said and stated that Chalco was mother and father of rulership, for the inhabitants of the various altepetl all had taken

their rulership from Chalco, where the rulers from everywhere were
endowed with nobility. But this was before the Mexica Tenochca
lord made war; [the Mexica Tenochca] were still in the middle of
the lake.[50]

Conquest and ethnic miscegenation were doubtless key factors contributing
to such a prideful and enduring association. Nevertheless, the vagaries of
politics and relative economic resources prevented unification and pre-
cluded any particular altepetl from becoming a permanent hegemon in the
early years.

FRIENDS BY AFTERNOON

The war between the Mexica and the Chalca, which lasted twenty years,
was legendary. Alvarado Tezozomoc devotes six chapters to the conflict and
tends to follow the same Nahuatl-language source used by Durán, while
furnishing more Nahua-specific substance, including Nahuatl terms and
place-names. Fray Diego allocates two chapters, rich in details and stirring
speeches, to the battles and machinations on both sides. Chimalpahin's
annals, episodic as they are, highlight some key events but tend to reiterate
the war's aftermath.[51] In the aggregate there is all the high drama of preparation for war: the marching of warriors in full battle dress (it is likely that
canoes were also involved for transportation and communication across the
lakes); the deviousness, as each side tried to dupe the other on several occasions; and the tense prolixity of Tlacaelel, who appeared to have something
to say about everything. The aftermath was fear, sorrow, and devastation for
the Mexica and Chalca as lives were lost and things changed forever, or so
the Chalca believed on their ultimate defeat.

The Mexica were methodical as they waged their battles against Chalco,
and it is apparent that they had no compunction when it came to initiating
hostilities against their foes at their most vulnerable; the Mexica attacked
during a famine when everyone was starving. Yet the Chalca were not the
only peoples of concern to the Mexica in these same years, for Tlacaelel
conducted battles resulting in victories across the land, along with infra-
structure improvements in the capital.

In Six Rabbit, 1446, on Tlacaelel's declaration of war, the Mexica were soon in full battle mode, with eagle and jaguar warriors at the ready. "All the men and youths between twenty and twenty-five years of age, and even the older ones of thirty, of forty, came out."[52] Indeed, all of Mexico Tenochtitlan hastened to bring together the necessary stores of supplies, including food and weapons, for the battle against Chalco. Finally, Tlacaelel led the troops out of the city, marching to Techichco, near Colhuacan and Cuitlahuac, where the Chalca were quartered. They were already well ordered in "files and squadrons" and "so numerous that they covered the entire plain."[53] As was his style, the Cihuacoatl held forth. With his weapons, sword, and shield in hand, he proclaimed, "O Mexica, behold! Observe what has brought you here, know that you are facing death, that death is your enemy. The Lord of the Earth, your mother, is waiting for you. Sell your lives dearly. . . . Therefore, let us go out into the field and let us show neither fear nor cowardice."[54] He then beat the drum that he carried on his back, and his warriors began to fight. By day's end, both sides agreed to use the night to regroup and to rest. The Mexica marveled at Chalca resilience, and they began to plan for a longer siege.

Some time later, the Chalca notified the Mexica of their intention to celebrate the festival of their deity Camaxtli and requested a five-day halt to the armed conflict. With great gall, they explicitly told the Mexica that they intended to propitiate their god with blood offerings from sacrificed Mexica captives. On learning of their impudence, Moteuczoma Ilhuicamina exclaimed that the Chalca alone would build Huitzilopochtli's temple. Horrified and angry at the loss of their fellow soldiers, the Mexica sought to retaliate immediately. Emulating Chalca military strategies, Moteuczoma Ilhuicamina decided to replenish his troops with new forces to intimidate the Chalca with a seemingly endless supply of soldiers in reserve. He recruited and trained boys, some as young as twelve, and ordered them, with their own captains and weapons, into the field. Once the fighting resumed, five hundred men, three hundred of whom were from Chalco's prime forces, were captured and delivered to Mexico Tenochtitlan. By order of Moteuczoma Ilhuicamina and Tlacaelel, they were to be sacrificed by fire, with a great bonfire on the temple floor and the Chalca warriors tossed alive into the flames. Before the men died, though, their hearts were extracted and offered to Huitzilopochtli. The Mexica then satiated themselves with the flesh of the Chalca.[55]

The remaining Chalca forces were beginning to wane but fought valiantly to hold their ground. Nevertheless, the Mexica never let up (*Auh yn Chalco manin yaoyotl*), and surely both sides were exhausted from the conflict. In Six Reed, 1459, two young nobles from Tlalmanalco Chalco—Necuametzin and Huehuetepoztli—went before Moteuczoma Ilhuicamina in Mexico Tenochtitlan to sue for peace. But Moteuczoma was not interested in a truce at this point, nor did he want to grant the Chalca any favors. Chimalpahin's sources blame the Acxotlan Tlalmanalco rulers, Totequixtzin the Teohuateuctli (r. 1418–43) and Cuateotl the younger the Tlatquic (r. 1413–44/46), for starting the war, although exactly what they could have done is uncertain since both men ruled before the major battles began.[56] However, the two nobles who had gone to see Moteuczoma Ilhuicamina to ask for peace were apprehended along with four of their associates once they returned to Chalco. Considered traitors and doubtless to set an example, they were taken to Amecameca and brutally punished for their betrayal. Their limbs were cut off, their necks were slashed, and their bodies were mutilated. Their executions were carried out on top of Mount Amaqueme at the temple of the deity (*yn icaya ynteocal intlacatecolocal*) of the Itztlacoçauhque in the presence of all twelve Chalco rulers, who had assembled for the occasion.[57]

Even before the fighting began, though, the Acxotlan king, Cuateotl the younger the Tlatquic, suffered a horrible demise. The annals are somewhat contradictory, but one source states that Cuateotl died in Four Flint, 1444. His tecpan was set on fire, and he was forced to flee through the door, where he was apprehended. His hands and feet were tied, and then he was stabbed through the navel so that he was eviscerated. The names of the three individuals who murdered him are furnished. He had certainly married well, for his wife, Matlalxochtzin, was a daughter of Acamapichtli, the first tlatoani of Mexico Tenochtitlan. Cuateotzin and Matlalxochtzin had three children. The annals indicate that five years earlier Moteuczoma Ilhuicamina had come to Chalco (probably to Tlalmanalco), and he and Cuateotzin had become friends. It is likely that the Tlalmanalco ruler was thought to have betrayed his own people by his friendship with the enemy.[58] It may have been a recollection of this early alliance that provoked the two Tlalmanalca noblemen to travel to see Moteuczoma Ilhuicamina and try to negotiate an accord for peace.

Fray Diego Durán furnishes a compelling narrative about the Mexica war against Chalco but collapses the two-decade undertaking into two short chapters without providing any real time frame. At some point after the fire sacrifices, the Mexica pressed deep into Chalco, through Tenanco Tepopolla in the west, to the outskirts of Amecameca. Moteuczoma and Tlacaelel, who were both in the field directing the battles, were confident of another favorable outcome and did not accompany their soldiers all the way to Amecameca. The Mexica had generally been successful over the long term because they continued to employ the Chalca's military tactics of replenishing and cycling their troops, and the Chalca were finally in retreat. But Chimalpahin reports that in the year Eleven Flint, 1464, fighting for their lives, the Chalca prevailed when they were able to surround and trap many Mexica warriors. There were, of course, casualties as the two sides brutalized each other in another fierce round of combat. But at the end of the day, three brothers of Moteuczoma Ilhuicamina and Tlacaelel lay dead in the field. It was a bitter loss, and Moteuczoma and Tlacaelel wept.

The king addressed his Cihuacoatl: "How does it affect you, Tlacaelel, seeing our brothers lying here dead"?

Tlacaelel callously replied, "O my lord, I do not marvel at such deaths, nor do they fill me with fear. This is how wars are fought! . . . How long and how deeply must we mourn the deceased? If we stay here weeping we shall not be able to accomplish more important matters!"[59]

Both sides had taken captives during the battle, and the Mexica decided to host another ceremonial sacrifice of Chalca soldiers, this time for the festival of the deity Xocotl. The Chalca too were going to have their own sacrificial rites with their captives but realized that a close relative of Moteuczoma Ilhuicamina, a nobleman named Ezhuahuacatl, was among their prisoners.[60] The Chalca consulted among one another and decided to free the man and offer him a kingship. But Ezhuahuacatl was thoroughly Mexica and cheered his fellow warriors: "I shall die with you, since I did not come here to reign but to fight and perish like a man."[61] Aware that the other captives were still going to be sacrificed to Camaxtli, the deity of the hunt, by being shot with arrows, he first tricked his Chalca captors by stating that he wanted to celebrate his good fortune. Ezhuahuacatl requested a long, tall log for what appears to be what is now known as a *volador* ceremony.[62] The log was brought in, and, celebrating with the traditional drum, dancing, and singing, Ezhuahuacatl ascended to a platform on top of the log. The Mexica noble then leaped to his death, proclaiming to his fellow warriors, "Brothers, the time has come. Die like brave men!"[63] The Mexica and Chalca were undone by his brazenness and the loss. Moteuczoma Ilhuicamina responded by telling Tlacaelel, "You have observed the death of our brothers and our kinsmen. It would be unjust if their deaths were not avenged. Therefore, without delay call together the Mexica army once more. Let us go to Chalco, where not a man, child, or adult will be left alive."[64] Personally leading their forces back to the site of the last battle in Amecameca, the two rulers addressed their soldiers: "Brothers, we have come to this place from which there is no return if it is not a victory; otherwise we shall remain here, dead. . . . This time it will be 'win or die.'"[65]

In the field, all were unnerved, especially as they listened to the hooting of owls through the night as the birds called out their messages of war. Another deity, Tecolotl, "Owl," then prognosticated for all to hear, "Chalco will disappear."[66] Tlacaelel took the god's message as a favorable omen for the Mexica, and the Chalca were clearly concerned. They decided to try to deceive their enemies and sent three warrior sons of the late Cuateotl the younger, the previous ruler of Acxotlan, to speak with Moteuczoma Ilhuicamina. The Chalca nobles pretended to switch sides and offered to lead the Mexica in the defeat of their own people. Tlacaelel was wise, though, and played his own trick. He greeted Cuateotl the younger's sons and treated them very well, furnishing them with lodging and even women. However, the three nobles were not allowed in battle the next day, which the Chalca quickly realized. Their commander was on the front line with his forces, and Tlacaelel took quick advantage, personally seizing the man in his arms and taking him captive. Troops from both sides charged in to protect their leaders, but it was another major loss for the Chalca.[67]

The battles continued until the next year, Twelve House, 1465, when Amecameca finally fell, along with the three other Chalco altepetl: Tlalmanalco, Tenanco, and Chimalhuacan. The Mexica fought fiercely, and in Amecameca, old men, old women, and children, who had been watching the battles from high in the hills, all tried to flee rather than surrender to their foes. Tlacaelel ordered his men to capture everyone but not to harm them. Remarkably, all the Amecameca kings fled in exile to Huexotzinco, where they had long-lasting ties. Moreover, there was not even a real regime change, as the Chalca kings left their heirs, their sons, to govern in their stead. Those left behind put down their arms and gave up, stating:

> O Mexica, we have done everything in our power to defend our-selves, and we can do no more. Now that we shall be your vassals we can serve you by providing you with wood for your buildings, stone, loads of earth, carved canoes, laborers to till your lands and masons for your works, brave spirited soldiers for your wars, and foodstuffs for your campaigns. These are the things we can give you.[68]

The Chalca also offered the Mexica their beautiful maidens.

As was expected, Chalco's lands were divided among the conquerors, with Moteuczoma first, Tlacaelel second, and "each leading warrior" receiving what was surely an ample reward. As an additional splendid benefit, Moteuczoma mandated that all who had served "should have their noses pierced as a sign of valor. In this way they could enter the city with feathers and golden jewels hanging from their noses, like mustaches." Then, demonstrating that his goodwill and generosity knew no bounds, he granted the same honor to the brave Chalca warriors.[69] Chimalpahin, a master of understatement, noted, "As the sun rose, they attacked us. By late afternoon, the Mexica had become our friends."[70]

TLACAELEL AND CHALCO

We may never know if Tlacaelel and his brother the king had a personal vendetta against the peoples of Chalco or if, instead, their grasping actions were no more than the royal prerogative of imperial inclusivity. Certainly, Chalco was an altepetl known as a rich source of foodstuffs, especially maize, and timber was also abundant, as was the coveted stone for sculpting and temple building. To finally have full access to an endless store of such assets as well as an impressive number of subject Chalca for labor must have been satisfying. But there also seem to have been old animosities dating back more than a century. Chalca sovereignty and patriotism were surely more than a mere annoyance for the Mexica.

For the conflict to have lasted twenty years seems unprecedented, because the other major encounters of any duration had been against the Tepaneca in the early decades of the century. But those were different sorts of battles against assorted polities, particularly once Maxtlaton was no longer involved. Formal martial strife between the Mexica and Chalca had begun with a flower war in 1324 that was followed by periodic sniping and assaults over many years; and then all-out war began in 1446. But were the Mexica particularly harsh toward the Chalca? Clearly, the Mexica were not above the practice of ritual human sacrifice of their war captives to their deities, but immolation by fire was extreme and cruel. It was also remarkably inappropriate, because Tlacaelel had important social and political ties in Chalco. Though he may have had several wives, his first and primary wife was from Amecameca, Chalco. And judging by his age and the status of his successor upon his death, it is likely that he married her before the onset of the long-drawn-out twenty years' war. Certainly he was concerned about providing for his family even in the early years, when he volunteered to singlehandedly take on Maxtlaton, the ruler of the Tepaneca.[71]

Chimalpahin reports that in Amecameca, Tlacaelel "asked for and took" as his wife a noblewoman by the name of Maquiztzin.[72] She was the daughter of Quetzalmaçatzin the elder the Chichimecateuctli of Itztlacoçauhcan, the highest ranked ruler in Amecameca (r. 1392–1410). Maquiztzin went with Tlacaelel to live in Mexico Tenochtitlan. There they had five children (fig. 16). Their first son was Cacamatzin, who became the Tlacochcalcatl. He married and had twelve children. Just one example of the esteem of the Tlacaelel royal line is that their first daughter married Nezahualpilli, the tlatoani of Tetzcoco. Their son, named Cacamatzin after his grandfather the Tlacochcalcatl, was certainly one of the most distinguished of his heirs, for he became tlatoani of Tetzcoco (r. 1516–20) and was in office when Hernando Cortés and his Spaniards arrived in central Mexico. Cacamatzin the Tlacochcalcatl's second child was named for his grandfather Tlacaelel, and he eventually became Mexico Tenochtitlan's third Cihuacoatl.[73]

Tlacaelel and Maquiztzin's second son was Tlilpotonqui, who succeeded his father upon his death and became the second Cihuacoatl in the capital.

Cacamatzin the Tlacochcalcatl = ♀
♂ Tlacaelel the younger the Cihuacoatl

♂ Tlacaelel = ♀ Maquiztzin

♂ Tlilpotonqui the Cihuacoatl (fourteen children)
♂ Toyaotzin (seven children)
♀ Achihuapoltzin = ♂ Coyolchiuhqui (of Huexotzinco)
♀ Xiuhpopocatzin

= ♀ —— ♀ Tollintzin

= ♀ —— ♀ Macuilxochitzin =
♂ Quauhtlapaltzin

= ♀ —— Xochiacamapichtli

= ♀ —— Xillomantzin

= ♀ —— ♂ Tezcatlteuctli = ♀
♂ Tlacotzin the Cihuacoatl = ♀²
♂ don Gerónimo Velásquez

= ♀ —— Itzpapalotzin

= ♀ —— Chiquatzin teuctli

= ♀ —— Totomochtzin³ =
♀   ♀   ♀ = ♂ don Tomás de San Martín
Quetzalmaçatzin the
Chichimecateuctli
♂ don Martín Mozoquineloatzin

= ♀ —— Tlacoachchimaltzin

= ♀ —— Toznenetzin

= ♀ —— ♀

= ♀ —— ♂ Chimalpantzin

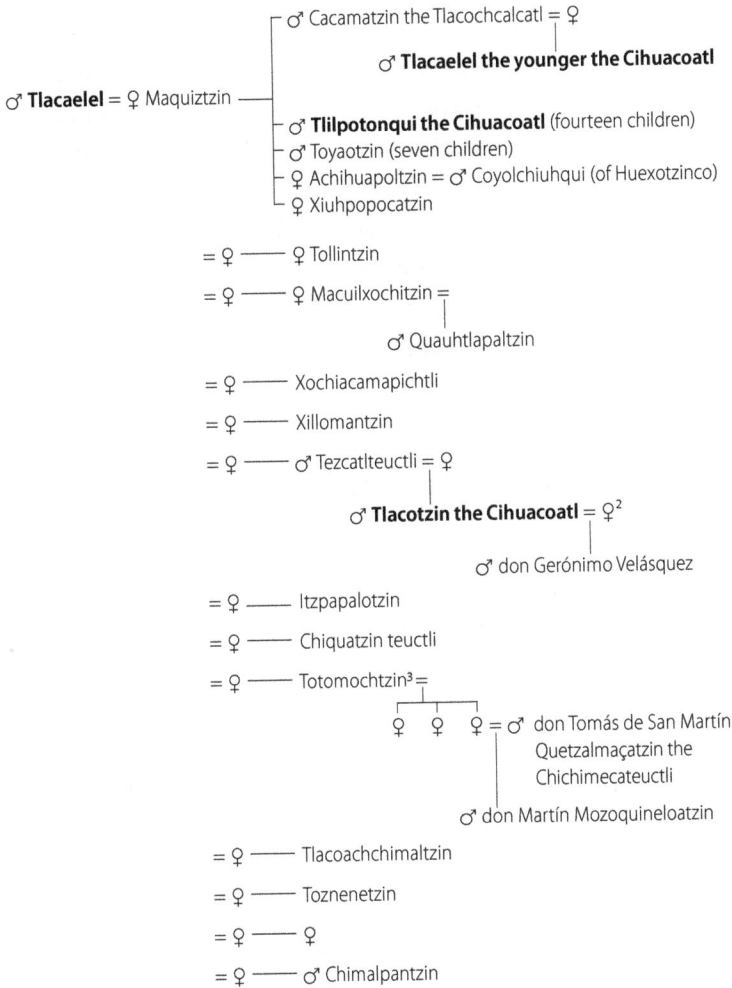

FIG. 16. Tlacaelel's children.[1]
Copyright © 2016, University of Oklahoma Press.

Boldface indicates which of Tlacaelel the elder's descendants became the Cihuacoatl.

1. CC 1:45, 143–45; DC 2:173. The names of Tlacaelel the elder's wives and children are furnished when known. That some were daughters is indicated.
2. Tlilpotonqui was succeeded by his nephew, Tlacaelel the younger, his brother Cacamatzin the Tlacochcalcatl's son. Tlacotzin, Tlacaelel the elder's grandson, was the fifth and last Cihuacoatl. AT, 120, states that a Tlilpotonqui was active in the war against Chalco, and surely he was the same Tlilpotonqui, son of Tlacaelel the elder and first successor to the office of the Cihuacoatl.
3. Or Totomotzin. See p. 66, n. 62.

Tlilpotonqui likewise married Chalca women, the first of whom was from Amecameca, like his mother, and the second from Acxotlan, the leading altepetl in Chalco. Tlilpotonqui was said to have had fourteen children. Tlacaelel and Maquiztzin's two older sons became major figures in Mexica life, and they carried on the traditions of their father and their uncle, King Moteuczoma Iluicamina, as they made their own contributions to the glory of the empire. Many of their descendants did well for themselves under Spanish rule. Their lives and activities are discussed more fully in chapter 4. One set of annals lists the names of seventeen of Tlacaelel's children, including the five he had with Maquiztzin. Other annals, though, state that he had a total of eighty-three offspring.

DURING AND AFTER CHALCO

While the battles were raging in Chalco and afterward, the Mexica attended to a multitude of other tasks. One had to do with their island and the succession of a new ruler in Tlatelolco after King Quauhtlatoatzin died (r. 1428–60). The Mexica Tlatelolca had maintained their own dynastic line to this point, yet for reasons that are not fully clear, Moteuczoma Ilhuicamina and his grandson Axayacatzin intervened and arranged for a Moquihuixtli of Acolhuacan (Tetzcoco), the son of Moteuczoma's older sister, to be installed on the throne (r. 1460–73).[74] Although he had an auspicious beginning, Tlatelolco's new king was to have a sorry end.[75]

Once well settled in office, in Three House, 1469, Moquihuix sent four of his nobles as envoys to Amecameca to speak with the nobles serving there as interim rulers (*quauhtlatoque*). The messengers told the Amecameca rulers that Moquihuix wanted to attack the Mexica Tenochca and asked if they would help.[76] Even though now subjects of the Tenochca and not happy about it, the Amecameca leaders captured the men from Tlatelolco, tied them up, placed them face-down in canoes covered with bundles of reeds, and took them at night through the lagoon to Axayacatzin, who was by then tlatoani in Mexico Tenochtitlan. The Tlatelolco messengers were subsequently killed, roasted in an oven, and served at a banquet to Moquihuix and his Tlatelolca constituents, who did not know that they were dining on compatriots. Axayacatzin personally played the drum and went about encouraging the singing and dancing.[77] Five years of war between the Tenochca and Tlatelolca followed, even though Moquihuix was still married to Axayacatl's sister, Chalchiuhnenetzin. They had two children, but Moquihuix treated his wife horribly, preferring his mistresses instead and taking all the gifts and revenue that were hers. It was said that she was too thin and flat-chested and had bad breath. He cast her out of the palace to live with the servants amid the metates. Chalchiuhnenetzin had notified her brother Axayacatzin that Moquihuix was abusing her and that he was planning to go to war against the Tenochca. Axayacatzin and his Tenochca were prepared for combat, which included the composition of a battle song, and the Tlatelolca ultimately were made to look like fools, or "quack like ducks," as Chimalpahin put it.[78] Tlatelolco never again enjoyed full sovereignty, nor did its royal lineage hold sway.

Tlacaelel, although getting on in years, was still playing an active role in Tenochca politics, and it is assumed that he was a key figure as the conflict played out. Fray Diego Durán's *History* furnishes even more information about the Tlatelolca situation, some of which revises the annals' information. He finds Moquihuix to be a valiant leader and places the blame for the conflict on the Mexica Tenochca. The implication is that many polities were antagonistic toward the Tenochca and willing to challenge their authority. Numerous rulers reportedly allied with the Tlatelolca, and the Mexica Tenochca and the Mexica Tlatelolca sent emissaries to one another to determine their intentions. Chalchiuhnenetzin, Moquihuix's wife, was initially loyal to her husband but befuddled by his inability to control his fellow noblemen. She went so far as to ask that she be allowed to speak to their countrymen, hoping to prevent the war. Finally, though, she contacted her brother Axayacatl and notified him that an attack was imminent.

There were unpropitious omens, too, predicting doom for the Tlatelolca, and when Moquihuix's insubordination was no longer tolerable, it was the old veteran Tlacaelel who personally took his weapons and climbed to the top of the Tlatelolca's pyramid, calling out: "Sons and brothers, do not be faint, justice is on our side. . . . This time we shall not have to go far from our boundaries to fight. Our enemy lies right behind our houses. . . . Imagine that you are just brushing flies from your bodies."[79] He then gave the signal to attack the Tlatelolca warriors. Drums were played, along with trumpets, horns, and other instruments. The fighting was fierce, and Moquihuix would not surrender. Tlatelolca women got into the fray, naked, and squirted milk from their breasts to rout their enemies. Axayacatl and his soldiers prevailed, killing Moquihuix and his nobles. No longer would Tlatelolco be exempt from tribute obligations. Every eighty days thereafter they would deliver to the Tenochca "mantles, breechcloths, feathers, jewels, precious stones, weapons, and slaves." Their homes were plundered, their rulership was terminated, and they were thereafter subjects on their own island.[80] The Tlatelolca's version of this war differs, of course.[81] It is probable that the Mexica Tenochca, in truth, coveted the Tlatelolca's profitable port and market, and war was ultimately the only means to gain control of this valuable resource.

After the final battle in Chalco and the division of the spoils, the Mexica had returned to the capital and dedicated eighty days to grieve for their kinsmen lost in the conflict.[82] The doleful ceremony was followed by a respite of peace, which was cut short, according to Durán and Alvarado Tezozomoc, when the Tepeaca killed some imperial merchants who had been visiting their altepetl.[83] Their actions precipitated one more Mexica call to arms, and men and supplies came from across the realm. Yet another military victory was expected, which promised to bring Tepeaca, Tecalli, Cuauhtinchan, and Acatzinco into the fold.[84] As in their prime, Tlacaelel and Moteuczoma Ilhuicamina took to the field, and the battle was over almost as soon as it began. There were the customary riches to be divided among the king and his Cihuacoatl and, this time, the royal council. The conquered altepetl were admonished to travel to Mexico Tenochtitlan in order to pay homage and thereafter worship the Mexica deity Huitzilopochtli.[85]

Durán furnishes a rich description of the rank and file of the priestly bureaucracy that was to participate in the sacrifices that were now a part of each successful armed endeavor. Moteuczoma Ilhuicamina and Tlacaelel were duly feted, and then Tlacaelel benevolently informed the Tepeaca, because of the essential location of their altepetl, that they were now charged as gatekeepers, through which no end of travelers with valuable merchandise would be passing. Moreover, their home was to be the site of an important marketplace that was to showcase all the precious imperial wares.[86]

In some ways, the Tepeaca can be thought to have gotten off easy, for war soon followed against the Huaxteca, then against the peoples of Ahuilizapan, then against the Coixtlahuaca, in the Mixteca, and then beyond. Vast numbers of warriors with supplies from all the subject altepetl were commissioned to participate. The fighting was severe and devastating, but the spoils were splendid and plentiful. The Mexica also established outposts, with particular noblemen serving as governors to oversee the collection of tribute thereafter.

In the meantime, improvements to the great temple continued, and Tlacaelel reminded Moteuczoma Ilhuicamina of the need for a new, grand altar, which was to serve for the sacrifices of the many captives from the battles. In this instance, sculptors were to fashion a piece to commemorate the Mexica's defeat of the Tepaneca in Azcapotzalco. Durán adds that Tlacaelel, in addition to "being bold and cunning in the artifice of war, also invented devilish, cruel, and frightful sacrifices."[87] In short order, a *temalacatl*, which means 'stone wheel,'" was delivered.[88] It was placed on a platform slightly taller than the height of a man. The festivities began on the feast day of Tlacaxipehualiztli, and fray Diego details the gory gladiatorial rituals and sacrifices that were conducted in the presence of a plethora of guests, who were eating and drinking their fill during the ceremony. On this occasion, it was the Huaxteca captives who died.

THE LAST YEARS OF MOTEUCZOMA ILHUICAMINA

Tlacaelel was aging and no longer led the Mexica warriors in the field. His dotage, however, did not interfere with his avid interest in ceremonial sacrifice. For the Coixtlahuaca captives, he proposed the creation of a *cuauhxicalli*, or "eagle vessel," which was to be a huge, round stone with a basin to contain the sacrificial blood, and it was to be sculpted in the likeness of the sun.[89] Additional carvings were to commemorate the Mexica's most recent military conquests. Finely worked and very pleasing to Moteuczoma Ilhuicamina, the sculpture was placed on a tall platform with four ascending staircases positioned to reflect the four cardinal directions leading to the sun. Moteuczoma made a point of showing his guests the magnificent work, and it was of course admired by all.[90]

Moteuczoma Ilhuicamina and Tlacaelel were featured in the ceremony to inaugurate the sun stone. Durán's *History* describes how in preparation both men in tandem blackened their bodies with soot and pitch so they glowed, which seemed to set off their feathered and bejeweled gold crowns, their golden arm-shields, their jewel-encrusted jaguar sandals, and their exquisitely woven breechcloths and mantles. Their nose plugs were also of fine jewels. Carrying knives and accompanied by five priests, Moteuczoma and Tlacaelel took different stairs as they ascended to the altar and the stone, where each man cut open the chest and extracted the heart of four men at a time until all the warriors from the Mixteca had been killed.[91] The hearts were placed in the central cavity of the stone, with the blood sprinkled toward the sun.[92] The ceremony was elaborate and it was followed the next day by another, the two events serving as examples for the visiting noblemen regarding how they too should begin to build new temples, train their priests, create new military orders, and establish schools to educate youths in the art of celebratory singing and dancing.[93] It should be noted too that thereafter a Mexica administrator was to be posted in the newly conquered territory to ensure the delivery of tribute on schedule to Mexico Tenochtitlan.

Distinguishing social class was an ongoing concern, and it was increasingly important that one not mingle with anyone of inferior standing. For example, in the palace rooms were separated by social rank, and only individuals of high position were permitted to wear sandals. The tribunals for justice were elaborately tiered, and the eating of human flesh was privileged and limited to members of the order of the Knights of the Sun, who were "allowed to keep as many women as they could support." Moteuczoma Ilhuicamina and Tlacaelel continued to confer about all matters of state.[94]

The wealth that flowed to the capital was nearly beyond description, since each polity in Mexica dominions was required to deliver quantities of whatever might be unique to its area. For example, feathers and chocolate were received from specific regions, while gold and silver were quarried elsewhere. Woven cloth was always a coveted commodity, as were foodstuffs, such as the essential maize and beans, which were part of most tribute requirements.[95] Talented artisans crafted exquisite clothing and beautiful luxury items, such as jewelry, sacred images, palace and temple furnishings, and the like.[96] Manufactured goods, such as armor, weapons, paper, and utilitarian products could be expected too. Moreover, the natural fauna of the empire came to be a part of the capital, as wildlife from all parts were captured, brought to the king, and put on display for his pleasure in a zoo and aviary.

But the polities found to be lacking desirable riches paid the greatest price: "maidens, girls, and boys, all slaves . . . were divided among the lords."[97] Such bounty for Mexico Tenochtitlan was understood, naturally, to be well deserved because of the ingenuity and diligence of the Mexica's eminent men, with Tlacaelel listed as first among all.[98]

The capital must have served as an enormous redistribution center, judging by the abundance and quality of the items that were produced. That such goods were regularly delivered from distances as great as the coastal shores and deep into southern territories was testimony to the Mexica's awesome reach. The comfort and security that came with the self-replenishing were epitomized in the sumptuous display of it all in the capital in the person of the nobility and their lifestyle, but it was also available to allies who distinguished themselves by their service and loyalty.

Luxuriating in relative tranquility and resplendent wealth, Moteuczoma Ilhuicamina, perhaps to ensure that the bounty endured and to manage the capital's burgeoning population, subsequently imposed rigid new ordinances. The rules were based on social stratification and designed to regulate everything from courtly attire and civil deportment to education and priestly activities. Claiming that the rules were divinely inspired, Moteuczoma and Tlacaelel doubtless sought to gain even greater control. Moreover, the new policies were not limited to the capital but were to be realized across the empire. The regulations were strict; they targeted even the number of stories on one's home and the type of clothing and jewels that could be worn. The court system was again elaborated, and schools were established to teach comportment, while other laws were drafted to prevent adultery and stealing, with severe punishment set for violators.[99]

The pleasure of peace and abundance may also have been cause for introspection on the part of the two Mexica leaders, for the king began to reflect on his peoples' origins and, especially, their deity, Huitzilopochtli, and the fact that the god's mother, from hundreds of years in the past, was still waiting for her son to return to her in Chicomoztoc. Moteuczoma Ilhuicamina determined to send some of his most stalwart warriors on a quest for the homeland. But the always loquacious Tlacaelel had reservations and cautioned his king:

O powerful lord, your royal chest is not moved, not governed, by your
own reasons, nor is your heart moved by human motives; without
doubt this has been proposed to you by some eternal deity. . . . You
must know, O great lord, that what you have determined to do is not
for strong or valiant men, nor does it depend upon skill in the use
of arms in warfare. . . . Your envoys will not go as conquerors but as
explorers.[100]

Tlacaelel explained that Chicomoztoc was no longer a lush and easy place
to live, or at least as they knew it from the lore of their forefathers. Since
the Mexica's departure the landscape had become harsh and foreboding
and difficult to navigate. The Cihuacoatl urged the king to send "wizards,
sorcerers, and magicians . . . to discover that place," as well as to deliver a
trove of luxurious gifts to whomever might be inhabiting Chicomoztoc in
those days. There were also presents for Coatlicue, Huitzilopochtli's mother.
Moteuczoma Ilhuicamina sent sixty sorcerers, who, although considered
to be learned men, would gain even greater wisdom as they came to con-
template the folly of avarice and hubris in the person of the eternally vital
overseer of the famed Chicomoztoc. They also met with Coatlicue, who in
a way was glad to hear of the exceptional prestige of her son, yet still and
forever felt her loneliness in his absence. Nevertheless, she sent along a gift
for her offspring and a warning to all of the transience of their fame and
fortune. Immortality, Moteuczoma and Tlacaelel learned, was not to be their
lot or that of their god.[101]

Chastened somewhat, the king and his Cihuacoatl tried to verify Coatlicue's prognostication but were soon distracted by the murder and robbery
of some of their envoys as they returned from Coatzacoalco. The men were
transporting gold and finely worked items from the coast. Other travelers,
this time men from Chalco, saw the remains of the slaughtered porters and
hastened to Mexico Tenochtitlan to report to the king the deaths as well as
the loss of the goods. Individuals from Oaxaca were said to be the villains.
Moteuczoma promptly consulted with Tlacaelel, who advised his brother
to delay avenging the deaths until the construction of the new temple was
completed. Once it was ready, he said, all the warriors taken in battle in
Oaxaca could be sacrificed during the temple's inauguration ceremony.

What followed can only be described as another cavalcade of sumptuous ceremonies and outlandish slaughters.

Work began immediately on the temple, with subject altepetl across the realm furnishing supplies and laborers. With plentiful materials and workers, the structure, with its chamber for Huitzilopochtli on top, was completed in short order, which meant that everyone would then begin to make ready for war. All of Oaxaca was to be destroyed, and the Mexica and their allies were in a hurry to do it. The destruction was equivalent to what the Romans did to Carthage, although without the symbolic scattering of salt upon the soil, doubtless because the Mexica planned to cultivate it at some time in the future. Consequently, the Mexica sent notices to neighboring polities, warning them of their fate if they challenged Mexica authority. The victorious warriors were ecstatic because of the plethora of captives from which they would profit as capital or slaves. Indeed, such plenty was exactly what the audacious old veteran Tlacaelel had anticipated.

Nevertheless, even after the captives had been paraded through Mexico Tenochtitlan and presented to Moteuczoma Ilhuicamina, each one kissing the king's feet, Tlacaelel was not prepared to inaugurate Huitzilopochtli's temple. He wanted a polished mirror to be finished, and there was a "pointed stone on which the sacrificial victims are to be thrown to have their hearts cut out" that was also not ready.[102] Yet while he saw to the finishing touches on the temple, disingenuous to the end, he was already plotting new battles to procure even more prisoners and treasure, reportedly for Huitzilopochtli. These too were to be peoples who were not a part of Mexica dominions. Exposing Tlacaelel's insatiable appetite, Durán stated that the Cihuacoatl equated the soon to be conquered men with "maize cakes hot from the griddle—tortillas from a nearby place, hot and ready to eat whenever [the god] wishes them. Let our people, let our army, go to this market place to buy with our blood, with our heads and hearts, and with our lives the precious stones, jades, and rubies, and splendid long shining feathers for our wondrous Huitzilopochtli." Tlacaelel had decided against more combat in distant places, such as Oaxaca, because "our god does not like the flesh of those barbarous people. They are like hard, yellowish, tasteless bread in his mouth." Getting to the new "human market," as he called it, would not tax his warriors, because the Cihuacoatl was looking east to nearby polities such as Cholula, Huexotzinco, and Tlaxcala as his next source of "warm tortillas," that is, human flesh. Moteuczoma Ilhuicamina and the royal council were to be consulted about his plan.[103]

Durán goes on to reiterate that although Tlacaelel was elderly, he was still in charge of affairs of war. Apparently, he was also preoccupied with the propitiation of the Mexica deities, which meant to him more sacrifices. The friar added, "He had acquired a taste for human flesh since the lords ate it frequently." Was he making excuses for the old man when he explained that the devil had influenced Tlacaelel, who was "now inventing a thousand cruel acts, all of which he made into law before his death. He was obeyed so blindly that everything he ordained was done."[104]

His brother the king was willing to execute the Cihuacoatl's proposal to establish military marketplaces in six polities to the east of the capital to ensure a steady supply of human flesh for the god. The market wars would also furnish Mexica warriors with honor in the field and bring them magnificent presents from Moteuczoma Ilhuicamina. As part of the promotion, Tlacaelel enumerated a dozen or more harsh penalties for any soldier who refused to participate. Then, perhaps to further intimidate the old guard, he opened the ranks to offspring of nobility born outside the royal lineage, granting them inheritance rights, high social standing, and extraordinary gifts when they distinguished themselves in combat.[105]

Finally, Tlacaelel ordered that Oaxaca be colonized with groups from all the major altepetl. He promised the colonists land and that he would send some six hundred families from his own polity (probably Acatlan). His cousin, Atlazol, was to be their governor. Moreover, the settlers would no longer have tribute obligations, and Moteuczoma offered supplies, such as metates and labor from neighboring towns to build their homes, to get them started. They were assured safe passage and good governance once established there. The settlers agreed to the conditions because, Durán commented, "wherever death awaited them, whether it be here or there, in the end it was, after all, the same death."[106]

Moteuczoma and Tlacaelel were feeling their age, and the king resolved to create a lasting personal tribute to signify all that he and his brother had accomplished in their lifetimes. He decided that having their images carved in stone at Chapoltepec was a suitable memorial, and sculptors carved likenesses so agreeable that they were immediately rewarded with fine gifts and then titles that were used to distinguish their families for another hundred years. Durán included an illustration of the Chapoltepec sculpture in his *History*, but it features only the king, a curious omission since he had invested so much of his work to exalting Tlacaelel and pairing the two (see fig. 11).

Once he was satisfied with his legacy in stone, Moteuczoma spoke personally with his brother and asked him to succeed to the throne upon his death. He reminded Tlacaelel of the extraordinary things that had been realized in Mexico Tenochtitlan during their tenure and admonished him to be the next Mexica tlatoani. Moteuczoma Ilhuicamina wanted none other of his relatives to follow him. Tlacaelel, while gratified, advised the king that there was more yet to be done, that he wanted another memorial in Moteuczoma's honor. This one was to be in Oaxtepec at a place where Moteuczoma would go to relax and take pleasure. There were to be gardens filled with wonderful vegetation, all brought from Cuetlaxtla and possibly beyond. Exotic and lovely plants and surely other living things were going to be transplanted to the central portion of the realm. Springs and waterways were dammed, creating a resort, and the flowers bloomed within three years. One wonders if this might have been a last-ditch effort on the part of Tlacaelel to furnish healing waters for an ailing king.[107]

Moteuczoma Ilhuicamina died in Two Flint, 1468.[108] Durán states that the funeral, probably arranged by Tlacaelel, included the obligatory gifting and mourning and the sacrifice of many captives and slaves to honor the old king appropriately. Tlacaelel convoked the nobility and the royal council and spoke fondly of his brother in tribute.[109] The annals state that Moteuczoma had many children but only one son, Iquehuac the Tlacateccatl. Moteuczoma's daughters, from what is known about them, tended to marry well, and one, Mazaxochtzin, initiated a rulership in Tepexic Mixtlan, her husband's town.[110] Another set of annals claims that there were two sons of Moteuczoma, Iquehuac the Tlacateccatl and Machimalle, both of whom came to despise their nephew Axayacatl because he succeeded to the throne and they did not. In spite of his prestigious title and office, which should have afforded him membership in the Council of Four, Iquehuac and his brother led lives of crime and great dishonor.[111]

In yet another set of annals, another of Moteuczoma Ilhuicamina's daughters, Atotoztli, married an uncle, Tezozomoctzin the elder, the son of former tlatoani Itzcoatl. Although identified as a tlatocapilli, or royal noble-man, Tezozomoc never ruled. But with Atotoztli he had three sons who did. Axayacatl (r. 1469–81), Tizocic (r. 1481–86), and Ahuitzotl (r. 1486–1502), respectively, succeeded to the throne formerly occupied by their grandfa-thers Itzcoatl and Moteuczoma Ilhuicamina as high kings (*huehueyntin tlatoque*) of Mexico Tenochtitlan.[112] Chimalpahin, compounding the confu-sion regarding the king's heirs, adds that Moteuczoma, on recognizing that not all of his sons would rule, created various professions, such as "the [art of using the] bow, the lapidary art, wood sculpture, painting. All of his sons became public officials."[113] Recall that Moteuczoma Ilhuicamina had already institutionalized the Mexica office of sculptor by granting formal titles to the men who carved his portrait at Chapoltepec. Surely Tlacaelel's legislation to professionalize and legitimize offices with high social rank hearkens back to when he and the king decreed that merit, not birthright, would determine a man's eligibility for noble standing. Early on, Tlacaelel and Moteuczoma Ilhuicamina may have realized that neither Iquehuac nor Machimalle was fit to rule.

Reflecting Tlacaelel's—no doubt unexpected—popularity across Mexica society, Chimalpahin states that the commoners wanted Tlacaelel to be the next ruler, while Durán claims that it was the nobles and then "all the old men, the young men, the women, and the children" who asked him to serve next.[114] Either way, Tlacaelel refused. Rather, he consulted with tlatoque Nezahualcoyotl of Tetzcoco and Totoquihualiztli of Tlacopan, and all agreed that Tezozomoctzin the elder's youngest son, Axayacatzin, should be crowned, and he was, with all the pomp appropriate for a high king.[115] As an aside, the Nahuatl terminology, *huey tlatoani*, "great king," or "emperor," was associated specifically with the five rulers dating from the time of Moteuczoma Ilhuicamina to Moteuczoma Xocoyotl.[116]

AXAYACATL AND TLACAELEL CARRY ON

Axayacatl was installed on the throne in Three House, 1469, "on the day count Two Quiahuitl, 'Rain,' the second of August"; his older brother Tizocic became the Tlailotlac; and another brother, Ahuitzotl, was made the Tla-cochcalcatl.[117] Furnishing some hint of courtly behavior on the part of subject altepetl, Chimalpahin noted that four tlatoque—from Tlamanalco, Chalco, *tocolhuan*, "our grandfathers," namely Yacacoltzin, Macuilxo- chitzin, Huilotzin, and Icualtzintli, traveled to Mexico Tenochtitlan to pay homage to the new king, Axayacatzin, as was the Tlalmanalca tradition.[118] As noted, Axayacatl was already despised by his jealous uncles, Iquehuac and Machimalle, but there was also deep animosity toward him on the part of his brothers, who insulted him and made fun of his prowess as a warrior. But Axayacatl had already distinguished himself in battle in Huexotzinco.[119]

It has also been noted how well Axayacatl handled the conflict with his brother-in-law Moquihuix, the ruler of the Mexica Tlatelolca.[120] Reportedly, the pretext for that war was Moquihuix's sorry abuse of Axayacatl's older sis- ter, Chalchiuhnenetzin, as well as his attempts to recruit the rulers of Chalco, Colhuacan, and elsewhere to join forces with him against the Tenochca.[121] The Tlatelolca were not only soundly defeated but also humiliated when they were conquered in Seven House, 1473. Yet the annals blame Axayacatl: "It has already been said that Axayacatl brought it about. It was done still in the time of the lord named Tlacaeleltzin [the] Cihuacoatl, conqueror of the world."[122]

Even before the fall of Tlatelolco, though, Axayacatl had taken to the field. In fact, during his rule hardly a year passed when the Tenochca did not conquer one or more altepetl. The annals list many of these polities; to give only a few examples, in Four Rabbit, 1470, it was the Cuextlaxteca; and in Five Reed, 1471, Xochitlan, Tepeticpac, Tonallimoquetzayan, and the Mazahua of Xiquipilco. In Seven House, 1473, Chiapan fell.[123] The brave king was captured by enemies in Eight Rabbit, 1474, but saved by a fellow tlatoani, Quetzalmamalitzin of Teotihuacan.[124] Four years later, in Xiquipilco, 6,020 died on the battlefield and 10,000 were taken captive. Axayacatl was reportedly wounded but survived.[125] This king was such a great warrior that the Chalca performed a celebratory war song for him. It was presented in front of his palace, and Chimalpahin used the occasion to glorify his hometown, Amecameca. He reported that the event began with a young man from Tlamanalco singing and dancing. The young man fal- tered, though, and a man from Amecameca saved the day with his skillful performance. Axayacatl, in his palace with his wives, was greatly flattered and rewarded the singer handsomely, taking the song, the *Chalca yaocihua-cuicatl*, for himself.[126]

Fray Diego furnishes the context for some of the battles. In Toluca, for instance, Tlacaelel had created a ruse to get into the territory by requesting materials that were not natural to the region. When excuses were made, Tlacaelel, who by this time was carried about on a litter, encouraged Axayacatl to go to war if for no other reason than to prevent the Matlatzinca from joining forces with enemies in Michoacan. The Mexica and their allies marched toward Toluca, demanding peaceful surrender of their foes, since "it was well known that the Mexica were like fire that burned the fields of grain and the fruit trees, that consumed with its heat the maguey plants and the houses."[127] But it was a fight to the finish, with the customary slaughter and destruction. Axayacatl was wounded (again?) before the Matlatzinca of Callimanyan fell, in Eleven House, 1477.[128] When Tlacaelel was notified that the Mexica were once more victorious, he arranged for a lavish reception of the warriors, the injured tlatoani, and the extraordinary treasure. He also urged the king to proceed forthwith with preparations for the feast of Tlacaxipehualiztli, so that the captives could be sacrificed. Scheming, he warned Axayacatl, "My son, you see my white hair, my old age. I beseech you not to tarry in setting up the altars, the stones, for sacrifice. . . . If you delay in preparing these things I may be dead tomorrow or some other day soon, and I shall not be able to take with me the memory of this happy event.[129] Durán commented, "All this was said by that evil old man, who never had enough human flesh to satisfy him."[130]

Massive stone altars were moved to the top of the temple, and summons were sent across the land. In many ways, it was a festival of horror because so many captives were sacrificed, and the invited guests were seriously alarmed, although they seem not to have refused any of the lovely gifts that were presented to them. But they had hardly begun to depart the capital when Tlacaelel advised Axayacatl that a new sculpture, the sun stone, was ready to be officially presented. Now all that was necessary was to decide where to obtain the next group of captives.[131]

They decided to go to war against Michoacan in order "to paint the temple red with the blood of those people."[132] Allied soldiers and supplies joined with the Mexica, totaling some twenty-four thousand men at arms. Axayacatl traveled with his soldiers to Michoacan but was greatly dismayed to learn that the Tarascans numbered forty thousand. Obviously, the combat did not go well for the Mexica and their allies, and they were forced into retreat, having lost twenty thousand men in combat.[133] On hearing the news, Tlacaelel arranged for what could only have been a dirge, played upon drums and conchs as the survivors entered the capital. Axayacatl grieved the loss of his men, but Tlacaelel counseled him, "Son, do not be faint, let not your heart feel dismay! Have courage: your subjects did not die working at the hearth, nor spinning like women, but on the battlefield, fighting for the glory of your heart and for the love of the country. . . . But I do not know why I have been spared."[134] He then set about organizing the ceremonies to honor the fallen, which Durán discusses in great detail.

However, hardly had the mourning ended when Tlacaelel launched another war to obtain captives to inaugurate the sculpted stone. Warriors from Tliliuhquitepec seemingly had that distinction, and Tlacaelel and Axayacatl, appropriately "dressed in magnificent clothing," taking turns, extracted the hearts of their prisoners until they exhausted themselves. The king, though, was ill, reportedly from the festivities and because the blood had "a bad sour odor."[135] He asked Tlacaelel to arrange to have his likeness carved in stone next to that of his grandfather, Moteuczoma Ilhuicamina. Having seen the image, he died on his litter as he was being carried back to his palace.

Axayacatl died in the year Two House, 1481.[136] During his rulership there were two eclipses of the sun, in Ten Flint, 1476, and in Twelve Rabbit, 1478, frightening everyone. On the latter occasion, fierce *tzitzimime*, "devils" or "spirits," were said to descend from the trees. There was also an earthquake (Nine Reed, 1475) that damaged many structures.[137] Ominous warnings to some, perhaps, but nonetheless Mexico Tenochtitlan prospered mightily during the rulership of Axayacatzin and his able adviser. And Tlacaelel was still organizing funerals, his great-nephew the reason for another wondrous, lavish commemorative tribute.

The annals add that Axayacatl left seventeen children. Some went on to rule in other polities, but two, his seventh and eighth sons, Moteuczoma Xocoyotl (r. 1502–20) and Cuitlahuac (r. 1520), acceded to their father's Tenochca throne.[138]

TLATOANI TIZOCICATZIN AND TLACAELEL IN HIS LAST YEARS

Within days of the final funeral ceremonies honoring Axayacatl and after the participants and guests had departed, it was made known that Tizocicatzin Tlachitonatiuh was the next huey tlatoani of Mexico Tenochtitlan. Tlacaelel himself, now in his eighties, made the decision to put the eldest son of his brother Moteuczoma Ilhuicamina on the throne.[139] Tlatoque from all the major altepetl hastened back to the capital for the customary rituals of kissing the king's hand, rendering obedience, and gifting. Nezahualpilli, king of Tetzcoco, presided over the coronation, which included not only Tizocic's investiture with a crown, jewels, and magnificent robes but also autosacrifice, offerings to the gods, and formal installation on the throne. These activities were followed by eloquent orations celebrating both the office and the man, as well as his duties. Nezahualpilli set the standard, and his speech was followed by those of the ruler of Tlacopan and subsequently the kings from across Mexica dominions. It would seem, as was typical, that Tlacaelel was behind the scenes orchestrating the pageant.[140]

Hardly had Tizocic been crowned when it was decided that another celebration in his honor was warranted, one that brought into play "a great sacrifice of men."[141] Metztitlan was to be the target: soldiers were solicited from the many subject altepetl, and they were in the capital within days. Tlacaelel was in charge, and as he sent the warriors toward the meeting place (either Atotonilco or Itzmiquilpan), he commanded the military leaders to take good care of the king, since he was young and inexperienced in combat.

Once beyond the reach of Tlacaelel, though, an emboldened Tizocic revealed that he had a plan for battle and encouraged his men to fight. He promised to provide backup when necessary. But their enemies were prepared and fought well, killing many of Tizocic's forces. The king then ordered the youngest soldiers, his reserve troops, into the fray, and they were able to rout their foes. The Mexica had taken a mere forty captives, but, considering that there were only three hundred Mexica casualties and that they were eventually victorious, Tizocic thanked all the men and sent them home. Tlacaelel was duly notified, and while he mourned the loss of the warriors he promptly set about arranging for the welcome-home ceremonies with the traditional music and incense, and with their veteran warriors (the "*Cuauh Huehuetque*") outfitted in full battle dress, weapons and all, as greeters. The captives and brave young soldiers first honored Huitzilopochtli and then went to the royal palace to meet Tlacaelel and enjoy a fine feast.[142]

Tizocic and his entourage had also arrived, and they made their way to the palace, where the king sat on his throne to receive well-wishers. Even the widows of the fallen were included in the ceremony. However, Tlacaelel let little time pass before he proceeded with his arrangements for what he now considered would be an official inauguration ceremony for the king. He again summoned the court nobles and told them to send notice to every polity that was subject to the Mexica that they were to come to Mexico Tenochtitlan. When everyone was in attendance, Tlacaelel seated himself next to Tizocic, and the visitors were ordered to present themselves and their gifts to the king. The palace and city were lavishly decorated with flowers, and it was a festival to end all festivals. The guests not only brought wonderful treasures for their sovereign, but in turn the nobles, warriors, and even the poor received presents from the king. The ceremony lasted four days. The captives were finally sacrificed, and all the guests were then allowed to depart.[143]

In spite of Tlacaelel's grandiose efforts to establish Tizocic as a bona fide high king, both Alvarado Tezozomoc and Durán make short shrift of the man and his reign. It was Tlacaelel who had been adamant that Tizocic rule, but he turned out to be "cowardly," it was said, and the king was consequently killed by certain Mexica in his attendance.[144] Tizocic was cremated before the image of the Mexica deity, Huitzilopochtli, and everyone once again came from afar. Remarkably, even that sort of information was recorded in the pictorial manuscripts, as evidenced by Chimalpahin, who lamented that "the elders do not show if the kings of Chalco returned immediately to Mexico Tenochtitlan for the burial of Tizoc." We must assume that they did since Tizoc, as huey tlatoani, was responsible for reinstating the royal lineages in Chalco and, in reality, restoring a modicum of entitlement and dignity.[145] During the cremation procedures, though, horrifying figures, some emulating a god, were charged with the ordeal, but they were so terrifying that all those watching were intimidated. Was this also staging by Tlacaelel? The rites concluded with the killing of the "slaves and hunchbacks and dwarfs" with all the slaves attending in Tizocic's palace, and all his precious possessions were buried along with his remains. As Tlacaelel and the Mexica nobles bade farewell to everyone who had come to pay their respects to Tizocic, they were reminded that very soon there would be an announcement of the next tlatoani, essentially a notification to be ready for another grand celebratory spectacle.[146]

Chimalpahin's annals are more generous than Durán is regarding Tizocic and his legacy. They state that it was indeed Tlacaelel who selected the eldest of his brother Moteuczoma Ilhuicamina's grandsons to succeed Axayacatl, but since the new king was "little disposed to be warlike," the Mexica were unhappy, and for that reason they poisoned him.[147] The accounts vary as to the length of his rule, ranging from four to six years.[148] Nevertheless, another set of annals credits Tizocic with having conquered four altepetl, including finishing off one conflict that Axayacatl had started, but overall successfully waging war. Four battles, it should be noted, was also the number attributed to his younger brother and successor, Ahuitzotl.[149] Of primary interest to Chimalpahin, though, was that Tizocic restored most of the rulerships in Chalco. The year was Twelve Rabbit, 1478, and the thrones had been without tlatoque for twenty-two years. Only quauhtlatoque, "interim rulers," had been in charge of the many altepetl. But the tlatoani Tizocicatzin remembered the rulerships of Chalco (*Auh yn tlahtohuani Tiçocicatzin oc yehuatl quilnamic yn tlahtocayotl Chalco*), and he ordered that a search be conducted to identify the rightful rulers, or tlatocapipiltin.[150] He then officially installed as rulers (*motlahtocatlallique yn tlatoque Chalco*) several of the descendants of the tlatoque who had gone into exile so many years before. Within days of completing this exceptional task, Tizocic died.[151] For Chimalpahin, the golden age of Chalco had ended with the Mexica conquest in Twelve House, 1465, but a semblance of dignity and order was gained with rightful rulers on Chalca thrones once again.

The annals make a point of listing Tizocic's descendants. Chimalpahin obviously had several sets of Mexica annals and genealogies at his disposal, for he provides different, often conflicting, information about the king's offspring. Tizocic married the daughter of Xiconocatzin the elder of Temazcaltitlan.[152] He did not have to travel far to find this wife. Chimalpahin described the location when he wrote of the Mexica's arrival so many years before: "they came to and arrived at a certain site called Temazcaltitlan in the middle of this great lagoon of Tenochtitlan, where there [now] is the church of [our] Lord St. Paul."[153] He was assuredly referring to San Pablo Teopan, which constituted the southeastern quadrant of the Mexica Tenochtitlan capital. Tizocic's wife's name is not known, but they had two sons, Tezcatl Popocatzin the elder and Mauhcaxochitzin the elder.[154] Other annals, however, state that he had many esteemed sons (*tlatocapipiltin*), two of whom were particularly prominent: the aforementioned Tezcatl Popocatzin, and the prestigiously titled Tepehuatzin the Tlacochcalcatl.[155] The latter died tragically during the festival of Toxcatl in Two Flint, 1520, when a great many Mexica nobles were slaughtered by Pedro de Alvarado and his men.[156]

For present purposes, though, and looking forward, it is Tezcatl Popocatzin the elder, also from San Pablo Teopan, and Mauhcaxochitzin the elder, who are important to our story of Tlacaelel and the Mexica over the years. King Tizoc's family line—prestigious and enduring—is surely but one example of the vast familial and entitlement network enjoyed by the descendants of the Mexica royal house over the course of many decades. The genealogies are particularly rich with information about the offspring of Tizocic's two sons and their marriages. Several of the descendants did well for themselves over succeeding generations, with some daughters, many of whom were named María or doña María, marrying rulers. Most of Tizocic's descendants were baptized as well. Tezcatl Popocatzin the elder married a noblewoman from Tzaucyocan, although a note was added to the text stating that she was actually "just a servant of his."[157] That she was of lower rank is improbable, considering Mexica protocol for succession and eligibility to rule by this time.[158] Together they had a son, don Diego de San Francisco Tehuetzquititzin the Tlacateccatl, who held an important title and also eventually officiated in San Juan Tenochtitlan, the Nahua capital in the colonial era.

Tehuetzquititzin was apparently among the impressive and influential Mexica nobles negotiating with Hernando Cortés and his interpreter, Malintzin, during the conquest battles and afterward. Moreover, it is likely that he was among those imprisoned and tortured while Cortés searched for gold and other treasure. Certainly, he was a member of the same cohort that the conqueror took on his long journey to Honduras, where he planned to confront his former lieutenant Cristóbal de Olid, who had rebelled against him. The sitting tlatoani, Quauhtemoc, and Tlacotzin the Cihuacoatl, Tlacaelel the elder's grandson, among others, were also a part of that horrendous undertaking. Quauhtemoc, as is known, was hanged, and Tlacotzin, by then baptized don Juan Velásquez Tlacotzin the Cihuacoatl, was installed as the next tlatoani only to die on the trip home.[159] Somehow, Tehuetzquititzin, baptized don Diego de San Francisco Tehuetzquititzin the Tlacateccatl, made it back to Mexico City. He was installed in Ten House, 1541, as the second *gobernador*, "governor" (r. 1541–54) in the capital. His authority was such that his painted image appears in at least two extant colonial pictorial documents.[160]

One of don Diego's first deeds in office was to accompany Viceroy don Antonio de Mendoza (r. 1535–50) to Xochipillan, where he distinguished himself in battle.[161] His ability in warfare carried on the tradition of his predecessors, the valiant Mexica warrior-kings. Once back in the capital, he ruled in San Juan Tenochtitlan until he died at vespers on the feast day of San Juan Bautista on the twenty-third of June, in Ten Rabbit, 1554.[162] One final tribute—and in some ways the most important of all his accomplishments—is due to don Diego for helping to collect Mexica manuscripts and then, along with relatives, imparting that knowledge to don Hernando de Alvarado Tezozomoc, one of the principal authors and sources for this study of Mexica history: "I, don Hernando de Alvarado Tezozomoc, . . . listened to the rulers don Diego de Alvarado Huanitzin, my parent, don Pedro Tlacahuepan, my uncle, don Diego de San Francisco Tehuetzquititzin, and other highborn noblemen who indeed rightly understood the ancient ones' accounts. Here I took their statements."[163]

But the story of Tizocic's royal lineage did not end there. Don Diego had married "in holy wedlock" his first cousin doña María, the daughter of his uncle Mauhcaxochitl the elder. They had two sons, both of whom died young. Don Diego had at least two more "wives" and four more sons, along with five daughters. The years of those marriages and births are not furnished, but the implication is that Tehuetzquititzin had plural wives during the colonial era. Elsewhere, Chimalpahin states that *"ypan in yhcuac tzintic yn nenamictiliztli"* (in this year Eleven House, 1529, the sacrament of marriage began), and Nahua rulers across the land were forced to select only one of the women in their households to marry in the church.[164] Tehuetzquititzin, as prominent as he was, doubtless ultimately conformed to the new mandate.

It is the tenth of Tehuetzquititzin's children who leads us back to the Tlacaelel family line. Named doña María, too, she married her cousin don Jacobo, the son of Tehuetzquititzin's brother-in-law, and together they had a son, don Juan (fig. 17). But doña María, at some point widowed, had a second son, who, the annals state, was "considered important."[165] This was Miguel

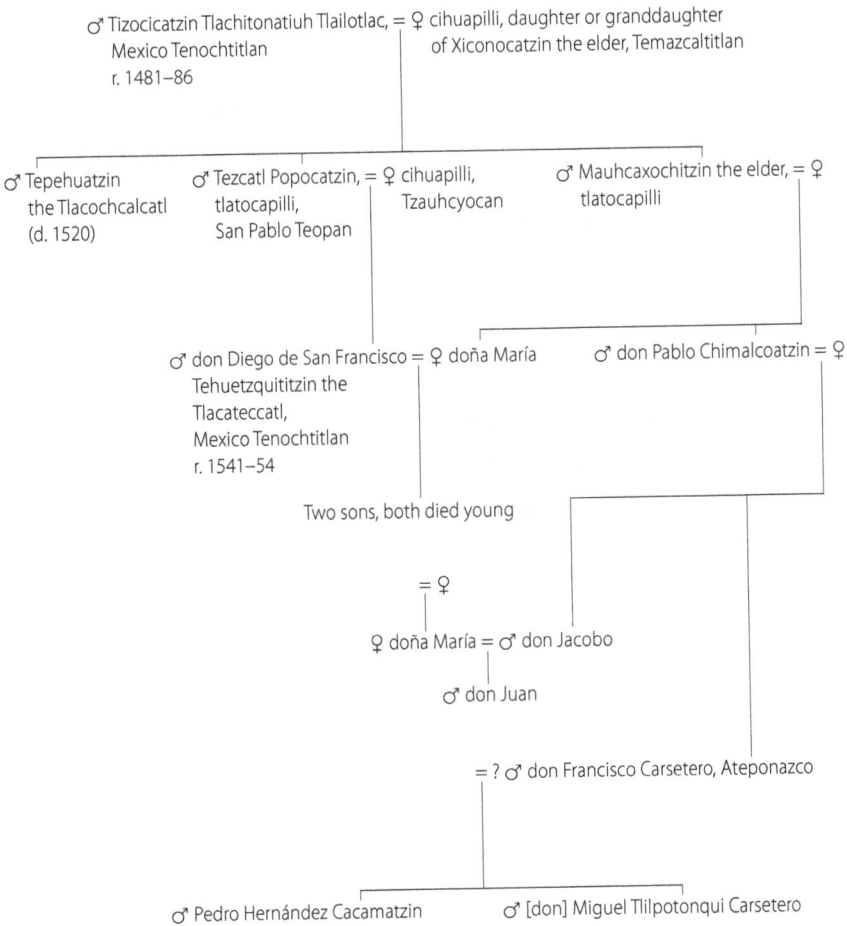

FIG. 17. Tlacaelel family ties to Mexica royalty in the colonial era.

Tlilpotonqui, a "natural son," who reportedly resembled the "legitimately begotten sons [sic], and could not be called a bastard son."[166] Another genealogy corrects this information by stating that doña María actually gave birth to Pedro Hernández Cacamatzin, "[an event] of which they made much," and then don Miguel Tlilpotonqui Carsetero, "an illegitimate son."[167]

"Illegitimate" may not be the best term to identify this child, nor would it be acceptable under any circumstance. But doña María's late husband, don Jacobo, had a brother, don Francisco Carsetero, of Atepanazco (Acatlan). It may be that the levirate dictated this arrangement, or that doña María had a relationship with don Jacobo's brother and their child was given his Spanish surname.

The names of the two sons are a sure indication of a connection to the Tlacaelel noble line. Tlilpotonqui was the name of the old Cihuacoatl's second son, and it is close to impossible to find the name elsewhere. Moreover, Cacamatzin was the name of Tlacaelel's eldest son, and Hernández was the Spanish surname used by the Tlacaelels in the seventeenth century.[168] Moreover, the Carseteros were from Atepanazco, next to, or a part of, Acatlan, the home polity of the Tlacaelel family (see map 2).[169]

Tizocic's prestige was such that the family's fame continued into the seventeenth century, to Chimalpahin's time, for don Diego de San Francisco Tehuetzquititzin's eleventh child, doña Cecilia, had married don Diego Quauhpotonqui, the ruler of Ecatepec (r. 1547–?), where their daughter, doña María, was still living "now in the year 1616."[170]

AHUITZOTL: TLACAELEL THE CIHUACOATL'S FINAL CHARGE

Hardly four days had passed after Tizocicatzin's funeral ceremonies when Tlacaelel convened his officials to select a successor to the throne.[171] In fact, Tlacaelel had already determined that the next king would be his nephew, Ahuitzotl, the second of his brother Moteuczoma Ilhuicamina's three sons. He knew that the boy was young and untested, but he would have no other as tlatoani. Mexico Tenochtitlan officials thought otherwise, and they insisted that the next king be a man of experience and proven leadership. At an impasse, both sides agreed that the decision should be made by Nezahualpilli, the ruler of Tetzcoco, who himself had acceded to the throne as a boy.[172] Undeterred, the indomitable Cihuacoatl sent back-channel messengers to Tetzcoco to tell King Nezahualpilli what to do. The king, not wishing to anger either Tlacaelel or the Mexica council, worked out a compromise of sorts: Tlacaelel was to be the king, essentially the regent, and Ahuitzotl would grow up and learn by his example.

Durán states that everyone, as on previous occasions, wanted Tlacaelel to be their tlatoani, and the officials returned to the capital "shouting their approval."[173] Tlacaelel, though, protested at length:

> O my sons, I am grateful to you and to the king of Tetzcoco. But come here! I wish to ask you, what have I been during the eighty or ninety years since the war with Azcapotzalco took place? What position have I had? Have I been nothing? Why have I not put the diadem upon my head, why have I not worn the royal insignia? When I have been a judge, when I have issued commands, have I been ignored? Have I executed the delinquent or pardoned the innocent without cause? Have I not been able to appoint chieftains or to remove them, as I have done? Have I acted wrongly, have I broken the laws of the republic in wearing the mantles, the breechcloths and sandals, golden armbands, anklets, labrets of gold and jade, and fine ear and nose pendants? Have I broken the law in entering the royal palace and the temple shod, as I have done up to now? For no one can do these things but the king. Have I done wrong in wearing the garments, the symbols, of the gods, showing myself as their image, and as a god taking up the knife to sacrifice men? If I could do these things, and I have been doing them for eighty or ninety years, and I am then a king and you have held me as such. What more of a king do you wish me to be?[174]

The council and other administrators had no choice but to accept Ahuitzotl, and Tlacaelel promptly sent envoys across the realm to notify the Mexica's subjects of the new king and to prepare for his installation in office. More immediately, however, Tlacaelel oversaw the investiture of the boy, with the rulers of Tetzcoco and Tlacopan duly placing a crown on his head, perforating his nasal septum, and outfitting him with jewels and the proper regal attire. They also counseled the young king on his duties.[175] Next, Ahuitzotl was taken before the image of Huitzilopochtli, where he performed the prescribed rituals. Finally, he was visited and officially recognized by all of Mexico Tenochtitlan's dignitaries, each of whom made an honorific pronouncement and kissed the tlatoani's hand.

All of these formalities were in anticipation of Ahuitzotl's proper coronation, which Tlacaelel was already planning. In truth, he was plotting another war in order to obtain another bounty of sacrificial victims. Warriors were requisitioned from near and far, and young Ahuitzotl, although uninitiated, was taken along to battle, which was to be against the peoples of Chiapa and Xilotepec, among others. Seven altepetl were ultimately conquered and ravaged, and a suitable number of captives was obtained for sacrifice. Tribute thereafter would be paid to the conquerors, and workers would be sent to Mexico Tenochtitlan.

News of another victory was sent along to Tlacaelel, and he, as always, arranged for the welcoming festivities for the victorious soldiers. After his reception and the usual speeches, Ahuitzotl, following protocol, first went to the temple to honor Huitzilopochtli and then to his palace, where he greeted Tlacaelel, who "was carried in on a man's shoulders because of his extreme age."[176] They celebrated the king's success, and Tlacaelel set the date Ce Cipactli, or One Alligator, for Ahuitzotl's coronation. Reportedly, everyone was to attend, and all were to bring goods, specialty items from their home regions to be certain that there was both an abundance and a variety of food and other wares. Doubtless, Tlacaelel intended a display of conspicuous consumption heretofore unprecedented. In part, too, Durán adds, the occasion was to dazzle and intimidate the Mexica's old enemies, the peoples in the east in and near Cholula, Huexotzinco, and Tlaxcala. The rulers in these polities were invited to attend, but most refused. Moreover, the coronation was also a potlatch of sorts with reciprocal, lavish gifting and everyone in their finery, with no end of flowers, tobacco, singing, and dancing. Delicious food was served, with a repast of chocolate. Durán speaks of "all the lords, noblemen, the chieftains and warriors, the priests and ministers of the temples," indicating male exclusivity at these sumptuous affairs.[177] Did women participate, other than as the laborers behind the scenes? Because female deities and royal women were held in high esteem, it is assumed that they, at least, celebrated along with their male counterparts. But the absence of mention of the presence of women at the celebratory festivities in the chronicles is striking.[178]

One thousand captives were sacrificed after four days of feasting and ceremonies, and, finally, the guests were allowed to depart. Some time later, though, Tlacaelel notified Ahuitzotl of an insurrection among the Huaxteca, and it was necessary to send forces to quell it.[179] Tlacaelel was the wizard behind the war, but the young tlatoani was in charge of it, commanding the squadrons and taking to the field. Once again, he proved himself a man a valor, and the Mexica's foe again was vanquished, with abundant spoils for Ahuitzotl's warriors.[180]

Durán states that the war against the Huaxteca occurred in Eight Reed, 1487, the second year of Ahuitzotl's reign. The annals credit Tizocicatzin with carrying out the major work of construction and adornment of the great temple, but it was his successor who was charged with its inauguration.[181] But first Ahuitzotl added his own finishing touches to the edifice by bringing in stonemasons who quickly completed their work. Tlacaelel was said to be very pleased that Ahuitzotl had turned his attention to the temple, surely because, once ready, it would be cause for another grand celebration.

Again, rulers and their entourages throughout the realm were contacted with invitations and notice to bring captives for the dedicatory ceremony. Tlacaelel's old grudges toward Tlaxcala and the other eastern polities were festering for having refused to attend Ahuitzotl's investiture, among other provocations. He reminded Ahuitzotl of the affront, and the king therefore sent gift-bearing emissaries in secret to contact those distant rulers and invite them to the inauguration of the temple mayor. And then the Mexica leader feted his adversaries, once they were in Mexico Tenochtitlan. Everything was done in secret, because Tlacaelel and Ahuitzotl did not want their own warriors to know that foes were among them in case there was a need to go to battle in the future.

The ceremonies in honor of Huitzilopochtli's temple were as spectacular as ever, and they were observed by the Mexica's vast imperial constituency, along with representatives from various rival factions. The capital was magnificently arrayed, and the royal gifts for rich and poor were generous. But amid all the festivities were the long, solemn lines of captives brought for the

occasion to be sacrificed at the top of the temple.[182] The rulers of the triumvirate, outfitted in their finest mantles, sandals, loincloths, and jewelry, served
as the principal executioners of the 80,600 individuals put to death over the
course of four days.[183] The next day, humbled, the guests left for home, laden
with gifts from their host and indelible memories of Mexica hegemony.

Chimalpahin states that Tlacaelel died in this same year, but the annals
do not include whether he was the mastermind of the prodigious inauguration of the temple and the grotesque slaughter. The grandiosity does have
his stamp, though. Durán, likewise, is not specific with his blame, or credit,
but Alvarado Tezozomoc does not hesitate to make a point of Tlacaelel
the Cihuacoatl and Ahuitzotl as the instigators and star performers.[184] The
Spanish-language chronicles, on the other hand, compress events and time,
with Ahuitzotl going off to wage more battles, one as far away as Tehuantepec. Ahuitzotl repeatedly demonstrated his success as a warrior and leader,
often showing benevolence toward those he conquered, and he was greatly
appreciated at home. He was at least as pious and dutiful to the deities as his
predecessor, and he was mindfully generous to those of his court, opening
his treasure stores and showering all with gifts.[185] The altepetl was for the
moment enjoying peace, and it was said that the king was calm. Durán notes
that it was at this time that Ahuitzotl lost Tlacaelel, his stalwart adviser. The
friar reported that the cause was both illness and the man's venerability.[186]
Rather, might his passing have been hastened by the unfamiliar serenity that
suddenly prevailed? It was the end of an era.[187]

❀

During Tlacaelel's tenure as principal adviser and "second king" to five
high tlatoque, Mexico Tenochtitlan was transformed from an ignominious
town to an imperial state. Once a desolate island devoid of resources, it
had become an entrepôt of treasure, its subjects channeling what seemed
an endless supply of coveted raw and finished materials into the capital for
display and consumption or preferential distribution among allies. Mexica
politics and economics were defined by protracted warfare, and Chalco—
Chimalpahin's home altepetl—became a classic example of their unyielding
violence and cruelty. Society was rigidly stratified but with exceptions for
some of the children of rulers born outside the royal household. The capital

and the court were surely burgeoned with royal favorites who afforded access to exotic goods and security abroad. Little is said of women during the five regimes, other than their being gifted to victors as war booty. Royal wives, daughters, and sisters certainly continued to build and ensure the expanding confederation of imperial altepetl through royal marriages. Durán and Alvarado Tezozomoc's histories make the case that religion was the force driving Mexica expansionism. Since the early years, the Mexica had followed the dictates of their god, Huitzilopochtli. That the scale of devotion would reach such extremes of expropriation of resources, slaughter, and cannibalism could hardly have been foreseen. Could one man have been responsible for so much?

CHAPTER 4

TLACAELEL'S SUCCESSORS IN THE COLONIAL ERA

❀

The old man died happy.

Durán

His obsequies had been performed as a person of his rank
deserved, according to his eminence, in the same way
they were carried out for the kings.

Durán

All those who succeeded him took this [special] name of
Cihuacoatl and gloried in being called Cihuacoatl, and
it remained consecrated as the highest title and rank in
the world after that of emperor.

Chimalpahin

He [don Miguel Sánchez Huentzin, a noble of Acatlan] was the
only one left, so that with him ended the line of the late lord
Tlacaelel the elder, the Cihuacoatl, high constable in Mexico
Tenochtitlan. With the said dead person the nobility of
Acatlan came to an end, he terminated it once and for all.

Chimalpahin

After Tlacaelel's death, the Cihuacoatls of Mexico Tenochtitlan carried on
as the masterminds of warfare, temple building, and ritual human sacrifice. They orchestrated the official policy and protocol during the course
of each huey tlatoani's reign. In so doing, they took note of and integrated

each succeeding ruler's personal preference and style. Tlacaelel had made certain that the royal dynasty would prevail. He was obsessed with ensuring that his brother Moteuczoma Ilhuicamina's grandsons should assume the throne, and when they did, one after the other, they never strayed far from traditional governance. Even the last of the preconquest tlatoque, Moteuczoma Xocoyotl (r. 1502–20), Tlacaelel's great-great-nephew and a masterful statesman in his own right, persisted in the growing of the empire and the economy while rigorously refining court society.

Upon the death of Moteuczoma Xocoyotl, the Cihuacoatls stepped up first as ardent defenders of the homeland and then as diplomats and mediators between the Spaniards and the tlatoque, overseeing the reconstruction and repopulation of large sections of what was becoming Mexico City. The Cihuacoatl suffered the extremes of torture and privation along with his ruler, with one, Tlacotzin, Tlacaelel's grandson, becoming a favorite of Hernando Cortés, only to die soon thereafter. Tlacotzin was the last of the infamous Mexica Cihuacoatls, and one would expect that with his death the Tlacaelel noble line also came to an end.

By the late sixteenth century, though, the Tlacaelel family was large. Some members married Spaniards, others entered the church, and still others became influential politicians. The Spaniards had implemented a system of government that in many polities allowed traditional rulers to hold sway in local governments. The Moteuczomas continued as a family of note in their familiar quarter, Atzaqualco, and the Tlacaelels stayed on in Acatlan, active in politics to the end.

TLACAELEL THE CIHUACOATL AND HIS SUCCESSORS

Tlilpotonqui, the Second Cihuacoatl (r. 1487–1503)

Tlacaelel Xocoyotl, the Third Cihuacoatl (r. 1503–ca. 1520)

Matlatzincatzin, Interim and the Fourth Cihuacoatl (r. 1520)

Tlacotzin, the Last Cihuacoatl (r. ca. 1520–1526)

It is hard to imagine that anyone could conceive of carrying on the tradition of Tlacaelel and his office, for he had been the man behind the throne of five great Mexica monarchs and had orchestrated the extraordinary evolution of his altepetl. But the Mexica were fully invested in Tlacaelel, who had institutionalized the position of the Cihuacoatl, the success of which was measured in its subsequent generations. His children, who were heirs to Tenochca, Tetzcoca, and Chalca interdynastic marriages, continued the customs and glory of the Cihuacoatl while elaborating prestigious and beneficial familial ties that served them well, even among Spaniards, into the seventeenth century.

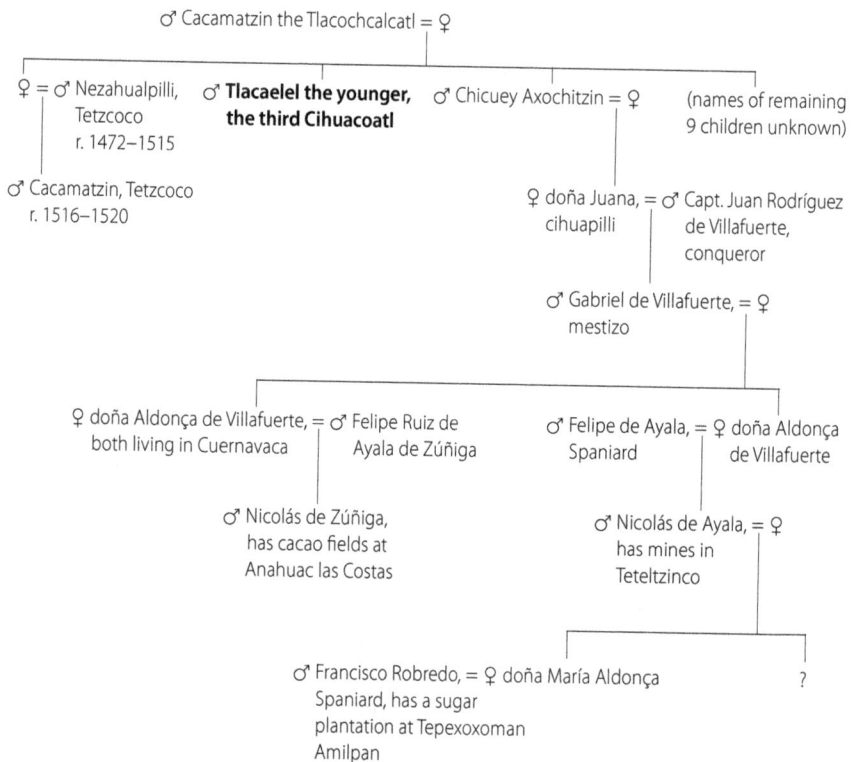

♂ Cacamatzin the Tlacochcalcatl = ♀

♀ = ♂ Nezahualpilli, Tetzcoco r. 1472–1515

♂ **Tlacaelel the younger, the third Cihuacoatl**

♂ Chicuey Axochitzin = ♀

(names of remaining 9 children unknown)

♂ Cacamatzin, Tetzcoco r. 1516–1520

♀ doña Juana, = ♂ Capt. Juan Rodríguez cihuapilli de Villafuerte, conqueror

♂ Gabriel de Villafuerte, = ♀ mestizo

♀ doña Aldonça de Villafuerte, = ♂ Felipe Ruiz de both living in Cuernavaca Ayala de Zúñiga

♂ Felipe de Ayala, = ♀ doña Aldonça Spaniard de Villafuerte

♂ Nicolás de Zúñiga, has cacao fields at Anahuac las Costas

♂ Nicolás de Ayala, = ♀ has mines in Teteltzinco

♂ Francisco Robredo, = ♀ doña María Aldonça Spaniard, has a sugar plantation at Tepexoxoman Amilpan

?

FIG. 18. Cacamatzin the Tlacochcalcatl's lineage.
Copyright © 2016, University of Oklahoma Press.

Boldface indicates which of Tlacaelel the elder's descendants became the Cihuacoatl.

TLILPOTONQUI:
THE SECOND CIHUACOATL

A man surely content with himself, Tlacaelel died at the age of ninety in Eight Reed, 1487: "At this time the very great war leader (chief, guide, and captain) and president over all the great noblemen, the lord Tlacaelel [the] Cihuacoatl, the great lord of Tenochtitlan, died."[1] Chimalpahin added that he was "superior to the great noblemen in what was proposed or was completely superior to the great noblemen as judge overlords (president or supreme superior judge), the lord Tlacaeleltzin [the] Cihuacoatl, the great lord of Tenochtitlan," and he left a capital that was sumptuous in its beauty, wealth, royalty, and orthodoxy. Ahuitzotl, the third son of tlatocapilli Tezozomoc and cihuapilli Atotoztli, daughter of Moteuczoma Ilhuica-mina, and grandson of Itzcoatl, had been installed on the Mexica Tenochca throne the year before, and he arranged appropriately lavish funeral cer-emonies for his co-ruler and honorable uncle, cremating his remains and interring his ashes adjacent to the royal sepulcher of the Mexica tlatoque.[2] Ahuitzotl, fulfilling his vow to take care of Tlacaelel's sons, who were his cousins, in accord with his royal council immediately installed Tlilpoton-qui as the Cihuacoatl, who then assumed the duties of his office. Durán states that the Cihuacoatl title had been bestowed by the gods.[3] Fray Diego claims that Tlilpotonqui was Tlacaelel's eldest son, but Chimalpahin's annals show that his firstborn son was Cacamatzin the Tlacochcalcatl (see figs. 16 and 18).[4]

Presumably, either Tlacaelel or Ahuitzotl had decided to divide the burden of the old man's duties between two of his sons, Cacamatzin and Tlilpotonqui, and Cacamatzin took on the military command, assuming charge of the troops in the field. He later died in Michoacan, after the Taras-cans took him as a captive. Tlacaelel's second son, Tlilpontonqui the Cihua-coatl, seemed to be exclusively involved with domestic duties, an enormous mandate in its own right. There is evidence that he had proved himself as a warrior during the Mexica-Chalca war (1446–65).[5] He was by this time "President of the Supreme Council of the Mexica Empire."[6] Chimalpahin described Cacamatzin and Tlilpotonqui as "great, brave warriors" who used the quetzal feather device as their insignia, which they bore on their backs.[7]

Ahuitzotl, who had gone to battle alongside his cousins, confirmed their status.[8]

Ahuitzotl died in Ten Rabbit, 1502, and Tlilpotonqui, as was customary for the Cihuacoatl, arranged for the king's funeral. Alvarado Tezozomoc wrote that Tlilpotonqui sent notice across the realm to be certain that everyone attended, and it is assumed that royal dignitaries came from far away.[9] Prominent in the obsequy to King Ahuitzotl were King Nezahualpilli of Tetzcoco and Totoquihuaztli, ruler of Tlacopan, who both stayed on for the royal council meeting to select the next Mexica king. As expected, Tlilpotonqui the Cihuacoatl presided: he spoke eloquently, praising the valiant candidates—all sixteen legitimate grandsons of the late King Moteuczoma Ilhuicamina—and urging the council to select the most suitable of the lot. It appears, though, that the Cihuacoatl favored the then-Tlacochcalcatl, Moteuczoma Xocoyotl, to be the next ruler and ensure the continuation of the royal lineage, and he was approved unanimously.[10] More specifically, "the great president Tlilpotonqui the Cihuacoatl himself and at the demand of the community chose a son of Emperor Axayacatl named Moteuczoma to be emperor."[11]

The Cihuacoatl also continued to serve as primary adviser and oversaw numerous transformative social reforms at the court and across the empire, many of which concerned the education and comportment of the young nobles who attended Moteuczoma Xocoyotl. According to Durán, "Through his [Tlilpotonqui's] hands passed all things connected with the government."[12] By the time of Moteuczoma's rule, due especially to the concerted efforts of previous rulers to confederate the empire by means of plural wives and interdynastic marriages, the court was likely close to being overwhelmed with an assortment of well-connected but superfluous attendees.[13] Purging his dominions of hangers-on from the days of Ahuitzotl and possibly earlier, when Tlacaelel and Moteuczoma Ilhuicamina opened the ranks for non-nobles, and making certain that their replacements were of legitimate and noble birth, properly educated, and fastidiously loyal, Moteuczoma Xocoyotl aimed for solidarity as well as an environment of patrician and eloquent uniformity. Durán summarized and quoted Moteuczoma Xocoyotl: "Just as precious stones lose their value when mixed with common, inferior stones, people of royal blood do not look well when they are among those who are of low birth." All courtiers were to be nobles of the finest lineages, well spoken, properly attired, of a certain stature, and dignified in manner. All were to treat the women of the court with respect, and even those individuals charged with the most menial tasks were to be in compliance. And "all were to be young boys because it is easier to give them good advice."[14] The boys were to become mainstays of the palace service personnel. Of course, most were Moteuczoma's kin.[15] Tlilpotonqui was to ensure that there was universal conformity, and anyone who failed to measure up was shot with arrows or burned to death. Reportedly, everyone who had previously served Ahuitzotl was killed.[16] And at this point fray Diego editorializes, stating that Moteuczoma Xocoyotl "showed himself to be the greatest butcher that ever existed, in order to be feared and held in awe."[17] The palace came to be fashioned as the "house of the god," and the emperor was held as a deity incarnate. "If any commoner dared to lift his eyes and look upon him [Moteuczoma Xocoyotl], the king ordered that he be slain." For that reason, "when he passed, everyone prostrated himself on the ground."[18]

Alvarado Tezozomoc fails to distinguish carefully between Tlilpotonqui, the second Cihuacoatl, and those who followed him. He has one man, Tlilpotonqui, or, instead and more commonly, "the Cihuacoatl," carrying out all the duties of the office and, most important, serving as adviser and imperial administrator.[19] Under Moteuczoma Xocoyotl, he was referred to as Moteuczoma's "lugartiniente,"[20] and when the king went to war the Cihuacoatl was charged with doing all that was necessary to govern and administer the republic efficiently.[21] Then, upon receiving word of success in the field and having already arranged for the festivities, the Cihuacoatl was in Xoloco when the king and his troops returned from battle; and, as expected by this time, he oversaw the spoils of war and distributed them in accordance with their tradition.[22] Alvarado Tezozomoc describes Tlilpotonqui as the "second king."[23]

Warfare continued apace, but Tlilpotonqui was cosseted in the capital, managing the government and planning Moteuczoma Xocoyotl's inauguration ceremony, which featured now-familiar pomp: grandiose oratory and gifting, feasts, and the sacrifice of captives. Typically, Tlilpotonqui, as had his father, wore the clothing of a woman styled after the attire of the goddess Cihuacoatl, described as "eagle garments," especially when he marched in

procession with Moteuczoma Xocoyotl.[24] On other occasions, when Tlilpotonqui worshiped alongside the king at the temple of Huitzilopochtli, the
king entered a sacred chamber and performed the requisite ceremonies
before the images of all the deities from across the land in order to inaugurate each new sacred precinct. From there, the two men moved on to the
place where sacrifices were to be performed.[25] When he served as priestly
executioner with Moteuczoma Xocoyotl, the Cihuacoatl and the king were
outfitted as high priests, anointed with "divine bitumen," and both men
"wore gold diadems on their heads."[26] Accompanied by the music of conch
shells, flutes, whistles, and drums and working in tandem, Moteuczoma and
Tlilpotonqui sliced open the captives' chests; extracted the hearts, raised
them to the sun, and placed them before the images of the gods; and then
toppled the bodies down the stairs. Thousands were sacrificed on any one
occasion.[27] On the other hand, when grieving the loss of Mexica warriors
after a battle, Tlilpotonqui and Moteuczoma wore their cloaks of eagle

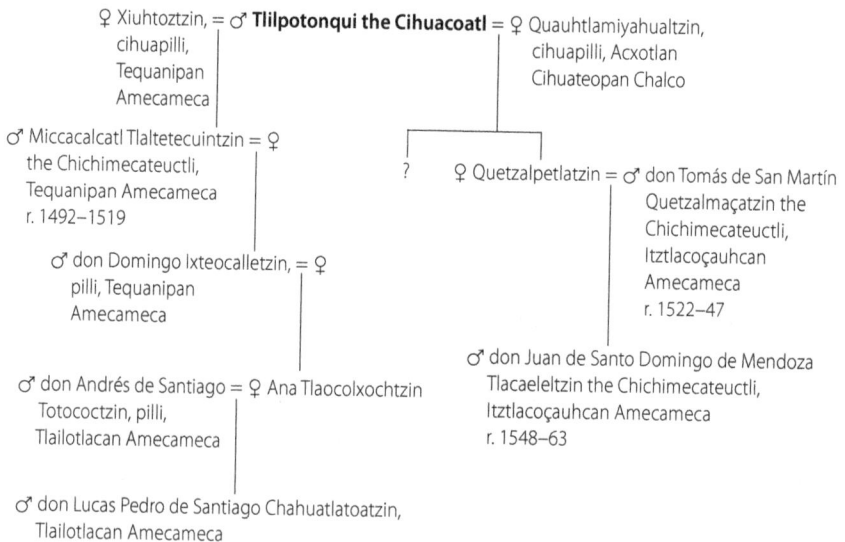

♀ Xiuhtoztzin, = ♂ **Tlilpotonqui the Cihuacoatl** = ♀ Quauhtlamiyahualtzin,
cihuapilli,   cihuapilli, Acxotlan
Tequanipan   Cihuateopan Chalco
Amecameca

♂ Miccacalcatl Tlaltetecuintzin = ♀
the Chichimecateuctli,
Tequanipan Amecameca
r. 1492–1519

                                                            ?   ♀ Quetzalpetlatzin = ♂ don Tomás de San Martín
                                                                                         Quetzalmaçatzin the
                                                                                         Chichimecateuctli,
    ♂ don Domingo Ixteocalletzin, = ♀   Itztlacoçauhcan
    pilli, Tequanipan   Amecameca
    Amecameca   r. 1522–47

                                                            ♂ don Juan de Santo Domingo de Mendoza
♂ don Andrés de Santiago = ♀ Ana Tlaocolxochtzin   Tlacaeleltzin the Chichimecateuctli,
Totococtzin, pilli,   Itztlacoçauhcan Amecameca
Tlailotlacan Amecameca   r. 1548–63

♂ don Lucas Pedro de Santiago Chahuatlatoatzin,
Tlailotlacan Amecameca

FIG. 19. Tlilpotonqui the Cihuacoatl and his Amecameca descendants.
Copyright © 2016, University of Oklahoma Press.

Boldface indicates which of Tlacaelel the elder's descendants became the Cihuacoatl.

feathers as they stood at the entrance of the temple, solemnly greeting the few survivors as they returned from afar.[28]

Chimalpahin recorded that Tlilpotonqui had fourteen children. According to his annals, Tlilpotonqui married two women from Chalco, which may not have been unusual since his mother was from there (fig. 19). His first wife was a noblewoman (cihuapilli) named Xiuhtoztzin, daughter of the interim ruler (quauhtlatoani) Yaopaintzin (r. 1438–65 or later) of Huixtoco Tequanipan, a tlayacatl altepetl in Amecameca.[29] Xiuhtoztzin went to live with Tlilpotonqui in Mexico Tenochtitlan, and in 1483 their son Miccacalcatl Tlaltecuintzin was born. In Thirteen Flint, 1492, at the age of nine, Miccacalcatl Tlaltecuintzin was installed as ruler of his mother's altepetl (r. 1492–1522) and given the title of the Chichimecateuctli, which was unique to him in Huixtoco Tequanipan and certainly the most prestigious title and office in Amecameca.[30] Nevertheless, upon the arrival of the Spaniards in 1519 Miccacalcatl Tlaltecuintzin left his kingship and went to join Moteuczoma Xocoyotl and his own Mexica relatives in Mexico Tenochtitlan.[31] However, we know nothing of his role in fighting the Spaniards.

The second of Tlilpotonqui's wives was a noblewoman from the highest-ranked Chalco polity, Acxotlan Cihuateopan. Her name was Quauhtlamiyahualtzin, and she was a member of the royal court there. The couple had a daughter, Quetzalpetlatzin, who married don Tomás de San Martín Quetzalmaçatzin the Chichimecateuctli (r. 1522–47), ruler of Itztlacoçauhcan, the premier polity in Amecameca, Chalco.[32] Quetzalpetlatzin was obviously don Tomás's primary wife, since their son, don Juan de Santo Domingo Mendoza Tlacaeleltzin (r. 1548–63), succeeded his father as the tlatoani and as the Chichimecateuctli upon his death and ruled Itztlacoçauhcan Amecameca for fifteen years.[33] The Nahua surname Tlacaelel is a cognominal reminder of Amecameca's prestigious ties to Mexica royalty. Doubtless, it was because of those ties that two of Tlilpotonqui's Amecameca sons came to assume that altepetl's highest title and office.

Tlilpotonqui reportedly had eleven sons and three daughters, and, like his father, Tlacaelel, he surely had wives other than the noblewomen from Amecameca.[34] His fifth child, Tzihuacxochitzin, was one of these daughters, and although the name and affiliation of her mother is unknown, she must have been from one of the best families. Tzihuacxochitzin married

Moteuczoma Xocoyotl, her distant cousin, and they had two daughters: doña Leonor de Moteuczoma and doña María de Moteuczoma, the latter dying as a young girl. Doña Leonor, it can probably be said, fared better. Enjoying the enormous influence and wealth of both the Tlacaelel and Moteuczoma dynasties, she married a Spanish conquistador, don Cristóbal Valderrama, and received an encomienda in Ecatepec.[35] Their daughter, doña Leonor Valderrama de Moteuczoma, identified by Chimalpahin as a mestiza, also married a Spaniard, don Diego de Sotelo,

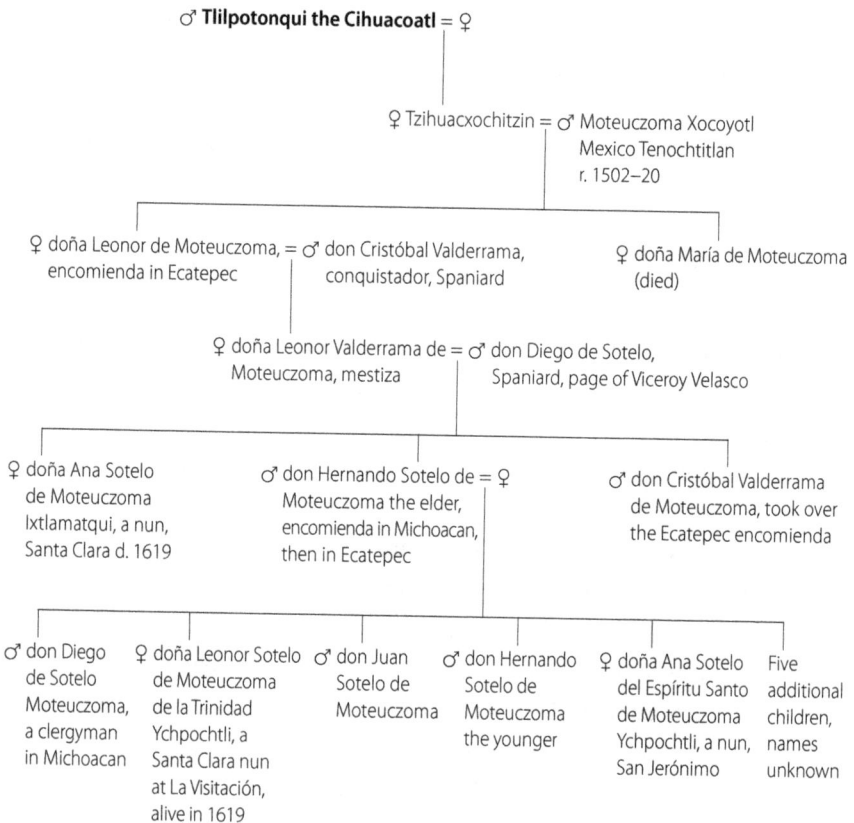

♂ **Tlilpotonqui the Cihuacoatl** = ♀

♀ Tzihuacxochitzin = ♂ Moteuczoma Xocoyotl
Mexico Tenochtitlan
r. 1502–20

♀ doña Leonor de Moteuczoma, = ♂ don Cristóbal Valderrama,
encomienda in Ecatepec   conquistador, Spaniard

♀ doña María de Moteuczoma
(died)

♀ doña Leonor Valderrama de = ♂ don Diego de Sotelo,
Moteuczoma, mestiza   Spaniard, page of Viceroy Velasco

♀ doña Ana Sotelo
de Moteuczoma
Ixtlamatqui, a nun,
Santa Clara d. 1619

♂ don Hernando Sotelo de = ♀
Moteuczoma the elder,
encomienda in Michoacan,
then in Ecatepec

♂ don Cristóbal Valderrama
de Moteuczoma, took over
the Ecatepec encomienda

♂ don Diego
de Sotelo
Moteuczoma,
a clergyman
in Michoacan

♀ doña Leonor Sotelo
de Moteuczoma
de la Trinidad
Ychpochtli, a
Santa Clara nun
at La Visitación,
alive in 1619

♂ don Juan
Sotelo de
Moteuczoma

♂ don Hernando
Sotelo de
Moteuczoma
the younger

♀ doña Ana Sotelo
del Espíritu Santo
de Moteuczoma
Ychpochtli, a nun,
San Jerónimo

Five
additional
children,
names
unknown

FIG. 20. Tlilpotonqui the Cihuacoatl and his Mexica descendants.
Copyright © 2016, University of Oklahoma Press.

Boldface indicates which of Tlacaelel the elder's descendants became the Cihuacoatl.

and they had two children, a daughter who became a nun at the Santa Clara convent and a son who had four children, three of whom entered the church (fig. 20).[36]

By all the evidence, Tlilpotonqui's offspring did well for themselves. They found prestigious partners and maintained the family name and status in Mexico City society. Chimalpahin reports that "all are now Spaniards, because their mother was a Spaniard and their aforementioned father was a quadroon."[37] It is not known, however, if the majority continued to reside in Acatlan, the Tlacaelel family home.

TLACAELEL XOCOYOTL: THE THIRD CIHUACOATL

Tlilpotonqui died in Eleven Reed, 1503, having worked with Moteuczoma Xocoyotl for only one year but nevertheless having accomplished a great deal. At this point, the histories by Durán, Alvarado Tezozomoc, and even Sahagún are increasingly vague regarding the Nahuatl personal and family names of the Cihuacoatl, referring only to the office. But Chimalpahin keeps carefully to his annals and genealogies and records that Tlacaelel the younger, the son of Tlilpotonqui's brother Cacamatzin, immediately succeeded to the office of the Cihuacoatl.[38] Tlacaelel the younger served Moteuczoma Xocoyotl, attending, most notably, the funeral for his brother-in-law, King Nezahualpilli, in Tetzcoco. Of all the many royal dignitaries present, the Cihuacoatl was the first to offer gifts of feathers, gold, jewels, mantles, and slaves and a funeral oration, holding the deceased Nezahualpilli's hand as he spoke.[39] The ceremonies lasted for eighty days. Alvarado Tezozomoc adds that Moteuczoma Xocoyotl and the Cihuacoatl consulted with the Tetzcoca nobles who came to Mexico Tenochtitlan regarding the successor for the Tetzcoca throne, and apparently it was Tlacaelel the younger who crowned the new monarch and then returned to Mexico Tenochtitlan to tell Moteuczoma about the coronation.[40]

The eponymous grandson served with Moteuczoma until the arrival of the Spaniards and probably until the king's death in 1520. Although Sahagún fails to mention the Cihuacoatl as one of Moteuczoma Xocoyotl's attendants when he went to meet Hernando Cortés for the first time in

Xoloco, Chimalpahin specifies that the Tlacaelels were among the delegation of Mexica nobility on that momentous occasion.[41] Totomotzin, another son of Tlacaelel the elder, was there, however, and one would expect that the Cihuacoatl stayed behind in the palace, possibly for strategic purposes.[42] Even before Cortés's arrival, though, temple building, warfare, and commemorative ceremonies continued at an inexorable rate, for the annals list a great many military conquests during Moteuczoma's reign and Tlacaelel the younger's tenure with him.[43]

Tlacaelel the younger's nephew Cacamatzin also distinguished himself but came to a tragic end. Tlacaelel the younger's older sister had married King Nezahualpilli (r. 1472–1515), and their son Cacamatzin eventually succeeded his father to the throne in Tetzcoco (r. 1516–20). He was the sitting king when the Spaniards invaded Mexico Tenochtitlan.[44] Cacamatzin had accompanied Moteuczoma Xocoyotl, positioned at the emperor's left side, when he met Cortés in Xoloco, and he was killed along with Moteuczoma by the Spaniards in Two Flint, 1520.[45] Chimalpahin states simply, "And it was also at that time, in the aforesaid year [Two Flint, 1520], that Moteuczoma had been put in irons; this was by action of the Spaniards. In that place lord Cacamatzin, ruler of Tetzcoco, died with him. He had ruled for five years."[46]

Doubtless it was Tlacaelel the younger who was part of Moteuczoma's royal council as they listened to the early and alarming reports of the Spaniards along the Veracruz shore. Sahagún, in particular, offers a great deal of information about Moteuczoma's interactions with the invaders and how the emperor consulted with any number of specialists to determine the best course of action to thwart their advance. Sahagún is incorrect, however, when he lists Tlilpotonqui as the Cihuacoatl and principal adviser to the emperor at the time, since he had died sixteen years earlier.[47] Rather, even after the Spaniards had occupied the capital and while they were living in the royal palace for several months, it was Tlacaelel the younger who served as go-between. And considering the high standing of the authoritative Cihuacoatl, it is entirely possible that Tlacaelel the younger was killed along with Kings Moteuczoma Xocoyotl and Cacamatzin.[48] At any rate, the slaughter of the rulers helped to precipitate a rebellion against the Spaniards that eventually forced them to flee the island and seek a safe haven with their allies in Tlaxcala.

MATLATZINCATZIN:
INTERIM AND FOURTH CIHUACOATL

During the respite from Spanish occupation, on September 16, the first day of Ochpaniztli, Two Flint, 1520, the Mexica promptly installed Moteuczoma Xocoyotl's younger brother Cuitlahuac on the throne, and he became the tenth tlatoani and the twentieth man to lead the Mexica since the early years. He was also Tlacaelel's great-great-nephew. Cuitlahuac had formerly been ruler in Iztapalapan. A man named Matlatzincatzin became the Cihua-coatl.[49] At one point, Chimalpahin asserted that all the Cihuacoatls were descendants of Tlacaelel the elder.[50] However, Matlatzincatzin was said to be Cuitlahuac's brother, although likely born of a different mother, not a primary wife, and not of the line tracing directly to former King Huitz-ilihuitl. Therefore, Matlatzincatzin, though a relative of Tlacaelel, was not an immediate descendant of that family lineage, or at least as far as can be determined. But Matlatzincatzin the Cihuacoatl stepped down from his office in December, some eighty days after assuming his duties, when Cui-tlahuac died of an epidemic disease brought by the Spaniards.

TLACOTZIN: THE LAST CIHUACOATL

In Three House, 1521, Quauhtemoc, cousin to Moteuczoma Xocoyotl and Cuitlahuac, succeeded to the Mexica throne. Family connections definitely influenced his appointment, for Quauhtemoc's aunt, Chalchiuhnenetzin, was married to King Moquihuix of Tlatelolco (r. 1460–73). Chalchiuhne-netzin was also the sister of three Mexica emperors, Ahuitzotl, Tizoc, and Axayacatl, and Moquihuix was foolish enough to abuse and neglect his wife and their son. To make matters even worse and more ridiculous, he was planning to attack Mexico Tenochtitlan, although it is possible that the Tenochca already had imperial pretensions for the island and wanted to bring Tlatelolco to heel.[51] At any rate, Chalchiuhnenetzin was rescued by her family, but the rest ended badly: the Tenochca overwhelmingly defeated Moquihuix, compromising the rulership permanently and causing great humiliation for the Tlatelolca.[52] An interim ruler, Itzquauhtzin Tlacoch-calcatl (r. 1475–1520), instead was appointed by the Tenochca king, and

the altepetl was never fully sovereign again.[53] Nevertheless, and in spite of
Tlatelolco's diminished status, King Ahuitzotl later married Tecapantzin,
a noblewoman and daughter of Epcoatzin, a tlatocapilli of Tlatelolco. They
had one child, Quauhtemoc, who later became ruler of Tlatelolco and
Tenochtitlan.[54] That Quauhtemoc may have been something of a pretender
to the Tlatelolca throne is revealed in the Nahuatl annals describing his
rather sudden interest in the place:

> *iii. calli xihuitl 1521. años. ypan in yn axihuac yn mexicayotl. yn
> tenochcayotl. çan nauhpohualihuitl onmatlactli ynic axihuac ynic
> cehuico yaoyotl. ypan cemilhuitlapohualli ce cohuatl yc niman yquac
> ompa motlallito yn tlacatl quauhtimoctzin in tlatilolco*

The year Three House, 1521. At this time the Mexica state, the
Tenochca state, lasted for only ninety days. It endured [until] the war
ceased on the day count One Serpent. It was then, at that time, that
the lord Quauhtemoctzin went to settle in Tlatelolco.[55]

It was not untypical for a son to assume the throne at the home polity of his
mother; granted, the mother was usually the daughter of the local king.[56]
Tlatelolco's rulership was now subject to Tenochca oversight and it is likely
that the royal genealogy was no longer functional. On the other hand, it is
possible that Quauhtemoc finally went to settle in Tlatelolco as Tenochtitlan
had been besieged militarily by the Spaniards. And it is possible that some
Tlatelolca resented his becoming tlatoani, considering his official affiliation
with Mexico Tenochtitlan, for in only a few years one of them falsely accused
Quauhtemoc, resulting in his death.

Tlacotzin, nephew of Tlilpotonqui and grandson of Tlacaelel the elder,
became the Cihuacoatl.[57]

> *1521. iii. calli xihuitl, ypan in motlahtocatlalli yn tlacatl quauhte-
> moctzin tlahtohuani mochiuh tenuchtitlan . . . ytlan cihuacoatl mochi-
> uhca yn tlacotzin*

1521, Three House. At this time the lord Quauhtemoctzin was
installed as ruler; he became tlatoani of Tenochtitlan . . . with him
Tlacotzin was made the Cihuacoatl.[58]

If his predecessor and cousin, Tlacaelel the younger, ever required his dip-lomatic skills, Tlacotzin must have been prepared for the challenge, having been witness to Mexica and Spanish machinations since the Spaniards first arrived. Cortés early on and to his credit, though, held him in great esteem and wrote of his attempt to come to an accord with Quauhtemoc and end the bloodshed. Hoping to discuss a treaty, the captain reported, he asked to speak with the king. Instead, Tlacotzin the Cihuacoatl appeared, with Cortés describing him as "one of the most important persons in the city[,] . . . cap-tain and governor of them all [who] directed all matters concerning the war." Tlacotzin, though, told him that Quauhtemoc would not meet with him, and Cortés believed that Tlacotzin regretted it.[59]

During the final siege, according to Sahagún, Tlacotzin again took to the field, one of two eagle warriors and two jaguar warriors who led an attack against the Spaniards' allies as they constructed obstacles and planned to rob Mexica commoners. The warriors appeared out of nowhere on the lake, vigorously poling their canoes as wind instruments resounded, and successfully defeating their enemies, for the time being.[60] And in the ultimate moments of battle, it was Tlacotzin the Cihuacoatl who called out to rally Mexica patriotism: "O Mexica, O Tlatelolca, is there nothing left of the way it was in Mexico, of the way the Mexica state was, which was said to be the envoy of Huitzilopochtli that he sends against people, as he used to send the fire serpent, the fire drill at our enemies? O Mexica, you are taking his envoy the dart; you are to aim it only at our enemies. . . . And if one or two of them are hit, or if one or two of our enemies are captured, then it is truly our fate that for a little while longer we will [find favor], while our lord so wishes."[61] In Sahagún's *Historia*, when the fighting is over, the brave warriors of Tlatelolco are ranked first, as one would expect in this account, but Tlacotzin the Cihuacoatl is listed in preference after the king among the Tenochca.[62]

The battle lost, Quauhtemoc assembled his warriors for their counsel regarding what to do next, how to arrange to pay tribute to Cortés, and how to go about surrendering. They decided that Quauhtemoc should depart the island in a canoe with two attendants. It is noteworthy that Tlacotzin was not with the king; rather, he stayed behind with other warriors to guard the gold, surely recognizing that it was their most valuable asset in transactions

FIG. 21. Tlacotzin the Cihuacoatl, King Quauhtemoc, and warrior
Motelchiuhtzin before Hernando Cortés and a Franciscan friar (or an
executioner). They are probably calling for torture by fire. Codex Mexicanus,
pl. 77. Bibliothèque Nationale de France, nos. 23–24.

with the Spaniards.[63] Afterward, it was with Tlacotzin that Malintzin
and Cortés negotiated regarding the disappearance of the gold, which
had reportedly fallen into the Tolteca Canal during the Spaniards' Noche
Triste retreat from Tenochtitlan. By now, Quauhtemoc and his warriors
and advisers had been taken into custody by Cortés, whose only concern
was finding the gold. Tlacotzin reminded the captain that the Spaniards
had emptied the palace storeroom of its gold and taken it for themselves,
which Malintzin and Cortés acknowledged. But the gold had been lost as
they fled the capital, and Tlacotzin, prescient and speaking loyally for the
Mexica Tenochca, righteously denied that the Tenochca had taken any of
it. He instead accused the Tlatelolca of being the culprits. But Quauhtemoc
spoke up to challenge his Cihuacoatl and denied wrongdoing on the part of
the Tlatelolca. Tlacotzin then changed his tactic to divert the attention and
blame from his noble cohort and onto the commoners: "Perhaps someone
of the common folk took it away." He promised to locate it, while adding,
"Perhaps some poor woman put it into her skirt."[64] The *Codex Mexicanus*
depicts the high rank and authority that Tlacotzin the Cihuacoatl enjoyed

as he, Quauhtemoc, and warrior Motelchiuhtzin, as associates, were being sentenced to torture by fire by Cortés and what appears to be an executioner (fig. 21).[65]

Cortés shackled Quauhtemoc along with the rulers of Tetzcoco and Tlacopan, Tlacotzin, and two other high officials. He kept them at Coyoacan, where his men tortured them by fire and burned their feet in hot oil to force them to produce the lost gold and other treasure. While in captivity, Tlacotzin served as spokesperson. He explained to Cortés, among other things, the nature of imperial lands and revenues and that the Mexica did not actually cultivate their own crops but rather enjoyed and depended on those of their subjects, such as the Xochimilca, Acolhuaca, and Chalca.[66] The captain was surely ecstatic to learn of such a vast, sophisticated, and profitable enterprise. How long the rulers were imprisoned is not known, but the kings and Tlacotzin must have been doing everything in their power to ensure that their subjects supplied the Spaniards with everything they wanted. Cortés, suggesting that he had come to understand the Cihuacoatl's authority regarding domestic operations in the capital, commented to Holy Roman Emperor Charles V in his fourth letter, dated October 15, 1524, that he had put Tlacotzin in charge of rebuilding the capital, adding, "I charged a captain general whom I had known in the time of Mutezuma [sic] with the task of repopulating it [the city]. And so that he should have more authority I gave back to him the title he held when his lord was in power, which was that of Ciguacoatl [sic], which means lieutenant to the king."[67] Cortés remarked that he had returned several nobles to their previous governing positions and made a point of stating that he gave Tlacotzin and the other men "such lands and people as were necessary for their sustenance, although not as much as they had owned before, nor enough to make them dangerous at any time."[68] The Cihuacoatl, the second wealthiest man in Mexica dominions, had lost his estate but would recoup much-needed support and revenue so he could see to everything the Spaniards demanded of him.

However, Chimalpahin corrects Cortés and his secretary, Francisco López de Gómara, by recording that the conqueror had in truth put Tlacotzin in charge of rebuilding and repopulating his home district, "called Xoloco and Acatlan, where the church of San Antonio Abad, the glorious and most holy patriarch of the friars, now stands," then and now in the southeastern quarter of Tenochtitlan. Moteuczoma Xocoyotl's son, don Pedro Moteuczoma Tlacahuepan, was to oversee the reconstruction of Atzaqualco, the indigenous northeastern quarter of Tenochtitlan, where the Moteuczoma family lived and continued to exercise influence.[69]

During these first postconquest years, Tlacotzin the Cihuacoatl's métier in urban affairs apparently served him well. Barbara Mundy reiterates his important relationship with Cortés. She states that Tlacotzin was influential in establishing what came to be a rather short-lived market (*tianquiztli*) called "Tianguis de Juan Velázquez."[70] The market was purportedly located next to Tlacotzin's residence in the western sector of the city, a distance from the Tlacaelels' patrimonial home in Acatlan.[71]

During the course of the reconstruction of the capital, Cortés decided to undertake an expedition to Honduras to capture and punish one of his lieutenants, Cristóbal de Olid, but also to claim for himself what was rumored to be yet another wealthy indigenous polity. He took Malintzin; Quauhtemoc; the rulers of Tetzcoco and Tlacopan, Coanacochtzin and Tetlepanquetzal, respectively; Tlacotzin the Cihuacoatl; and selected other Nahua noble officials, in addition to three thousand Indians to serve as porters and laborers.[72] Along the way, according to Cortés and Malintzin, Quauhtemoc conspired to kill the Spaniards. The native sources, including Chimalpahin, state that the accusation was false, something drummed up by a fellow Tlatelolca named Cristóbal Cotztemexi, who, except for his villainy, is hardly known in Tlatelolca history.[73]

Quauhtemoc must have been dispensable by this time, for Cortés first baptized the kings (including the Cihuacoatl), assigning them Spanish Christian names and surnames, and then hanged the Mexica ruler and his counterpart Tetlepanquetzatzin of Tlacopan at Acallan, although not all accounts agree that Quauhtemoc accepted Christianity. Needing a replacement for Quauhtemoc, Cortés immediately installed the newly baptized don Juan Velásquez Tlacotzin the Cihuacoatl as the first full-fledged colonial Nahua king of Mexico Tenochtitlan.[74] The Nahuatl wording, "*auh yc niman yehuatl ompa quitlahtocatlallica yn marques yn Don Juan velasquez tlacotzin cihuacoatl,*" is explicit and affirms that Tlacotzin the Cihuacoatl was installed as a tlatoani and not an interim ruler (quauhtlatoani), gobernador, or an officer of inferior standing.[75] Having performed a yeoman's task as negotiator and administrator, don Juan Velásquez Tlacotzin was also granted the privilege to outfit himself as a Spaniard (*quiespañolchichiuh*)—that is, to wear Spanish attire, carry a sword and dagger, and ride a white horse—which became a common and familiar way for the Spaniards to reward Nahua favorites.[76] It did Tlacotzin little good, though, since he was still in Honduras.[77] And when Cortés finally decided that his mission there had been fulfilled, he traveled home by boat while Tlatoani Tlacotzin made the long trek by land. Along the way, in Nochiztlan Quatzontlan, he became ill with cocoliztli (sickness) and died.[78]

yn onmiquillico yn tlahtohuani Don Juan velasquez tlacotzin cihuacoatl

The tlatoani don Juan Velásquez Tlacotzin the Cihuacoatl died.[79]

He had been ruler for no more than one year and one month. Chimalpahin lamented, "There the office of the Cihuacoatl came to an end; then no one was once again installed [as the Cihuacoatl]."[80] The year was Eight Rabbit, 1526, and it would seem that Tlacaelel and his Acatlan dynasty had come to an end.[81] Nevertheless, the ancient tradition of maintaining records of the royal genealogy (*tlatocatlacamecayotl*) to demonstrate its enduring importance and the longevity of the imperial house continued in the sixteenth century. The dynastic tradition is realized in pictorial representational style in the Codex Aubin, where Tlacotzin, with his Cihuacoatl glyph, is depicted wearing a rulerly *xiuhhuitzolli* and sitting on a throne in an official robe with the gloss *nican vnmotlatocatlalli yn çivacovatzintli tlacotzin*, "at this time the Cihuacoatl Tlacotzin was installed as tlatoani."[82] In the Humboldt Fragment II, Tlacotzin the Cihuacoatl is once again included among other leaders in a long sequence of rulers of Mexico Tenochtitlan, although he is not shown wearing a xiuhhuitzolli, a curious omission.[83]

ACATLAN AND THE TLACAELELS IN THE LATER YEARS

Acatlan and Xoloco were tlaxilacalli, or subdistricts, of Tenochtitlan altepetl tlayacatl, located in the southeastern part of the island.[84] Alfonso Caso reproduced the 1789 Alzate "Plano de Tenochtitlan," which shows Acatlan as a large polity adjacent to the lake and on the western border of the colonial subdivision of (San Pablo) Teopan.[85] Xoloco is close by but minuscule in comparison and definitely part of the higher-ranked quarter of San Juan Tenochtitlan. Caso's more modern 1954 rendering of the map refers to the tlaxilacalli as "barrios" (map 2). Xoloco is where Chimalpahin's much-heralded San Antonio Abad church was located, and there was a *ciénaga*, or wetlands, and boulevard (now Pino Suárez) named after the church that connected the old causeway to the downtown part of the capital.[86]

The Tlacaelels held sway in Atepanazco Acatlan, and it was logical that Cortés would assign the repopulation and reconstruction of this part of the city to Tlacotzin, Tlacaelel's grandson.[87] Caso shows Atepanazco as a separate barrio in San Pablo Teopan, but, considering the manner in which Chimalpahin identifies and locates sociopolitical entities,[88] I would argue that Atepanazco was a principal subdistrict of Acatlan during the precontact years. Certainly, Acatlan had its own nobility, as becomes evident in the annals' references to "a noblewoman of Acatlan" who married don Diego de Alvarado Huanitzin of Ecatepec. He, as the new, first governor in the capital (r. 1538–41), was soon to be the highest-ranked, most prestigious Nahua in Mexico City.[89] Confirming the genealogical ties of the Tlacaelels with Mexica royalty, Chimalpahin traces five generations of the descendants of Mexica King Tizoc (r. 1481–86), noting that a don Miguel Tlilpotonqui Carsetero was the illegitimate son, or brother, of a Pedro Hernández Cacamatzin. The Carseteros were from Atepanazco, and most used the Spanish title "don," as would be expected of Tlacaelel scions. Tizoc's son, Tezcatl Popocatzin the elder was from San Pablo Teopan, and some of his descendants became active in the church there.[90] Cacamatzin and Tlilpotonqui are, of course, Nahuatl personal (and, possibly, family) names, and Hernández, in later years, would be a Tlacaelel colonial surname.[91] Don Miguel Tlilpotonqui, described as someone "considered important," suffered no discrimination because of the circumstances of his birth: "since he resembled the legitimately begotten sons, he . . . could not be called a bastard son."[92]

Even the Tlacaelels' title of Cihuacoatl came to be either a surname or, very possibly, an indication that the Mexica rulers had individuals occupying the second-in-rank position of the Cihuacoatl at imperial outposts.

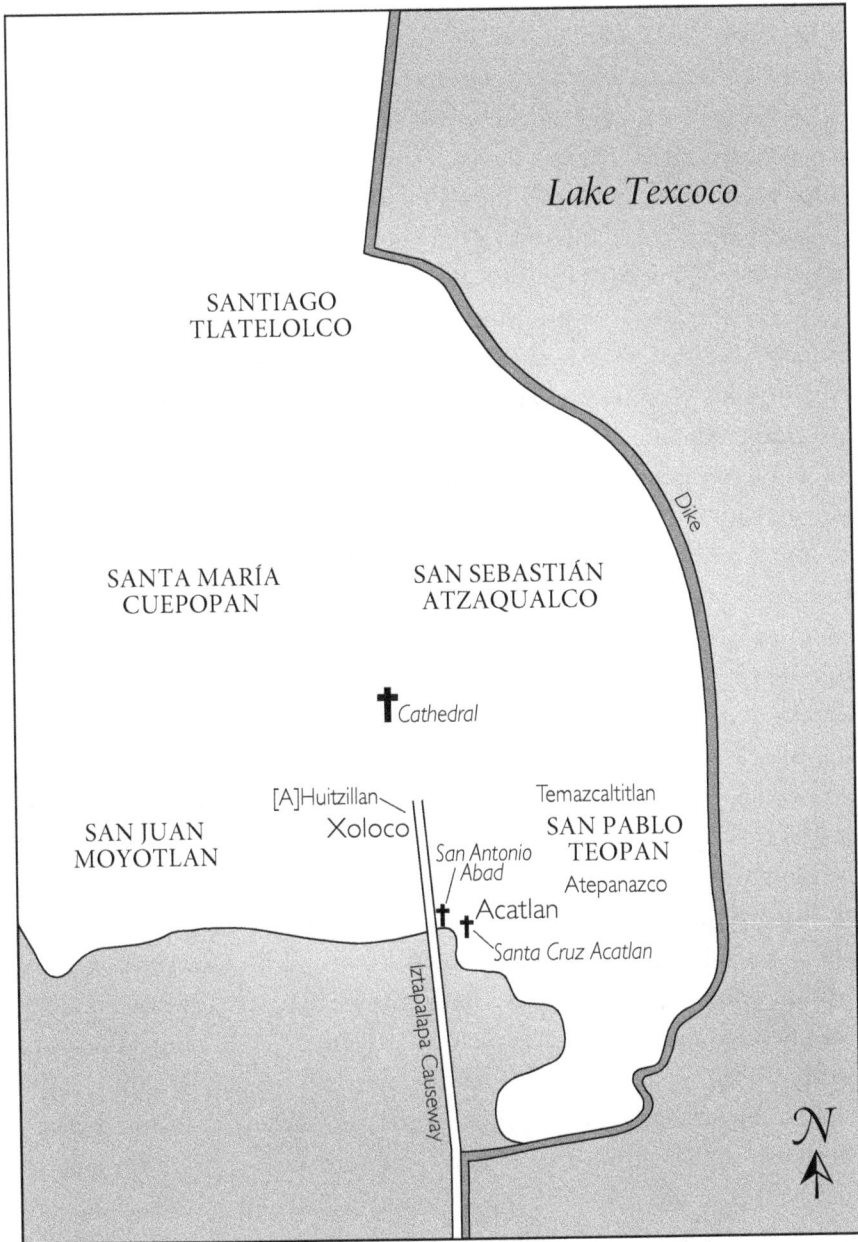

MAP 2. Xoloco and Acatlan in Mexico Tenochtitlan, after Alzate/Caso, 1789/1954, plate 2. Drawing by Jennifer Berdan Lozano. Copyright © 2016, University of Oklahoma Press.

Robert Haskett discusses a cabildo official in Cuernavaca in 1547 with "Ciguacoatl" as a surname, while Laura Matthew has identified a don Marcos Çiguacoatl serving as a governor of Xoconusco but then joining the Spaniards' invading forces in Guatemala in 1524. Forty years later, don Marcos related his role during those years of conquest.[93] Elsewhere, however, Haskett alludes to the primordial and theological role of the deity Cihuacoatl, and it is entirely possible that the references to individuals such as Cihuacoatl in Cuernavaca and Xoconusco are indicative of a temple or religious ritual relating to the deity and that these individuals, or their ancestors, served as Cihuacoatl deity impersonators.[94] Certainly, even into the seventeenth century, Cihuacoatl was an important deity in the incantations and ritual worship of native peoples as they were observed by curate Hernando Ruiz de Alarcón in his district of Atenango, south of Mexico City.[95]

Yet information about the Tlacaelels' tlaxilacalli in the seventeenth century is hard to come by. In the Mexicas' formative years, according to López de Gómara, one of their founding fathers, a man named Mixtecatl, established a place called Acatlan somewhere toward the South Sea (Pacific Ocean), and Chimalpahin mentions in his annals that an Acatlan was conquered in 1492, although there is no evidence that it was the same Tenochtitlan tlaxilacalli.[96] Peter Gerhard lists a dozen such toponyms in his work on central New Spain.[97]

Moreover, Acatlan and Xoloco are often listed as one entity, and it is likely that at one time that was the case. I would not be surprised if Xoloco was not a subpolity of Acatlan. We do know much more about Xoloco because Chimalpahin lived there and wrote about it. It may be that it separated from Acatlan as part of Franciscan redistricting. But early on Acatlan was probably a principal part, if not the principal quarter, in southeastern Mexico Tenochtitlan. Chimalpahin suggests as much when he interpolates the names of the native rulers in his "Conquista" history who were among Cortés's party when he returned to Spain in 1528. Of the fifteen nobles identified, it is worth noting that, adhering to his obsession with rank and order, after listing the three heirs and relatives of Moteuczoma Xocoyotl, the fourth man, also said to be related to the late emperor, was don Gaspar Toltequitzin of Xoloco Acatlan.[98] It may well be that Toltequitzin was representing Tlacaelel's lineage in his old town and still occupied a position of distinction in Nahua city society.

There are several references to Xoloco Acatlan in his many annals, but confounding the issue are such entities as Xoloco Oztocaltitlan, Oztocaltitlan Arcotitlan, Mexico Xoloco, San Antón Acatlan, Acatlan in Xoloco, San Antonio Abad Oztocaltitlan Xoloco, and San Agustín Xoloco.[99] The Nahua Cristóbal del Castillo, in the extant fragments of his annals, spoke of a Xoloco Acalotenco as the locale where Cortés went to greet the Franciscans upon their arrival in Mexico City in 1524.[100] Then, more specifically, he referred to a Tecuauhtitlan Acalotenco Xoloco. As with Chimalpahin, the order of the place-names suggests smaller sites within larger ones and Xoloco at the end being the definitive polity.[101] Alvarado Tezozomoc includes a "Xoloco which now is la Puente de Sancto Antonio."[102] Even in the nineteenth century, the famed lawyer and historian Carlos María de Bustamante identified Xoloco as "*donde hoy está S. Antonio Abad.*"[103]

Long an area of historic significance, what also made Xoloco special was that it was the site of the famous first meeting of Moteuczoma Xocoyotl and Hernando Cortés. Yet Sahagún tells us that the encounter was indeed in Xoloco but actually at Huitzillan, a little farther north, where Pedro de Alvarado's house and the beatas of Santa Mónica de Gracia were located.[104] Chimalpahin's annals state that the site of the first meeting, along with the exchange of gifts, was at Acachinanco—perhaps more precisely in Xoloco—which fray Diego Durán identified as "the gates of the Aztec city."[105] Sahagún adds that Acachinanco was a "landing place," and the Spaniards used it to launch the brigantines that they had assembled in Tetzcoco. From Acachinanco they "forced them down the road [canal] past Xoloco," moving on to an all-out attack on the Mexica.[106] The images in Sahagún's Book 12 are revealing of the physical structure of the place, with walls, surely retaining walls to hold back the lake waters, bordering both Xoloco and Huitzillan. They also show the landing of the brigantines and the fierce fighting that followed.[107] After the fall of the capital, Acachinanco was the same locale where Cortés assembled all the captured rulers and warriors of Mexico Tenochtitlan before taking them to Coyoacan to be tortured.[108]

In the seventeenth century, in spite of Chimalpahin's boosterism for his little church, Xoloco was home to a slaughterhouse, which was not a particularly desirable feature.[109] Today, Chimalpahin's Xoloco church of San Antonio Abad still stands facing west, as it has always, although it is nearly obscured by the close proximity of the traffic-burdened Pino Suárez highway. While the church has been closed for many years, Mexico's Consejo Nacional para la Cultura y las Artes (CONACULTA) is currently in the process of restoring the bell tower, and the church has a fresh coat of soft orange and gold-colored paint. Less than two blocks away to the southeast is the partially restored Santa Cruz Acatlan church. It currently serves as a parish church and faces south onto a shady park. Once a Franciscan *visita*, it was secularized in the early 1770s. Gerhard notes that Acatlan (Santa Cruz de los Rastreros) existed as a barrio into the eighteenth century.[110] Its noble line continued as well. Santa Cruz Acatlan was the home of Jesuit-educated don Domingo José de la Mota, an exemplary cacique and parish priest who was particularly notable for his literary career.[111]

There is a conspicuous gap in the Tlacaelel family history between the death of Tlacotzin in 1526 and what Chimalpahin records for the seventeenth century. Durán, though, mentions a son or grandson of Tlacaelel the elder who had gone to Yacapichtlan, in the hot country, and became the ruler there. He had fought bravely against Cortés, and his descendants continued as the leaders, or "lords," in that region.[112] A search for Nahuatl family names reveals that the Codex Osuna mentions a Tomás Tlilpotonqui, of San Juan [Moyotlan], who served as a witness in 1558. And Acatlan is mentioned twice in the Codex, which suggests that it continued to be a polity of some importance.[113] Indeed, in the so-called annals of Juan Bautista, in October 1564 there is a regidor Francisco Quauhtli of Acatla[n], with a footnote stating that at that time the barrio of Acatlan was part of the parcialidad of San Juan Moyotlan.[114] And in August of that same year Bartolomé Atenpanecatl died. He was in charge of the *tequihua*, "tribute collection," and was very old. There were celebrations in his honor in the capital upon his passing. Earlier, in Twelve Reed, 1543, "Atempanecatl Bartolome" had made an announcement at the temple, according to the Codex Aubin.[115]

The Nahua title Atempanecatl traces back to Tlacaelel the elder; it was the first title that he held in the days when the Mexica were still subject to the Tepaneca.[116] It is possible that the title was originally associated with the Tlacaelels' dynastic lineage in Atepanazco Acatlan, although in the 1560s old

Bartolomé Atenpanecatl was said to be a resident of San Juan Tequicaltitlan, a district in a subdivision of San Juan Moyotlan, the Mexico Tenochtitlan southwestern quarter.[117]

Tlacotzin, the first colonial tlatoani and the last Cihuacoatl, was not entirely lost to sixteenth-century history, though. Apparently, he had an estate dating to precontact times that passed to his son and heir, don Gerónimo Velásquez. A lawsuit in 1569 reveals that don Gerónimo had exchanged a house and its land in Mexico City (in or adjacent to Santa María Tepetlalcingo) with a Spaniard, Luis de Ávila, who then wanted to collect tribute from the renters. The Nahuas argued that the land was *mexicatlalli*, "Mexica land," and not subject to tribute, claiming rights and privileges from ancient times, which may well have been the case given the wealth and vastness of Tlacaelel the elder's holdings.[118] Still, the Tlacaelel Acatlan record is spotty at best during these years.

As noted, in Chimalpahin's annals Xoloco and Acatlan as barrio, or tlaxilacalli, names often overlap, doubtless because of parish and governmental districting conflicts. But by the seventeenth century, and making the case for Acatlan, he is meticulous when he speaks of the Tlacaelels, who, remarkably, were still prevailing in local politics. In Thirteen House, 1609, a don Miguel Sánchez Huentzin, a nobleman of Acatlan, was serving along with don Antonio Valeriano the younger as the cabildo alcaldes for San Juan Moyotlan in Mexico Tenochtitlan.[119] The next year, however, on September 20, One Rabbit, 1610, Huentzin died, and Chimalpahin wrote, "He was the only one left, so that with him ended the line of the late lord Tlacaelel the elder, the Cihuacoatl, high constable in Mexico Tenochtitlan. With the said dead person the nobility of Acatlan came to an end, he terminated it once and for all."[120] Earlier, in One House, 1597, another Sánchez, Diego, was serving as alcalde with a Nicolás Hernández as regidor.[121] Their affiliations are not furnished, unfortunately. Then, in Three Flint, 1612, Nicolás Hernández Tlacaelel, now of San Pablo [Teopan], appears as a litigant in a lawsuit,[122] and finally Hernández Tlacaelel is named again, this time on Sunday, at midday, March 24, Four House, 1613, when his mother died. His mother, doña Martina, was from Atepanazco [Acatlan], and Chimalpahin knew her. She was "one of the descendants, called the hair and fingernails, of one who lived long ago here in Mexico Tenochtitlan, who was held in great awe, and that was Tlacaelel the elder, the Cihuacoatl, a noble of the royal dynasty of Tenochtitlan."[123] Doña Martina was buried in the church of San Pablo, and it is likely that by this time Acatlan had become part of the San Pablo Teopan quarter and possibly part of the Augustinians' parish district. Certainly, when Chimalpahin's priest, fray Agustín del Espíritu Santo, died unexpectedly in 1624, it was Augustinian friars who immediately invaded and took over the little church of San Antonio Abad in Xoloco, causing city officials to close and padlock it. Chimalpahin was then unemployed, and his careful record-keeping came to an end.

❁

It is apparent that the official royal lineage of Acatlan had terminated upon the death of Alcalde don Miguel Sánchez Huentzin. But other branches of the Tlacaelel family continued to flourish, as can be seen in the activities and political office of don Nicolás, who also continued to use Tlacaelel as a surname. The aura of the Cihuacoatl in the halcyon years of the Mexica empire may have faded, but the family name, authority, and legacy were by no means forgotten. His royal descendants followed in the old man's footsteps as the alcaldes and regidores on the San Juan Tenochtitlan cabildo, the most influential indigenous political body in New Spain.

CONCLUSION
A LEGEND?

❀

Now we are living on the land that was once Mexico
Tenochtitlan.

Chimalpahin

A significant portion of Chimalpahin's intellectual formation was already
the stuff of legend. From the heroic exploits of Pelayo in rescuing Christian Spain from Muslim intruders (ca. 722) to the tumultuous but regal
Trastámara Dynasty of the Catholic Kings Isabela I of Castile and Fernando
II of Aragón (r. 1474–1504 and 1474–1516, respectively), Chimalpahin had a
keen appreciation of the epic dimension of Spanish history.[1] Indeed, from the
marriage of Isabela and Fernando's daughter Juana to Philippe, archduke of
Burgundy, Juana's succession to the Spanish throne as queen, and the accession to rule of first their son Carlos and then two royal generations of Feli-
pes—these events were largely cause for his proud and defensive chronicle of
his own Amecameca, Chalco.[2] He knew of Holy Roman Emperor Carlos V
(r. 1516–56), also a "huey tlatoani . . . emperador," and included information
about his son Felipe II (r. 1556–98) in his account. Felipe II, Chimalpahin
wrote, received two jaguars and a magnificently embroidered turquoise cloak
(*xiuhtilmantli*) from the Nahuas in Mexico City in April of Nine Flint, 1592,
and he recorded the Spanish king's death in Two Rabbit, 1598, even though
it had taken four months for the news to reach the capital.[3] As we would
expect in an annals template regarding the death of a ruler, even a Spanish
one, Felipe appointed his son Felipe III (r. 1598–1621) as his successor and

"gave him his rulership and crown so that he would govern the universal (*cemanahuac*) altepetl." There was a tolling of bells across New Spain, and "the Spaniards were all notified to fast and wear mourning clothes."[4] There was not the spectacle and high drama recorded for the deaths and funerals of the Mexica huey tlatoque, but Chimalpahin does invoke a somber tone.[5]

Of Felipe III, we know more, since Chimalpahin was well into the recording of events in his Mexico City annals during his reign. For example, he tells of everyone's exuberance on receiving word of the birth of the king's son and heir (Felipe IV, r. 1621–65) in Nine House, 1605, and of his issuing a royal cédula to implement *congregaciones* of the commoners and then revoking it two years later, in Ten Rabbit, 1606, even though it was too late to undo the damage.[6] There is also news about some of the interests of Felipe III's wife, doña Margarita of Austria, and then word of her passing, which this time was cause for a grand funeral ceremony in the capital and grieving across the land.[7] Viceregal appointees were also the mandate of the king, and he was involved in additional legislation affecting the colony.[8] These annals are not unlike Chimalpahin's annals about Mexica and Chalca royalty: tantalizing fragments of information but leaving the reader wanting more.

Knowing and writing the sweep of Spain's history from the Visigoths to the third generation of Hapsburg rulers, then, was little different from telling the history of the Mexica and their great rulers. Both were valid stories about good times and hard times. Does it matter that Chimalpahin may have written one before the other; for example, did he record the Spanish account to avoid sanctions against writing about the Mexica? His information about the Spaniards is sketchy, though, compared with what he recorded for the Mexica. Could his Nahuatl sources have been more plentiful, or, more likely, was there greater urgency to salvage and preserve what was extant? Moreover, did Tlacaelel matter to Mexica history? Certainly, it would have been a dull story without him, and who then to blame for all the savagery? Did the Mexica kings need a guiding light—or a scapegoat?

Chimalpahin's purpose was noble, and Tlacaelel's story is as much about family as it is about dynasty. It is a local truth for Nahuas but in a legitimate literary medium that would weather the test of time. Their patriotism and fame were such that Tlacaelel and Moteuczoma Ilhuicama were written into a Nahuatl pictorial Christian catechism that dates to the 1650s, reiterating the battles and accomplishments of the two valiant leaders.[9] The intersection of primordial Mesoamerican history and colonial Catholicism is a topic that warrants further research.[10]

Of course, Alvarado Tezozomoc and Durán also went to great lengths to produce long chronicles about the extraordinary Tlacaelel and the Mexica, which then came to be corroborated and complemented by Chimalpahin's Nahuatl annals. Among the three authors, there was awe and acceptance, although Durán apparently was not invariably approving. Theirs were histories of Mexica success: the challenge of settlement in the central basin; marriage alliances and dynasty; wars, conquest, and imperialism; extraordinary wealth; intellectualism and cultural flourishing; and religious fanaticism. It was a story that had to be told. The skeptics whose silence or denial regarding the life of Tlacaelel that might have been cause for censure or obscurity now seem shortsighted. Its central conceit notwithstanding, who might dare to claim that it is a tale too good to be true?

yn oquichihuaco yn oquitlallico yn intlillo yn intlapallo yn intenyo yn imitolloca yn imilnamicoca. yn oc ompa titzitihui ayc polihuiz ayc ylcahuiz

And what they came to do, what they came to establish, their writings, their renown, their history, their memory will never perish, will never be forgotten in times to come.[11]

GLOSSARY

Some definitions are based on the translations and definitions found in the texts themselves.

Acatl. Reed

Achcolli. Great-grandfather, ancestor; pl. poss. *tachcohcolhuan*, our grandfathers, our ancestors

Altepetl. Ethnic state; sometimes complex or confederated

Atempanecatl, Atecpanecatl, Atenpanecatl. Title held by government official; executioner

Azteca. Name of migrating peoples who later settled in central Mexico

Braza. Unit of measure, approximately two varas

Calli. House

Calpolli. Sociopolitical subdistrict of a **tlayacatl**

Casa de Águilas. House of Eagles

Centro histórico. Central historic district in Mexico City

Chalca. Peoples who settled in the southeastern part of central Mexico

Chalchiuitl. Greenstone, precious stone(s)

Chapolin, pl. Chapoltin. Grasshopper

Chichimeca. Peoples supposedly from the northern regions who lacked sophistication; a title of political office when combined with *teuctli*

Chinampa. Aquatic gardens

Ciénaga. Wetland, swamp

Cihuacoatl. Female Serpent, name of a deity and a political office

Cihuapilli. Noblewoman

Cihuatlatoani. Queen

Cipactli. Alligator

Cocoliztli. Sickness

Codex, códice. Book, painted book

Colli. Grandfather, ancestor, statesman; pl. poss. *tocolhuan*, our grandfathers

Congregación. The bringing together of disparate villages into a single town

Copilli. Crown

Crónica. Chronicle

Cuauh Huehuetque. Veteran warriors

Cuauhxicalli. Eagle vessel, batea, or similar thing made of wood

Elli. Liver

Fiscal. Native assistant to a Catholic priest

Gobernador. Governor

Gran suerte de tierra. Large plot of land

Historia. History

Huehue. Elder

Huehuetque. Ancients, ancestors

Hueltiuhtli. Elder sister; poss. *ynhueltiuh*, their older sister

Huey. Great, large

Huey tlatoani. Great, high king, emperor; pl. *huehueyntin tlatoque*, high kings

Huey yaotiyacauh. Valiant warrior

Macehualli. Commoner; pl. *macehualtin*; *macehualtzitzin*, poor commoners

Mexica. Migrating group of peoples who later settled on an island in central Mexico and then separated into two distinct ethnic groups: the Mexica Tenochca and the Mexica Tlatelolca

Mexicatlalli. Mexica land, patrimonial land

Nahua(s). A great variety of indigenous peoples who shared a common language

Nahualli. Sorcerer

Nahuatl. Language of the peoples of central Mexico that became something of a lingua franca for political and economic purposes

Nahuatlato, Nahuatlatoa. Interpreter

Nueve partes de tierras. Nine parcels of land

Papa mayor. Pope

Patrona. Patron, sponsor

Pehua. To vanquish one's enemies, to conquer someone

Pilli. Noble

Polihui. To perish, disappear, be defeated

Principal. High-ranking individual

Quauhtlatoani, pl. **Quauhtlatoque.** Interim ruler(s)

Quauhxicalli. See **Cuauhxicalli**

Quiahuitl. Rain

Quiespañolchichiuh. To be outfitted as a Spaniard

Regidor. Councilman

Relación. Account, story

Reportorio. Almanac

Tecolotl. Owl, deity

Tecpan. Palace; poss. *itecpanchan*, his/her palace residence, court

Tecpatl. Flint

Temalacatl. Stone wheel

Templo mayor. Great temple

Tenochca. One of two **altepetl** of Mexica living on an island in central Mexico

Tequihua. Nahuatl *tequitl*, tribute, tribute collection, tribute collector

Teuctlatoani. Lord ruler, titled lord; pl. *teuctlatoque*, lord rulers, titled lords

Tichalca. We Chalca

Timexica. We Mexica

Tlacatl. Person; pl. *tlaca*. people

Tlacateccatl. People-Lord; title of a political office, usually associated with the military

Tlacochcalcatl. Person at the armory; title of a political office, usually associated with the military

Tlailotlacteuctli. Title of a political office

Tlamacazqui. Offering priest

Tlatoani. Ruler, king, speaker; pl. *tlatoque*

Tlatocacihuapilli. Rulerly noblewoman

Tlatocapilli. Royal nobleman; pl. *tlatocapipiltin*

Tlatocayotl. Rulership

Tlatocatlacamecayotl. Royal lineage

Tlaxilacalli. Sociopolitical subdistrict of a **tlayacatl**

Tlayacatl. Sociopolitical subdivision of an **altepetl**

Tochtli. Rabbit

Tzitzimitl. Demon, devil; pl. *tzitzimime*, devils, spirits, statues

Tzompantli. Skull rack or platform

Visita. A church visited periodically by a nonresident priest

Volador. Ceremonial event where one or more individuals descend from a tall pole, appearing to circle and fly down to the ground

Xiuhhuitzolli. Crown

Xochiyaoyotl. Flower war

Xocoyotl. The younger, the youngest

Yaocihuacuicatl. Warrior woman's song

Yauh. To go (cease to exist)

Zopilote. (Nahuatl *tzopilotl*), buzzard

NOTES

LIST OF ABBREVIATIONS USED IN THE NOTES

AHT   Don Domingo de San Antón Muñón Chimalpahin Quauhtlehuanitzin, *Annals of His Time*, ed. and trans. James Lockhart, Susan Schroeder, and Doris Namala (Stanford: Stanford University Press, 2006).

AT   Don Hernando de Alvarado Tezozomoc, *Crónica mexicana*, ed. Gonzalo Díaz Migoyo and Germán Vázquez Chamorro (Madrid: Dastin, 2001).

CC   Don Domingo de San Antón Muñón Chimalpahin Quauhtlehuanitzin, *Codex Chimalpahin*, ed. and trans. Arthur J. O. Anderson and Susan Schroeder, 2 vols., (Norman: University of Oklahoma Press, 1997).

DC   Domingo Chimalpáhin, *Las ocho relaciones y El memorial de Colhuacan*, trans. Rafael Tena, 2 vols. (Mexico City: Cien de México, 1998).

Durán   Fray Diego Durán, *The History of the Indies of New Spain*, ed. and trans. Doris Heyden (Norman: University of Oklahoma Press, 1994).

THE WHO AND THE WHY OF TLACAEL:
An Introduction

Epigraph 1. Don Hernando de Alvarado Tezozomoc, *Crónica mexicana*, ed. Gonzalo Díaz Migoyo and Germán Vázquez Chamorro (Madrid: Dastin, 2001), 171 (hereinafter AT). This edition is reportedly a transcription of what is thought to be the earliest copy of Alvarado Tezozomoc's original manuscript, now housed at the Library of Congress in Washington, D.C., H. P. Krauss Collection, 117.

Epigraph 2. Fray Diego Durán, *The History of the Indies of New Spain*, ed. and trans. Doris Heyden (Norman: University of Oklahoma Press, 1994), 72 (hereinafter Durán). See also Códice Durán, Biblioteca Nacional de Madrid, MS, Vitrina 26-11. The manuscript is paginated successively, without titled volume or book divisions. I cite Heyden's English translation of this work throughout this study of Tlacaelel.

Epigraph 3. Don Domingo de San Antón Muñón Chimalpahin Quauhtlehuanitzin, *Codex Chimalpahin*, 2 vols., ed. and trans. Arthur J. O. Anderson and Susan Schroeder (Norman: University of Oklahoma Press, 1997), 1:47 (hereinafter CC). This portion of the original text by Chimalpahin is in Spanish, and hence the native Mexica are "mexicanos," which we translated into English as "Mexicans." Here and elsewhere I have restored the more accurate Nahuatl term, "Mexica."

1. H. B. Nicholson, book review, "The Aztecs," *American Anthropologist* 66, no. 6 (1964): 1408–11; Stephen A. Colston, "Tlacaelel's Descendants and the Authorship of the 'Historia Mexicana,'" *Indiana* 2 (1974): 69–72.

2. H. B. Nicholson, "Hugh Thomas' *Conquest:* Observations on the Coverage of the Indigenous Cultures," in *In Chalchihuitl in Quetzalli, Precious Greenstone, Precious Quetzal Feather: Mesoamerican Studies in Honor of Doris Heyden*, ed. Eloise Quiñones Keber (Culver City, Calif.: Labyrinthos, 2000), 129–36. See chapter 1 for discussion about the rather limited contribution of Juan de Tovar, S.J., to the Tlacaelel controversy.

3. For the Crónica mexicayotl, see Susan Schroeder, "The Truth about the *Crónica Mexicayotl*," *Colonial Latin American Review* 20, no. 2 (2011): 233–47.

4. Note that these authors and their works are discussed more fully in chapter 1.

5. Tom Cummins, "The Indulgent Image: Prints in the New World," in *Contested Visions in the Spanish Colonial World*, ed. Ilona Katzew (Los Angeles: Los Angeles County Museum of Art, 2011), 203–25, has suggested that the native authors of pictorial manuscripts formed "a community that participated in a global culture" because they were familiar with painting styles from published European books, which they compared with their own techniques. Might not the same be said for natives writing in Roman alphabetic script? While Alvarado Tezozomoc, Chimalpahin, and Durán represent individuals each writing his own history, collective endeavors were not unknown. See Amos Megged and Stephanie Wood, eds., *Mesoamerican Memory: Enduring Systems of Remembrance* (Norman: University of Oklahoma Press, 2012).

6. Even centuries later there were advantages to writing in one's own language, as evidenced by Sequoyah in the United States, whose syllabary "allowed Cherokees to protect, enact, and codify Cherokee knowledge and perspectives." Ellen Cushman, *The Cherokee Syllabary: Writing the People's Perseverance* (Norman: University of Oklahoma Press, 2011), 9–10.

7. *CC* 2:35.

8. Frances Karttunen, personal communication, February 29, 2012.

9. See pages 32 and 38–39 for further discussion of a possible crossover between the graphic representation of the office and the deity.

10. *CC* 1:49. The suffix *-tzin* is a reverential ending used by various Nahua authors.

11. Don Domingo de San Antón Muñón Chimalpahin Quauhtlehuanitzin, *Annals of His Time*, ed. and trans. James Lockhart, Susan Schroeder, and Doris Namala (Stanford: Stanford University Press, 2006), 239 (hereinafter *AHT*).

12. See don Fernando de Alva Ixtlilxochitl, *Obras históricas*, ed. Edmundo O'Gorman, 2 vols. (Mexico City: Universidad Nacional Autónoma de México, 1975, 1977), for a full treatment of Alva Ixtlilxochitl and his writings. See also the numerous articles dedicated to Alva Ixtlilxochitl, the man, his life, and his work,

in *Colonial Latin American Review* 23, no. 1 (2014): 1–101. For more than one hundred years, Alva Ixtlilxochitl's original manuscripts, along with a Nahuatl-language volume by Chimalpahin, were archived as part of the British and Foreign Bible Society Library in Swindon, England. In the 1980s the entire Bible Society Collection was relocated to Cambridge University Library, Cambridge, England, MS 374, 3 vols. In 2014 the volumes were purchased by a private party and are now housed in Mexico City at the Museo Nacional de Antropología.

13. Bibliothèque Nationale, France, Manuscript Mexicain, nos. 46–50, 51–53, 54–58. And see especially Dana Liebsohn, *Script and Glyph: Pre-Hispanic History, Colonial Bookmaking, and the* Historia Tolteca-Chichimeca (Washington, D.C.: Dumbarton Oaks Research Library and Collection, 2009), and Camilla Townsend, "From Old Worlds to New: The Creation of the *Historia Tolteca-Chichimeca*," paper presented at the American Society for Ethnohistory conference, New Orleans, September 2013.

14. See Richard L. Kagan, *Clio and the Crown: The Politics of History in Medieval and Early Modern Spain* (Baltimore, Md.: Johns Hopkins University Press, 2009), for an informative study of the writing of official history, a practice dating back centuries and still current and fashionable during Chimalpahin's time.

15. See Gaius Suetonius Tranquillus, *Lives of the Caesars*, trans. Catharine Edwards (New York: Oxford University Press, 2000), and also Gaius Suetonius Tranquillus, *The Twelve Caesars*, trans. Robert Graves (Baltimore, Md.: Penguin Books, 1957), 7, 8.

16. Cornelius Tacitus, *Tacitus: The Annals*, trans. A. J. Woodman (Indianapolis, Ind.: Hackett, 2004).

17. Peter B. Villella, *Indigenous Elites and Creole Identity in Colonial Mexico, 1500–1800.* Cambridge: Cambridge University Press, 2016, and Lori Boornazian Diel, "The *Codex Mexicanus* Genealogy: Binding the Aztec Past to the Colonial Present," *Colonial Latin American Review* 24, no. 2 (2015): 120–46. Even later and as far away as Tlaxcala, Villella, in "Indian Lords, Hispanic Gentlemen: The Salazars of Colonial Tlaxcala," *Americas* 69, no. 1 (2012): 1–36, has found that the Salazars, descendants of precontact Tlaxcalteca rulers, were exemplar intellectuals and leaders in that "their story is a vivid illustration of Spanish America's subtle yet consistent tendency, despite rigidly enforced norms and racially inflected epistemological and hierarchical norms, to co-opt and blend rather than fully erase or destroy," 36. And see especially Ethelia Ruiz Medrano, *Mexico's Indigenous Communities: Their Lands and Histories, 1500–2010*, trans. Russ Davidson (Boulder: University Press of Colorado, 2010), who finds real use of ancient histories by native peoples over the centuries to maintain the integrity of their customs and communities.

18. *AHT*, 155–57.

19. Ibid., 259.

20. Ibid., 295.

21. Ibid., 287.

22. Ibid., 153, 155. For an excellent discussion of issues relating to the Inquisition and its ongoing attempts to prevent translations of scripture into the vernacular,

including Nahuatl, see Martin Austin Nesvig, "The Epistemological Politics of Vernacular Scripture in Sixteenth-Century Mexico," *Americas* 70, no. 2 (2013): 165–201. In spite of the Inquisition's prohibitive regulations, some Nahuatl-language ecclesiastical texts continued to be produced and circulated, even by Chimalpahin, e.g., his version of the Sahagún-edited *Exercicio quotidiano*, in *CC* 2:130–83. For more on this topic, see David Tavárez, "Nahua Intellectuals, Franciscan Scholars, and the *Devotio moderna* in Colonial Mexico," *Americas* 70, no. 2 (2013): 203–35.

23. *AHT*, 177, 179.

24. By all appearances, fray Agustín del Espíritu Santo was a Nahuatl speaker who was deeply committed to the social and spiritual needs of his Nahua congregation. Chimalpahin frequently refers to him as *notlaçotatzin*, "my dear father." Notice of his death is found on endpapers in Bibliothèque Nationale, France, Fonds mexicains, 220.

25. Domingo Chimalpáhin, *Las ocho relaciones y El memorial de Colhuacan*, trans. Rafael Tena, 2 vols. (Mexico City: Cien de México, 1998) (hereinafter DC), 1:84.

26. *CC* 1:73. See also AT, 54.

27. William H. Prescott, *History of the Conquest of Mexico*, ed. John Foster Kirk, 2 vols. (Philadelphia: J. B. Lippincott Company, 1873).

28. Of note, fray Juan de Mijangos and fray Martín de León. See Barry D. Sell and Larissa Taylor, "'He Could Have Made Marvels in This Language': A Náhuatl Sermon by Father Juan de Tovar, S.J." *Estudios de Cultura Náhuatl* 26 (1996): 211–44.

29. See Susan Schroeder, *Chimalpahin and the Kingdoms of Chalco*. Tucson: University of Arizona Press, 1991. For extensive discussion of the Nahua altepetl, see James Lockhart, *The Nahuas after the Conquest: A Social and Cultural History of the Indians of Central Mexico, Sixteenth through Eighteenth Centuries* (Stanford: Stanford University Press, 1992), 14–58, and Frances F. Berdan, *Aztec Archaeology and Ethnohistory* (New York: Cambridge University Press, 2014), 44–46.

30. See Robert Graves, trans., in Gaius Suetonius Tranquillus, *Twelve Caesars*, 8, who speaks of the difficulties of meanings and translating terms such as the Latin *Imperator*, which initially meant "army commander," then a title of honor that a general might earn, then a title of honor after or before the name of a ruling Caesar, and then finally in an absolute sense as "Emperor." The huey tlatoque were the rulers associated with the rise and glory of the great Mexica state. *CC* 1:47 uses the terms empire and emperor freely: "This was the origin of the emperors" and "He was the beginning and origin of this monarchy. . . . For if it had not been for him . . . this Mexica Monarchy would not have been an empire." *CC* 1:45.

31. In the colonial period the four quarters became San Pablo Teopan, San Sebastián Atzaqualco, Santa María Cuepopan, and San Juan Moyotlan.

32. DC 2:186.

33. See James Lockhart, Introduction to *AHT*, 19, who, unaware of Chimalpahin's reference to Teopan as the first tlayacatl, asserts that Moyotlan was first [in rank], as, indeed it apparently was eventually, since Chimlpahin lists it first repeatedly elsewhere in his colonial annals.

34. *CC* 2:69.

35. Ibid., 2:83.

36. For a fuller discussion of what it meant to be conquered in the precontact and early colonial eras, see Susan Schroeder, "Introduction: The Genre of Conquest Studies," in *Indian Conquistadors: Indigenous Allies in the Conquest of Mesoamerica,* ed. Laura E. Matthew and Michel R. Oudijk (Norman: University of Oklahoma Press, 2007), 5–27.

37. Schroeder, *Chimalpahin and the Kingdoms,* 123–24, 176.

38. DC 2:326.

39. Lockhart, *Nahuas,* 15, 27.

40. DC 1:56.

41. Ibid., 1:56, 58.

42. Ibid., 1:64.

43. *AHT,* 270, 285.

44. For just a few examples of Chimalpahin's allegiance to both Chalco and Mexico Tenochtitlan, *AHT* (*titlaca Amaquemecan Chalco*) 186; DC (*ynic nican tomacuilcantian ticate Amaquemecan*) 2:348; *AHT* (*timacehualti [Mexico],* 180, (*yn Mexica timacehualtin*), 186; DC 2:368 (*tehuantin timacehualtin nican ypan Nueva España titlaca*).

45. *CC* 1:61. Chimalpahin took this section directly from a text by Alvarado Tezozomoc, to whom he gave full credit.

46. Cited in Schroeder, *Chimalpahin and the Kingdoms,* 31. See also Schroeder, "Truth about the *Crónica Mexicayotl,*" 237, for additional discussion.

47. DC 2:270–380.

48. Ibid., 2:294. This concern for accuracy among late sixteenth-century authors has parallels in ancient times. See Marshall Sahlins, *Apologies to Thucydides.* Chicago: University of Chicago Press, 2004.

49. Donald Lateiner, *The Historical Method of Herodotus* (Toronto: University of Toronto Press, 1989), 7, 8, 10. Herodotus was called the "Father of History" because "he created a subject and a method," 13.

50. See W. Kendrick Pritchett, *The Liar School of Herodotos* (Amsterdam: J. C. Geiben, 1993), 1, who states that Herodotus's critics claimed that his work was "a compilation of lies . . . concocted to amuse his audience."

51. Jill Lepore, *The Story of America: Essays on Origins.* Princeton: Princeton University Press, 2012.

52. Carlos María de Bustamante, *Necesidad de la unión de todos los mexicanos contra las asechanzas de la nación española y liga europea comprobada con La historia de la antigua república de Tlaxcallan* (Mexico City: Imprenta del Águila, 1826), 29.

53. Hasso von Winning, "Tlacaelel, Aztec General and Statesman," *Masterkey* 38, no. 2 (1964): 44–53, here, 49.

54. J. Rounds, "Dynastic Succession and the Centralizing of Power in Tenochtitlan," in *The Inca and Aztec States, 1400–1800,* ed. George A. Collier,

Renato I. Rosaldo, and John D. Wirth (New York: Academic Press, 1982), 63–89.

55. Miguel León-Portilla, *The Aztec Image of Self and Society: An Introduction to Nahua Culture*, ed. J. Jorge Klor de Alva (Salt Lake City: University of Utah Press, 1992), 98.

56. See William L. Barnes, "Secularizing for Survival: Changing Depictions of Central Mexican Native Rule in the Early Colonial Period," in *Painted Books and Indigenous Knowledge in Mesoamerica: Manuscript Studies in Honor of Mary Elizabeth Smith*, ed. Elizabeth Hill Boone (New Orleans: Tulane University, 2005), 319–44, here, 320–21. Barnes discusses the issue of whether an individual outfitted as a god was conceived as a *teixiptla*, a representative of the deity, or the god itself. See chapter 1 of the current volume for additional discussion of Cecilia Klein's scholarship on Tlacaelel in his role as the deity Cihuacoatl.

57. R.C. Padden, *The Hummingbird and the Hawk: Conquest and Sovereignty in the Valley of Mexico, 1503–1541* (New York: Harper Torchbooks, 1970), 22, 27.

58. For a fine study of the importance of native genealogies, see Eduardo de Jesús Douglas, "Our Fathers, Our Mothers: Painting an Indian Genealogy in New Spain," in *Contested Visions in the Spanish Colonial World*, ed. Ilona Katzew (Los Angeles: Los Angeles County Museum of Art, 2011), 117–31.

59. DC 2:296. According to Matthew Restall, Lisa Sousa, and Kevin Terraciano, eds., *Mesoamerican Voices: Native-Language Writings from Colonial Mexico, Oaxaca, Yucatan, and Guatemala* (New York: Cambridge University Press, 2005), 12, "the style and method of interpreting pre-Conquest-style codices could be extremely subtle and complex. . . . Thus, there was probably never one 'proper' reading, performance, or interpretation. It is unclear how interpretive the writing system was and to what extent memory and context guided the speaker/reader."

60. Of course, Alvarado Tezozomoc and Durán were not present at Tlacaelel's speeches, but their knowledge of what was said may have come from other accounts, including oral histories. The practice of including verbatim-like speeches in authentic histories is ancient, Tacitus himself, among others, employing the device.

61. See, especially, Eduardo Matos Moctezuma, "Symbolism of the Templo Mayor," in *The Aztec Templo Mayor*, ed. Elizabeth Hill Boone (Washington, D.C.: Dumbarton Oaks Research Library and Collection, 1983), 185–209, who believes that the templo mayor came to "represent the entire Mexica conception of the cosmos," 191.

62. David Carrasco, ed., *To Change Place: Aztec Ceremonial Landscapes* (Boulder: University Press of Colorado, 1991), and David Carrasco, *City of Sacrifice: The Aztec Empire and the Role of Violence in Civilization* (Boston: Beacon Press, 1999), as well as any number of his other works on Aztec religion; Michel Graulich, *Myths of Ancient Mexico*, trans. Bernard R. Ortiz de Montellano and Thelma Ortiz de Montellano (Norman: University of Oklahoma Press, 1997); and Rafael Tena, *La religión mexica*, 2nd ed. (Mexico City: Instituto Nacional de Antropología e Historia, 2012. And see DC 1:94–96, for more about the early relationship between Huitzilopochtli and the Mexica.

63. DC 1:94. See also Elizabeth Hill Boone, "The Image of Huitzilopochtli: Changing Ideas and Visual Manifestations of the Aztec God," in *The Imagination of Matter: Religion and Ecology in Mesoamerican Traditions*, ed. David Carrasco (Oxford: British Archaeological Reports, 1989), 51–82.

64. See Frances F. Berdan, "The Economics of Aztec Luxury Trade and Tribute," in *The Aztec Templo Mayor*, ed. Elizabeth Hill Boone (Washington, D.C.: Dumbarton Oaks Research Library and Collection, 1983), 161–83, for details about imperial revenues and trade goods.

1. THE MAN, THE OFFICE, AND THE DEITY:
The Sources

Epigraph 1. AT, 137.

Epigraph 2. CC 1:43.

Epigraph 3. Diego Durán, *Book of the Gods and Rites and the Ancient Calendar*, ed. and trans. Fernando Horcasitas and Doris Heyden (Norman: University of Oklahoma Press, 1975), 210.

1. AT, 348–49, states that Tlacaelel was more than 120 years old when he died. See also Miguel Acosta Saignes, "Los teopixque," *Revista Mexicana de Estudios Antropológicos* 8 (1946), 147–205, who is often cited as a source. It is Chimalpahin who states that Tlacaelel was ninety when he died in Eight Reed, 1487, CC 2:35.

2. Frances Karttunen explains that, contrary to popular thought, which most often defines Cihuacoatl as "Serpent Woman," the Nahuatl *Cihua-* modifies the noun *coatl*, hence, "Female Serpent," personal communication, February 29, 2012. Titles of office are treated thoroughly in the *Codex Mendoza*, ed. Frances F. Berdan and Patricia Rieff Anawalt, 4 vols. (Berkeley: University of California Press, 1992). See all volumes, but especially vol. 3. Among the Mexica, titles designated offices in the royal bureaucracy. In Chalco, a royal title was associated with each royal rulership and was always accompanied with the designation of *teuctli* (lord), i.e., Chichimecateuctli, Tlailotlacteuctli, etc. See Schroeder, *Chimalpahin and the Kingdoms*, passim. Zelia Nuttall, *The Fundamental Principles of Old and New World Civilizations: A Comparative Research Based on a Study of the Ancient Mexican Religious, Sociological and Calendrical Systems* (Cambridge, Mass.: Harvard University, 1901), 55–56, 60, 76–77, discusses the Cihuacoatl as both an office and a deity.

3. For example, CC 1:47

4. Cited in Hernando Cortés, *Letters from Mexico*, ed. and trans. Anthony Pagden (New Haven, Conn.: Yale University Press), 491n76; AT, 418.

5. Fray Bernardino de Sahagún, *Florentine Codex: General History of the Things of New Spain*, ed. and trans. Arthur J. O. Anderson and Charles E. Dibble, 12 vols. (Santa Fe, N.M., and Salt Lake City, Utah: School of American Research and University of Utah Press, 1950–82), book 8, Kings and Lords, 55.

6. CC 1:47.

7. Sahagún, *Florentine Codex*, book 2, The Ceremonies, 106; book 8:55, 77, states that the Atempanecatl were the king's executioners. Also spelled Atecpanecatl

and Atenpanecatl. Chimalpahin states that Tlacaelel already had the title of Atecpanecatl in Thirteen Reed, 1427, when Itzcoatl was installed as tlatoani. DC 2:69; and *CC* 2:33.

8. *CC* 1:45, 129, 231. And see pages 62–66, 67–68, and 86 for more about the Mexica's wars against Maxtlaton.

9. Ibid., 1:97–98.

10. Sahagún, *Florentine Codex*, book 6, Rhetoric and Moral Philosophy, 72, 75–76. He adds, "There is only one ruler, the heart of the city, and that there are two [assisting] dignitaries. . . . one is from the military, the Tlacateccatl; [and] one also is from the nobility, the Tlacochcalcatl," 6:110.

11. See page 124, which indicates when the military responsibilities of the Tlacochcalcatl were separated from that of the Cihuacoatl.

12. *CC* 2:95.

13. The Tlailotlacteuctli was the most prestigious title of the kings of Tenanco Texocpalco Tepopolla, second-in-rank of the four main altepetl of confederated Chalco. When a group of Tenanca separated from the mother altepetl and went to settle in Amecameca, the third-in-rank Chalca altepetl (based on chronology of settlement), they took the Tlailotlacteuctli title for their rulership and tlatoani and established Tzaqualtitlan Tenanco, the second-in-rank altepetl tlayacatl in Amecameca. Chimalpahin was a descendant of that exalted precontact royal lineage. See Schroeder, *Chimalpahin and the Kingdoms of Chalco*, 56–57, 104–6.

14. DC 2:313–17.

15. Sahagún, *Florentine Codex*, 8:55, 74.

16. Ibid., 8:77.

17. *CC* 1:145, states that Tlacaelel's sons were "great, brave warriors" who bore the quetzal feather crest device on their backs as their insignia in battle. This particular quetzal feather headdress is distinctive and worn by warriors and men of valor. It is worn by Moteuczoma in the Codex Rios, and see also the Codex Ixtlilxochitl. My thanks to Elizabeth Boone for the insight, August 18, 2014.

18. *Codex Mendoza*, 3:137, fol. 65.

19. Sahagún, *Florentine Codex*, book 9, The Merchants, 34; 8:43, 55.

20. See also Alfredo López Austin, *The Human Body and Ideology: Concepts of the Ancient Nahuas*, trans. Thelma Ortiz de Montellano and Bernardo Ortiz de Montellano, 2 vols. (Salt Lake City: University of Utah Press, 1988), 1:191–92, 198; 2:231–34, who describes the *el-* as a part of "the animistic centers" and that is "concentrated in the areas of vitality and feelings"—happiness and tranquility, love, anger, and hate. Hermann Beyer, in a section titled "El jeroglífico de Tlacaelel," discusses in considerable detail the graphic symbolism of the liver as it was associated with Tlacaelel. Hermann Beyer, *Mito y simbología del México antiguo*, special edition of *El México antiguo: Revista Internacional de Arqueología, Etnología, Folklore, Historia, Historia Antigua y Lingüística Mexicanas*, ed. Carmen Cook de Leonard (Mexico City: Sociedad Alemana Mexicanista, 1965), 506–8.

21. *Codex Mendoza*, 3:141, fol. 67. I am grateful to Elizabeth Boone for these insights about the representations of the liver. For more on Tzitzimitl iconography, see Elizabeth Hill Boone, "Coatlicues at the Templo Mayor," *Ancient Mesoamerica* 10 (1999): 189–206. Remarkably, and possibly intuitively, Justyna Olko, *Insignia of Rank in the Nahua World, from the Fifteenth to the Seventeenth Century* (Boulder: University Press of Colorado, 2014), does not discuss the insignia for Tlacaelel and the many offices he held other than when he describes them himself, 312, or when Chimalpahin describes his cape, 386.

22. Epigraph: Durán, *Book of the Gods*, 217. See also Durán, *Historia de las Indias de Nueva España e Islas de la Tierra Firme*, transc. Francisco González Varela, 2 vols. (Mexico City: Banco Santander, 1990, 1991).

23. Sahagún, *Florentine Codex*, book 8.

24. Ibid., book 1, The Gods, 11. Kay A. Read, in "More than Earth: Cihuacoatl as Mother, Warrior, and Inside Ruler," briefly treats aspects of the deity Cihuacoatl and touches on Tlacaelel the Cihuacoatl, but not definitively. Article is in *Códices y documentos sobre México: Tercer Simposio Internacional*, ed. Constanza Vega Sosa (Mexico City: Instituto Nacional de Antropología e Historia, 2000), 407–26.

25. Sahagún, *Florentine Codex*, book 1.

26. Ibid., 1:69–70. See especially Hernando Ruiz de Alarcón, *Treatise on the Heathen Superstitions That Today Live among the Indians Native to This New Spain, 1629*, ed. and trans. J. Richard Andrews and Ross Hassig (Norman: University of Oklahoma Press, 1984), 98, who found one reference to Cihuacoatl in the incantations of Nahuas in Atenango in the seventeenth century. Cihuacoatl in the incantation was referred to as *nohueltiuh*, "my older sister," a complex Nahuatl term with at least three distinct definitions. See Schroeder, "Chimalpahin and Why Women Matter in History," in *Indigenous Intellectuals: Knowledge, Power, and Colonial Culture in Mexico and the Andes*, edited by Gabriela Ramos and Yanna Yannakakis (Durham, N.C.: Duke University Press, 2014), 115–17.

27. Sahagún, *Florentine Codex*, 1:11.

28. Sahagún, *Primeros memoriales*, trans. Thelma D. Sullivan, ed. H. B. Nicholson, Arthur J. O. Anderson, Charles E. Dibble, Eloise Quiñones Keber, and Wayne Ruwet (Norman and Madrid: University of Oklahoma Press and Patrimonio Nacional and Real Academia de la Historia, 1997), 105–6.

29. See Sahagún, *Florentine Codex*, 6:151–58; 160–65, 179–81, for information about pregnancy and childbirth and Cihuacoatl's role in both.

30. Sahagún, *Florentine Codex*, 2:236–37. Compare his "Song of Cihuacoatl" in the *Primeros memoriales* (1997), 143–44.

31. Sahagún, *Florentine Codex*, 8:3.

32. Durán, *Book of the Gods* and *History*.

33. Durán, *Book of the Gods*, 210–20. See also "La historia de Tlatelolco désde los tiempos más remotos," in *Anales de Tlatelolco: Unos anales históricos de la nación mexicana y Códice de Tlatelolco*, ed. Heinrich Berlin (Mexico City: Editorial y Litografía Regina de los Ángeles, 1980), 70, for information about ritual activity at Tlillan.

34. Charles Gibson states that Xilonen was the corn goddess and that the "month" was dedicated to her. See George Kubler and Charles Gibson, *The Tovar Calendar* (New Haven: Memoirs of the Connecticut Academy of Arts and Sciences, 1951), 11:27. See also Sahagún, *Primeros memoriales*, facs. ed. (Norman and Madrid: University of Oklahoma Press and Patrimonio Nacional and Real Academia de la Historia, 1993), and *Primeros memoriales*, 1997, for additional discussion of Cihuacoatl and her various spiritual and iconographic iterations. Caution should be exercised regarding the precision of some of the dates in the many texts. As noted, there were inconsistencies and errors on occasion, perhaps because correlations with the Julian and Gregorian calendar adjustments had not been fully reconciled.

35. Durán, *Book of the Gods*, 217–18.

36. Ibid., 217.

37. *El libro del Ciuacoatl: Homenaje para el año del Fuego Nuevo, Libro explicativo del llamado Códice Borbónico*. ed. Ferdinand Anders, Maarten Jansen, and Luis Reyes García. (Spain, Austria, and Mexico City: Sociedad Estatal Quinto Centenario, Akademische Druck- u. Verlagsanstalt, and Fondo de Cultura Económica, 1991), 41–49.

38. In *El libro del Ciuacoatl*, Anders, Jansen, and Reyes García, alas, collapse the deity and office into one entity, presumably believing that the painted Cihuacoatl image is not merely a deity but one or another of Tlacaelel's descendants fulfilling his duties in the office of the Cihuacoatl. Images of Cihuacoatl are found in the *Códice Borbónico* facsimile (renamed *El libro*) on pp. 23, 26, 27, 28, 36, and 37. See, in the accompanying text, p. 42, a stone Cihuacoatl in relief excavated from the Templo Mayor. See also Elizabeth Hill Boone, *Cycles of Time and Meaning in the Mexican Books of Fate* (Austin: University of Texas Press, 2007), 211–12, who addresses the issue of provenience. She was of great assistance in clarifying various features of this image.

39. Pete Sigal, "Imagining Cihuacoatl: Masculine Rituals, Nahua Goddesses and the Texts of the Tlacuilos," *Gender and History* 22, no. 3 (2010): 538–63.

40. Cecelia F. Klein, "Rethinking Cihuacoatl: Aztec Political Imagery of the Conquered Woman," in *Smoke and Mist: Mesoamerican Studies in Memory of Thelma D. Sullivan*, ed. J. Kathryn Josserand and Karen Kavin (Oxford: British Archaeological Reports, 1988), 237–77. See especially Salvador Mateo Higuera, *Los dioses supremos: Enciclopedia gráfica del México antiguo* (Mexico City: Secretaría de Hacienda y Crédito Público, 1992), 139–48, for an interesting presentation of the variety of additional illustrations from codices and assorted ceramic pieces that are representative of Cihuacoatl. And see Cecelia F. Klein, "The Shield Women: Resolution of an Aztec Gender Paradox," In *Current Topics in Aztec Studies: Essays in Honor of Dr. H. B. Nicholson*, ed. Alana Cordy-Collins and Douglas Sharon, 39–64 (San Diego, Calif.: San Diego Museum of Man, 1993), 39–64, for certain primordial and militaristic aspects of Cihuacoatl.

41. See also Patrick Johansson K., "Tlahtoani y cihuacóatl: Una dualidad teocrática en México-Tenochtitlan," *Arqueología Mexicana* 23, no. 133 (2015): 22–29,

and "Tlahtoani y Cihuacoatl: Lo diestro solar y lo siniestro lunar en el alto mando mexica," *Estudios de Cultura Náhuatl* 28 (1998): 39–75, for additional discussion of duality issues relating to rulership and religion.

42. Epigraph: Sahagún, *Florentine Codex*, 6:226. See especially Cuauhtémoc Medina, "Beyond Sources," in *The Colors of the New World: Artists, Materials, and the Creation of the* Florentine Codex, by Diana Magaloni Kerpel (Los Angeles: Getty Research Institute, 2014), ix–xi, for a perceptive discussion of purpose and implementation of native-authored colonial Mesoamerican texts.

43. *CC* 1:63, 165, 171–73; *CC* 2:41, 101, 105. Huanitzin had more than one wife, and his offspring held a variety of prominent positions in local and regional governments.

44. This Nahua district was renamed San Sebastián Atzaqualco after the Spaniards established themselves in the capital. For corroboration of Atzaqualco as the traditional home of the Moteuczomas, see a sermon by Juan de Tovar, S.J., who also lived in the district, in Sell and Taylor, "'He Could Have Made Marvels,'" 211–44, "for here in Atzaqualco, the distinct place of San Sebastián, the royal eagle gave insignia to our altepetl of Mexico because it is the place of the very tlaxilacalli and childhood home of Moteuczomatzin," 234. I thank David Tavárez for bringing this source to my attention.

45. *AHT*, 67.

46. *CC* 1: 62–63, 64–65. For additional studies regarding Alvarado Tezozomoc, see especially Salvador Velazco, *Visiones de Anáhuac: Reconstrucciones historiográficas y etnicidades emergentes en el México colonial: Fernando de Alva Ixtlixóchitl, Diego Muñoz Camargo y Hernando Alvarado Tezozómoc* (Guadalajara: Universidad de Guadalajara, 2003); and José Rubén Romero Galván, *Los privilegios perdidos: Hernando Alvarado Tezozómoc, su tiempo, su nobleza, y su Crónica mexicana* (Mexico City: Universidad Nacional Autónoma de México, 2003). See pages 112–15 for more about Tehuetzquititzin.

47. For more than 150 years, there has been a misattribution of authorship regarding Chimalpahin's writings. See Schroeder, "Truth about the *Crónica Mexicayotl*," for the definitive work on this topic.

48. Don Domingo de San Antón Muñón Chimalpahin Quauhtlehuanitzin, *Chimalpahin's Conquest: A Nahua Historian's Rewriting of Francisco López de Gómara's* Conquista de México, ed. and trans. Susan Schroeder, Anne J. Cruz, Cristián Roa-de-la-Carrera, and David E. Tavárez (Stanford: Stanford University Press, 2010), 352.

49. *AT*, 72. Fortunately, Chimalpahin's Nahuatl annals exist in holograph and are located at the Bibliothèque Nationale, Paris, Fonds mexicains, 74 and 220; the Archivo Histórico, Instituto Nacional de Antropología e Historia, Mexico, vol. 256; and were at Cambridge University Library as part of the British and Foreign Bible Society Library Collection. MSS 374, v. 3, since 1827, until recently acquired by a private party in Mexico and subsequently housed at the Archivo Histórico at the Museo Nacional de Antropología de México. The earliest known copy of his Spanish-

language version of *Conquista de México* (1552) is the Boturini copy (1746), now in the Ayer Collection, Browning MS, Vault Folio Case MS 5011, at the Newberry Library, Chicago, Illinois. Also at the Newberry Library is Chimalpahin's manuscript copy of the "Exercicio quotidiano," by Sahagún, Ayer Collection, MS 1484.

50. "Exercicio quotidiano," *CC* 2:130–83.

51. Schroeder, *Chimalpahin and the Kingdoms*, 22–24. This quotation is excerpted from his account about Amecameca, Chalco.

52. *AHT*, 169.

53. See Schroeder, *Chimalpahin and the Kingdoms*.

54. *AHT*, 174n4, 175, 271. It is possible that they are two different men. Reportedly, there was an Hernando Durán who was a Franciscan. Clavigero confuses the names as well.

55. See, for example, Schroeder, "Chimalpahin Rewrites the Conquest: Yet Another Epic History?" in *The Conquest All Over Again: Nahuas and Zapotecs Thinking, Writing, and Painting Spanish Colonialism*, ed. Susan Schroeder (Brighton, UK: Sussex Academic Press, 2010), 101–23.

56. Alva Ixtlilxochitl, *Obras históricas*. See especially Alva Ixtlilxochitl's "Historia de la nación chichimeca," 2:177, for what appears to be a unique reference to Tlacaelel. I thank Amber Brian for this reference.

57. Ibid., 1:352, 371; 2:177.

58. The Jesuit Horacio Carochi (fl. 1645) stated that del Castillo was a mestizo but a "gran lengua Mexicana." Cited in Cristóbal del Castillo, *Historia de la venida de los mexicanos y otros pueblos e Historia de la conquista*, ed. Federico Navarrete Linares (Mexico City: Instituto Nacional de Antropología e Historia, 1991), 34.

59. Cortés's letters were written during the years ca. 1521–26. See Chimalpahin, *Chimalpahin's Conquest*, 362; and Cortés, *Letters from Mexico*, 321. For more about Tlacotzin the Cihuacoatl, see pages 132–44.

60. Bernal Díaz del Castillo, *The Discovery and Conquest of Mexico*, trans. A. P. Maudslay (New York: Da Capo Press, [1908] 1996), 310–11, 452, 454.

61. Bernal Díaz del Castillo, *The True History of the Conquest of Mexico*, trans. Maurice Keatinge (La Jolla, Calif.: Renaissance; Press, [1568] 1979), 404, where he implicates a "Tapia and Juan Velázquez," the latter signifying Tlacotzin after his baptism.

62. Francisco López de Gómara, *Historia de las Indias y Conquista de México* (Zaragoza: Agustín Millán, 1552), and Chimalpahin, *Chimalpahin's Conquest*, 183, 409. Little is known of Totomotzin, and note that Chimalpahin qualifies the relationship: "Totomotzin, said to be the son of the great captain general who was president of the supreme judicial council, or Chief Judge Tlacaelel [the] Cihuacoatl, founder of the Mexica empire." The annals do list a Totomochtzin, said to be the father of three daughters, one of whom married don Tomás de San Martín Quetzalmaçatzin the Chichimecateuctli, ruler of Itztlacoçauhcan, Amecameca, Chalco (r. 1522–47)—another Tlacaelel family connection with Chalco. See fig. 16.

63. Sahagún, *Florentine Codex*, especially books 1, 2, 6, and 8. Book 8, in particular, deals with rulerships of the tlatoque and their conquests. Tlacaelel would likely not, of course, be listed among the rulers, if Sahagún's purpose was essentially descriptive of the office. I thank Elizabeth Boone for this observation, August, 18, 2014.

64. Fray Gerónimo de Mendieta, *Historia eclesiástica indiana* (Mexico City: Editorial Porrúa, 1980), 108.

65. For example, fray Juan de Torquemada, *Monarquía indiana*, 3 vols. (Mexico City: Editorial Porrúa, 1975), 1:150, 170–71, 379, 571. See also *Anónimo mexicano*, ed. and trans. Richley H. Crapo and Bonnie Glass-Coffin (Logan: Utah State University Press, 2005), where there is repeated evidence of Torquemada's use of this particular Nahuatl source for his history, another example of the sharing of books and manuscripts among both Nahua and Spanish historians.

66. Fray Bartolomé de las Casas, *Apologética historia sumaria*, ed. Edmundo O'Gorman, 2 vols. (Mexico City: Instituto de Investigaciones Históricas, Universidad Nacional Autónoma de México, 1967), 2:382–83.

67. Although nearly impossible to prove, it is likely that Chimalpahin had the opportunity to see Las Casas's *Apologética*. Today the holograph of the *Apologética* is located at the Biblioteca de la Real Academia de la Historia, Madrid, MS A 73; vol. 46, Colección Muñoz. O'Gorman believes that a copy of the manuscript was at the friary of Santo Domingo in Mexico City and that both Mendieta and Torquemada made use of it, 1:xxxv.

68. Durán, *History*. Yet all the while, fray Diego was under the watchful eye of the Inquisition because of certain books in his possession. See Nesvig, "Epistemological Politics," 184.

69. Durán, *History*, 339.

70. Manuscritos, Vit. 26–11, Biblioteca Nacional, Madrid. See, especially, N. C. Christopher Couch, "Style and Ideology in the Durán Illustrations: An Interpretive Study of Three Early Colonial Mexican Manuscripts (Ph.D. diss., Columbia University, 1987), for a thorough study of the *History* and its illustrations. Couch, 339–40, traces precedents for the Durán illustrations to some of the finest Bibles being published in Europe at the time. For an excellent reproduction of the paintings, see Durán, *Historia*. Unfortunately, the text is derived from a flawed copy by José F. Ramírez in nineteenth-century Mexico.

71. Donald Robertson, "Paste-Over Illustrations in the Durán Codex of Madrid," *Tlalocan* 5, no. 4 (1968): 340–48; Elizabeth Hill Boone, "The Nature and Earlier Versions of Diego Durán's 'Historia de las Indias' in Madrid," unpublished manuscript, Summer 1978; and N. C. Christopher Couch, "Fragments of History: The Durán Paste-Over Illustrations," paper presented at the American Society for Ethnohistory conference, November 4, 1983.

72. Patrick Johansson K., "Tlahtoani y cihuacóatl" (2015), states that Durán's artist was mistaken in representing this figure as Axayacatl when most likely it

was high king Moteuczoma Ilhuicamina, Tlacaelel the Cihuacoatl's brother. He believes that the sacrifices marked the occasion of the dedication of *"la Piedra del Sol,"* 22. However, Durán wrote of two grand ceremonies where large, carved stones dedicated to the sun were held. Proposed by Tlacaelel, the first, under the auspices of Moteuczoma Ilhuicamina and Tlacaelel the Cihuacoatl, was to be a huge, round stone with a basin and to contain the sacrificial blood, sculpted in the likeness of the sun; the second, during Axayacatl's reign, with Tlacaelel still in charge, when a "Sun Stone" was inaugurated, 186 and 276–78, and see this volume, pages 98–99 and 107–8. However, the location of the painting in the manuscript relates specifically to the narrative about the great deeds of Tlatoani Moteuczoma Ilhuicamina, MS Vitrina 26–11, fol. 70r.

73. *El Códice de Huichapan*, plate 26. The Cihuacoatl (presumably Tlacaelel), with his title glyph, is seated along with King Itzcoatl and King Mixcoatl, each on his respective throne. I thank Frances Berdan for identifying the Mixcoatl figure. And see *Códice de Huichapan: Paleografía y traducción*, ed. Yolanda Lastra and Doris Bartholomew (Mexico City: Universidad Nacional Autónoma de México, 2001); and *El Códice de Huichapan*, vol. 1, *Relato otomí del México prehispánico y colonial*, ed. Manuel Alvarado Guinchard (Mexico City: Departamento de Lingüística, Instituto Nacional de Antropología e Historia, 1976).

74. Doris Heyden's edition of Durán's *History* unfortunately labels this painting, "The death of Tlacaelel. His body is being prepared for the funeral rites." But surely the corpse is that of King Tzotzomatzin of Coyoacan, who angered the Mexica tlatoani, Ahuitzotl, when he warned him of possible flooding if the Mexica redirected the springs toward the capital. Furious with his insubordination, Ahuitzotl ordered the man, who was wearing a royal diadem, to be strangled and his body cast onto the rocks. It appears that Tzotzomatzin did not go easily. As for Tlacaelel, he had already died and had the benefit of a funeral ceremony that was said to be as lavish and solemn as that of any of the kings that he served. The image is included because it is the only known extant image (however erroneous) where Tlacaelel is named.

75. Henrico Martínez, *Reportorio de los tiempos e Historia natural de Nueva España* (Mexico City: Secretaría de Educación Pública, [1606] 1948), 128–30.

76. DC 1:308.

77. Juan de Tovar, *Manuscrit Tovar*, ed. Jacques Lafaye (Graz, Austria: Akademische Druck- u. Verlagsanstalt, 1972); Juan de Tovar, *Codex Ramírez: Relación del origen de los indios que habitan esta Nueva España, según sus historias*, ed. Manuel Orozco y Berra (Mexico City: Editorial Leyenda, 1980); and especially Kubler and Gibson, *Tovar Calendar*, for a full description of the works of Tovar.

78. José de Acosta, *Natural and Moral History of the Indies*, ed. Jane E. Mangan, trans. Frances López Morillas (Durham, N.C.: Duke University Press, 2002).

79. Francisco J. Clavigero, *Historia antigua de México*, trans. J. Joaquín de Mora, 2 vols. (Mexico City: Editorial Delfín, 1944), 1:190–91.

80. Ibid., 1:191n1.

81. Charles Gibson has meticulously compared the two Tovar manuscripts, his "Historia" and his "Relación del origen de los yndios" (*Códice Ramírez),* and discusses the background and relationship of the Durán and Tovar histories in Kubler and Gibson, *Tovar Calendar,* 11:9–21.

82. Robert H. Barlow, "La Crónica X: Versiones coloniales de la historia de los mexica tenochca," *Revista Mexicana de Estudios Antropológicos* 7 (1945): 65–87; Ignacio Bernal, "Los calendarios de Durán: Más confusión alrededor de la Crónica X," *Revista Mexicana de Estudios Antropológicos* 9 (1947): 125–34; and Alfonso Caso, "Una fecha en el Códice Ramírez," *Revista Mexicana de Estudios Antropológicos* 7 (1945): 82–3.

83. Sylvie Peperstraete, *La "Chronique X": Reconstitution et analyse d'une source perdue fondamentale sur la civilisation Aztèque, d'après l'Historia de las Indias de Nueva España de D. Durán (1581) et la Crónica Mexicana de F. A. Tezozomoc (ca. 1598)* (Oxford: British Archaeological Reports, 2007), 590.

84. Ibid.

85. Ibid., 599.

86. Rafael Tena, "Revisión de la hipótesis sobre 'La Crónica X,'" in *Códices y documentos sobre México,* ed. Salvador Rueda Smithers, Constanza Vega Sosa, and Rodrigo Martínez Baracs, 2 vols. (Mexico City: Instituto Nacional de Antropología e Historia, 1997), 2:163–78.

87. Peperstraete, *La "Chronique X,"* 599–600.

88. *CC* 2:58–59.

89. Ibid., 2:118–20.

90. Ibid., 2:78–79.

91. Ibid., 1:62–63. And see Schroeder, "Truth about the *Crónica Mexicayotl,"* for discussion of Chimalpahin's abundant sources about the Mexica.

92. Schroeder, "Truth about the *Crónica Mexicayotl,"* 241.

93. *AHT,* 239.

94. Ignacio Bernal, "Durán's *Historia* and the *Crónica X,"* in Durán, *History,* 574.

95. Durán, *History,* 242–43. See also Patrick Thomas Hajovsky, *On the Lips of Others: Moteuczoma's Fame in Aztec Monuments and Rituals* (Austin: University of Texas Press, 2015), for more information about the Chapoltepec royal sculptures.

96. León-Portilla, *Aztec Image,* 37. See also León-Portilla, "Motecuhzoma Ilhuicamina," in *The Oxford Encyclopedia of Mesoamerican Cultures: The Civilizations of Mexico and Central America,* ed. David Carrasco, 3 vols. (New York: Oxford University Press, 2001) 2:343–44, who credits Tlacaelel as being a motivating force in the development of the Mexica Tenochca empire.

97. León-Portilla, *Aztec Image,* 98–99.

98. Klein, "Rethinking Cihuacoatl."

99. *CC* 1:145.

2. THE BEGINNINGS OF THE MEXICA HISTORIES, AND THE EARLY YEARS

1. Chimalpahin's manuscripts are located in England, France, Mexico, and the United States. While it has been possible to examine watermarks, paper, ink, and internal clues, the order of the production of his annals and other documents is still not established.

2. DC 1:64, 312–14. Simon Schama, *The Story of the Jews: Finding the Words, 1000 BC–1492 AD* (New York: HarperCollins, 2013), 152, credits Josephus for marking biblical time: "Now the number of years that passed from its first foundation which was laid by King Solomon, till this its destruction, which happened in the second year of Vespasian, are collected to be one thousand one hundred and thirty, besides seven months and fifteen days and from the second building of it which was done by Haggai in the second year of Cyrus the king till its destruction under Vespasian there were six hundred and thirty-nine years and forty-five days."

3. *CC* 1:45.

4. There are, as noted above, several other primary versions of early Mexica history. For two excellent pictorial sources, see *Codex Mendoza* and *Codex Telleriano-Remensis: Ritual, Divination, and History in a Pictorial Aztec Manuscript*, ed. Eloise Quiñones Keber (Austin: University of Texas Press, 1995).

5. Durán, 234.

6. *CC* 1:45.

7. Durán, 94.

8. DC 2:79.

9. While numerous Nahua personal names recur, no one else outside the royal family was named Tlacaelel, other than his heirs, although *CC* 2:73 has a Huehue Tezozomoctli Eleltzin of Colhuacan.

10. DC 2:53.

11. *CC* 1:105. *CC* 1:45 states that the Mexica were actually subject to Azcapotzalco, Colhuacan, Acolhuacan Coatl Ichan, and Chalco.

12. Ibid., 1:31, 209, 211. See pages 12 and 111–12 for discussion of Teopan as the first Mexico Tenochtitlan tlayacatl. There was a distance of at least several blocks between what is known of the location of Temazcaltitlan and the San Pablo church.

13. *CC* 1:31, 105, 109. Elsewhere, Chimalpahin states that it took 262 years to complete the journey from Aztlan; ibid., 1:31.

14. Ibid., 1:109. Chimalpahin lists the names of the founding fathers of Tlatelolco.

15. Ibid., 1:107; DC 1:215.

16. Ibid., 1:109

17. Reportedly, the volcano Popocatepetl "began to smoke" in the same year, *CC* 1:111. DC 1:223 has Seven House, 1368, as the date of Tenochtzin's death. For more about the formative years and migrations of the Mexica, see Susan Schroeder, "'Then They Pressed On': Indigenous Migration in the Nahuatl Annals of Chimalpahin," under review.

18. Huitzilihuitl the elder was said to be the first ruler of the Teochichimeca Mexica; *CC* 1:193, 195, 205; *CC* 2:69, 71. For his children and relatives, see *CC* 1:91; *CC* 2:75, 77. Note the conflict in dates in the different sets of annals.

19. Ibid., 2:77.

20. Huitzilihuitl's short-lived lineage was the original Mexica dynasty, *CC* 1:91. In another set of annals, DC 1:167n13, 169, 171, states that a son hid in the reeds and later went to live in Azcapotzalco.

21. *CC* 2:77.

22. Ibid., 1:91, 2:73.

23. Ibid., 2:75.

24. Ibid., 2:25, 29, 71.

25. Ibid., 2:29; Durán, 114.

26. *CC* 1:205; DC 2:35.

27. *CC* 2:29–31.

28. Ibid., 1:93, 205.

29. Chimalpahin typically distinguished between "cihuapilli" and "tlatocacihuapilli," the latter most often designating a noblewoman who either succeeds to the throne herself or whose heirs do. Unfortunately, Chimalpahin is not entirely consistent in his usage. See especially Schroeder, "Why Women Matter in History."

30. *CC* 1:92, 208; DC 1:357, 2:46.

31. Durán, 114.

32. DC 1:75.

33. Ibid., 1:74.

34. Ibid., 2:55.

35. For the Colhuacan lineage, see DC 1:223–25; and *CC* 2:63, 81–83, 89–91, 105–7.

36. *CC* 1:35; 2:91. See also *Anales de Cuauhtitlan*, ed. and trans. Rafael Tena (Mexico City: Cien de México, 2011), 115, which states that Ilancueitl departed with Acamapichtli from Tetzcoco [Acolhuacan] in Thirteen House, 1349. The annals continue, adding that in the next year, One Rabbit, 1350, Acamapichtli was installed on the throne at Tenochtitlan because of his wife, Ilancueitl. This occurred a full seventeen years before the time period in Chimalpahin's sources, which of course would greatly affect the succession chronology of all subsequent tlatoque.

37. *CC* 1:115. Note the eloquent use of the Nahuatl vocative.

38. Ibid., 1:117.

39. For an alternate version of this account, see ibid., 2:83.

40. Ibid., 1:39; Durán, 54, and see 115, where Durán states that Ilancueitl had a son.

41. DC 2:51; Durán, 57.

42. Durán, 55, 56.

43. Ibid., 57.

44. *CC* 1:229; DC 2:49.

45. DC 2:49.

46. *CC* 1:117–19; Durán, 57; DC 2:51.

47. *CC* 1:37; *CC* 2:95 states, though, that Itzcoatl and Huitzilihuitl the younger were born of the same mother (*ce ynantzin in*).

48. Ibid., 2:97.

49. Ibid., 1:37.

50. DC 2:51; *CC* 2:83 records that the daughter's name was Çocatlamihuatzin and that *she* was the mother of Huitzilihuitl the younger.

51. *CC* 1:39, 229. DC 55–9 states that Itzcoatl was the Tlacateccatl.

52. *CC* 1:39.

53. Charles Gibson, *The Aztecs under Spanish Rule: A History of the Indians of the Valley of Mexico, 1519–1810* (Stanford: Stanford University Press, 1964), 16–17, states that initially the Tepaneca "occupied the territory along the western edge of the lakes, between the Otomi to the north and the Xochimilca to the south."

54. AT, 65–66.

55. *CC* 1:119. Elsewhere, Chimalpahin's annals state that Huitzilihuitl the younger's primary wife and the mother of Chimalpopoca was Miyahuaxochtzin, daughter of Tlacacuitlahuatzin, the first tlatoani of Tiliuhcan Tlacopan. Ibid., 1:39; 2:83–85, 95. But *CC* 2:85 states that Huitzilihuitl married Matlalxochitzin, the daughter of surely the same Tlacacuitlahuatzin, ruler of Tiliuhcan Tlacopan, and that *she* was the mother of Chimalpopoca. To add to the confusion of names and places, *CC* 1:121–23 notes that Huitzilihuitl went to great trouble to seduce and later marry a Miyahuaxihuitl, daughter of Oçomatzin, tlatoani and sorcerer of Cuernavaca. See Susan Schroeder, "The First American Valentine: Nahua Courtship and Other Aspects of Family Structuring in Mesoamerica," *Journal of Family History* 23, no. 4 (1998,): 341–54, for more about this relationship. Durán's version, though, certainly makes for a better story.

56. Obviously, it had not been fifty years that the Mexica had been paying such tribute. Durán, 62–63.

57. *CC* 1:119–21, 123–25; DC 1:239–45.

58. Durán, 66.

59. *CC* 1:125; DC 1:239, 2:64–65. Or Four Tochtli, 1418. See pages 23–26 for discussion and illustrations of military titles.

60. *CC* 1:213.

61. Ibid., 2:57.

62. Durán, 67–68; DC 1:365–71.

63. *CC* 1:129; ibid., 2:95; Durán, 68.

64. *CC* 1:129; 2:33; DC 1:243 has Thirteen Reed, 1427, as the date of Chimalpopoca's death and that he ruled ten years.

65. *CC* 1:129, 2:95. AT, 70, has Teuctlehuac for the son's name. See also Durán, 69.

66. *CC* 1:131.

67. DC 1:370–71n5; 2:69.

68. *CC* 1:230–32.

69. Ibid., 1:129.

70. DC 1:365–67, 2:69n19.

71. DC 1:243–45. See also *Anales de Cuauhtitlan*, 137–39.

72. Durán, 86.

73. Ibid., 69–72.

74. Ibid., 72.

75. See Berdan, *Aztec Archaeology*, 138–41.

76. Tlacateotzin and the Tlatelolca were apparently allies of the Tenochca at this time, although he was stoned to death, or strangled, even before the battle began. His four legitimate sons, though, fought for the Mexica Tenochca and helped to bring about the fall of Azcapotzalco, CC 1:131, 231. DC 2:69 states that Tlacateotzin was killed by the Tepaneca Tlacopaneca, which was cause for war.

77. Durán, 74.

78. See pages 34–35 for this quotation.

79. Durán, 75.

80. Ibid., 77–78.

81. AT, 73–74.

82. Ibid., 71–73; CC 2:33.

83. Durán, 78–80.

84. Ibid., 80.

85. CC 1:45.

86. Durán, 80, 82; DC 2:71. It is not certain if it was strictly land that was won or the subjects and tribute from a given region.

87. Ibid., 83. But later great men such as Antonio Valeriano distinguished Azcapotzalco and were real evidence of a polity of importance through the sixteenth century.

88. As noted, Durán fails to identify the ruler of Azcapotzalco who had instigated the battle. Presumably, it was Maxtlaton, since he declared himself tlatoani upon the death of his father in Twelve Rabbit, 1426. Chimalpahin states that Maxtlaton returned to Coyoacan, although he soon went to Amecameca, Chalco, to ask the principal rulers for their assistance against the Mexica Tenochca, DC 2:73. See CC 1:213, which states that Maxtlatzin was ruling Azcapotzalco in One Flint, 1428, when it was conquered.

89. DC 1:365–75.

90. CC 1:231. The practice of feasting (on humans), gifting, and speech-making was likely all part of a strategy for consensus building that became institutionalized among Nahuas early on and served as an antecedent to war later with the Chalca, CC 2:49.

91. Durán, 91.

92. Ibid., 91–93.

93. Ibid., 71.

94. DC 2:67.

95. Durán, 81, 83, 104.

96. For a detailed treatment of the preliminaries and course of the final battles with Maxtlaton, see DC 1:365–93.

97. Durán, 89–90. See DC 1:390–92, for a variation of this account. Cuateotzin's partiality may be better understood when one considers that his wife, Ahua, was the daughter of Mexica Tenochca tlatoani Acamapichtli, DC 2:85. Around this time, DC 1:384 mentions a "Tezcacihuacohuati," apparently referring to a "Tezcacochitl," although the latter refers to a person while the former may pertain to the deity or a deity impersonator.

98. Schroeder, *Chimalpahin and the Kingdoms*, passim.

99. *CC* 1:115, 2:94.

100. Schroeder, *Chimalpahin and the Kingdoms*, 90, 92.

101. DC 1:390.

102. Ibid., 1:391. See Richard Conway, "Lakes, Canoes, and the Aquatic Communities of Xochimilco and Chalco, New Spain," *Ethnohistory* 59, no. 3 (2012): 541–68, for an excellent discussion of the importance of canoes and waterways in the lakes surrounding Mexico Tenochtitlan.

103. Durán, 95. Certainly, a lock of hair was less painful than the cutting off of a captive's ear for the same purpose. See page 54.

104. Durán, 83, 100.

105. In literal translation, the suggestion is that these were possibly malevolent sorcerers.

106. DC 1:393. Durán's sequence of altepetl conquests was Coyoacan, Azcapotzalco, Xochimilco, and Cuitlahuac. It is likely that the annals' date of Four Reed, 1431, refers to the final vanquishing of Maxtlaton, whose stubborn resistance precipitated numerous additional conflicts with the Mexica. *CC* 1:213 states that in Three Rabbit, 1430, the rulers of Azcapotzalco, Tlacopan, and Tenanyocan entered Mexico [Tenochtitlan], presumably as a final act of submission.

107. Durán, 101.

108. Ibid., 97.

109. DC 2:75 states that Tlacaelel gave up his Atempanecatl title at this time.

110. Durán, 97–99, 101–3. One is reminded of Malcolm in Shakespeare's "Macbeth," who upon defeating Macbeth and gaining the kingdom of Scotland, granted all his men the title of earl, "the first that ever Scotland in such an honor named." William Shakespeare, *The Unabridged Shakespeare*, ed. William George Clark and William Adis Wright (Philadelphia: Courage Books, 1989), 1006, act V, scene VIII.

111. AT, 97–99, also furnished the names of all the men who received royal titles.

112. Durán, 104.

113. Ibid., 105–6.

114. Ibid., 108–9.

115. Ibid., 109.

116. Ibid., 110.

117. DC 2:73

118. Durán, 112–13.

119. AT, 107; Durán, 117–18.

120. DC 2:77, 79.

121. Durán, 119.

122. Ibid., 120–21.

123. *CC* 1:45.

124. DC 2:73–75.

125. Durán, 121.

126. Ibid.

127. *CC* 1:41. See also *Anales de Cuauhtitlan*, 173, "Itzcoatl . . . y así comenzó definitivamente la gloria de los mexicas tenochcas."

128. *CC* 1:47.

129. For example, *CC* 1:71, 73, 79, 91, 95, 209. DC 1:83, 85, states that the deity was called Tetzauhteotl Yaotequi and that Huitzilopochtli was the god carrier and priest. See also DC 1:79–81. Ross Hassig, *Aztec Warfare: Imperial Expansion and Political Control* (Norman: University of Oklahoma Press, 1988), and *War and Society in Ancient Mesoamerica* (Berkeley: University of California Press, 1992), has exhaustively studied weapons and warfare in central Mexico and much has been gained from his work. Further treatment of the subject is not needed here.

130. *CC* 1:93, 97–99.

131. Ibid., 1:207.

132. Ibid., 1:209.

3. THE QUINTESSENTIAL ALTEPETL AND A GOLDEN AGE

Epigraph 1. Durán, 207.

Epigraph 2. DC 2:96.

Epigraph 3. *CC* 1:47.

Epigraph 4. Durán, 243.

1. Occasionally, though, the histories continued to identify Moteuczoma Ilhuicamina as the Tlacateccatl.

2. Durán, 123; DC 1:251.

3. See DC 2:89 for mention of Nezahualcoyotl's directing the construction of an aqueduct that was to bring water to Mexico Tenochtitlan from Chapoltepec. For more information about Nezahualcoyotl, see Chimalpahin's contemporary, don Fernando de Alva Ixtlilxochitl, *Obras históricas*.

4. Durán, 125.

5. Ibid.

6. See *CC* 2:33–35. Moteuczoma Ilhuicamina: 1398–1469, r. 1440–69; Nezahualcoyotl: 1402–72; r. 1431–72. Note Chimalpahin's error in stating that Nezahualcoyotl "ruled for 22 years."

7. Nezahualcoyotl was a grandson through his mother, Matlalcihuatzin, daughter of Mexica tlatoani Huitzilihuitl the younger, DC 2:53, 75. And see DC 2:89, where Chimalpahin states that Moteuczoma Ilhuicamina was Nezahualcoyotl's uncle. Nezahualcoyotl's son and successor, Nezahualpilli Acamapichtli, was the product of his union with Huitzilxochtzin, the daughter of Temictzin, a tlatocapilli in Tenochtitlan, another of Nezahualcoyotl's uncles, DC 2:97. However, *CC* 2:111

states that Nezahualpilli was the child of Nezahualcoyotl and a wife named Itzpapalocihuatl. She was the third child of Huehue Tezozomoc of Azcapotzalco, who married Tzihuacxochitzin, daughter of Huitzilaztatzin, a *teuctlatocapilli*, "lordly nobleman," of Quauhtepec Malinalco.

8. See page 93 for discussion of Tlacaelel's son, Cacamatzin, and his marriage.

9. Durán, 127.

10. Ibid., 128.

11. Sahagún, *Florentine Codex*, book 8, Kings and Lords, 9.

12. Durán, 127.

13. See AT, 113–14, which tells of the submission of Nezahualcoyotl and the Tetzcoca to Moteuczoma Ilhuicamina and Tlacaelel, followed by the *gran suerte de tierra* that went to Moteuczoma Ilhuicamina and then *nueve partes tierras* for the Cihuacoatl, with two to three each for the brave soldiers.

14. *CC* 2:45.

15. *CC* 2:49. There is a problem with the annals' date here, since Nezahualcoyotl died in Six Flint, 1472. The reference may be to his son Nezahualpilli (r. 1472–1515), who immediately succeeded his father as tlatoani, although he was still a child.

16. DC 2:75.

17. Ibid., 2:87.

18. *CC* 1:45.

19. Durán, 121.

20. Ibid., 130.

21. *CC* 1:233.

22. DC 2:82–83; *CC* 1:233.

23. DC 2:85.

24. Ibid., 2:93–95.

25. Ibid., 1:252n17, 252–53.

26. Ibid., 1:257; 2:87–89.

27. This is probably a reference to part or all of Tlalmanalco. It is not clear. The final conquest was not until 1465.

28. DC 2:89. The reference is surely to some part of the confederated altepetl that had lost a battle. The significance of the Nahua concept of "conquest" was discussed earlier, pages 13–14.

29. Durán, 238–41.

30. Ibid., 238–40.

31. *CC* 1:233; DC 2:89.

32. Durán, 130.

33. DC, 1:394.

34. Ibid., 1:255, 397. Note that all tlatoque are ranked, as was standard for Chimalpahin. Durán, 130–31.

35. DC 1:253.

36. Durán, 132–33. To be consistent, here and elsewhere I have substituted "Mexica" for "Aztecs" in Heyden's translation of Durán.

37. Ibid., 134.

38. Ibid., 134–35.

39. DC 1:141.

40. Ibid., 2:11–15, although they may have come from Chicomoztoc as well, see DC 2:21.

41. See Schroeder, *Chimalpahin and the Kingdoms*, for a full treatment of the early years in Chalco.

42. The Itztlacoçauhque were challenged by the Tzaqualtitlan Tenanca, Chimalpahin's own people, in Eleven House, 1269. Today, the hill is known as Sacromonte, DC 1:199–201.

43. See Schroeder, "Why Women Matter in History," 115–17, for more about Nahuas and their older sisters.

44. DC 2:11–13.

45. Ibid., 2:46.

46. *CC* 1:209; DC 2:37, and noted here, page 74.

47. DC 2:55–57.

48. *CC* 2:51–55. Chimalpahin's annals are in error here, for they refer to Itzcoatl as the father of Moteuczoma Ilhuicamina. Itzcoatl was his uncle. One set of annals states that it was Cuateotzin the Tlatquic, tlatoani of Itzcahuacan Tlacochcalco, who set the prisoners free. DC 2:71.

49. DC 1:391, and see this volume, page 66. DC 2:71–73 states that Maxtlaton went to Amecameca first to ask for help.

50. *CC* 2:52–53.

51. AT, chapters 23–28, pp. 115–33; Durán, chapters 16–17, pp. 130–48. The information regarding the war with Chalco in Chimalpahin's annals is scattered through his many texts.

52. Durán, 135.

53. Ibid., 133–35.

54. Ibid., 135–36.

55. Ibid., 135–41.

56. DC 1:255–57, 261.

57. Ibid., 2:90–91.

58. Ibid., 2:85.

59. Durán, 142; DC 1:261; 2:93.

60. Ezhuahuacatl in fact is not a personal name but rather the title and office of one of the principal figures on the king's royal council. For example, the Ezhuahuacatl was among the cohort who offered the rulership of Mexico Tenochtitlan to Tlacaelel on the death of Moteuczoma Ilhuicamina, as will be seen. AT, 189.

61. Durán, 142

62. Commonly known as the pole-flying ceremony, one or more participants ascend a tall pole and then, secured by a rope, leap from the top and circle the pole as they descend, as if they were flying.

63. Durán, 143.

64. Ibid.

65. Ibid., 144.

66. DC 1:263, 2:95, Durán, 144–45.

67. Durán, 145–46.

68. Ibid., 147. See also AT, 132–33, which describes the generous remuneration of prime polities and land that Tlacaelel took for himself, after Moteuczoma received his share, of course.

69. Durán, 147.

70. DC 2:97.

71. See this volume, pages 34–35.

72. See Schroeder, "The Noblewomen of Chalco," *Estudios de Cultura Náhuatl* 22 (1992): 45–86, for information regarding the Nahuatl-language terminology for marriage arrangements. Maintaining the alliance with Amecameca, a daughter of Totomochtzin (another of Tlacaelel the elder's sons), was one of several wives of don Tomás de San Martín Quetzalmazatzin the Chichimecateuctli, tlatoani in Itztlacoçauhcan, Amecameca (r. 1522–47); DC 2:173.

73. *CC* 1:141–45.

74. *CC* 1:133; DC 2:93. See Durán, 249–62, for a different perspective on Moquihuix's origins and various events in his life.

75. DC 2:99–101, 103, adds that later the Chalca joined the Tenochca in the fighting against Tlatelolco.

76. Ibid., 2:99–101.

77. *CC* 2:47–48 states that "a song was composed, how in song the ruler Axayacatzin chanted about them." Some of the lyrics are included in the *Codex Chimalpahin*.

78. *CC* 2:93, and see DC 1:403–5, DC 2:99–101.

79. Durán, 258–59.

80. Ibid., 261. But *CC* 2:51 lists the tribute as "four golden [objects] like wigs, which they named *tlacototzonilli*, and an eagle, and eight wicker baskets as tall as a man, and as wide, four hundred pots full of chia [racemes] pinole, and pulverized tobacco, required in war as food rations. These were paid yearly in tribute."

81. See, especially, *Anales de Tlatelolco*, ed. and trans. Rafael Tena (Mexico City: CONACULTA, 2004).

82. Durán, 149–53.

83. Ibid.

84. Ibid., 155–56.

85. Ibid., 155; AT, 133–37.

86. Durán, 156–59. See also Berdan, *Aztec Archaeology*, 132, who describes the Tepeaca market as designed to serve "guild-organized merchants [who] traded only within imperial bounds, carrying high-value, low-bulk goods from market to market in pursuit of economic gain."

87. Durán, 169.

88. Fray Alonso de Molina, *Vocabulario en lengua castellana y mexicana y me-*

xicana y castellana (Mexico City: Editorial Porrúa, 1970), 97, translates "temalacatl" as *muela, o rueda de piedra.*

89. Molina, 87v, has *quauhxicalli,* "batea, o cosa semejante hecha de madera."

90. Durán, 183, 188.

91. Ibid., 183–89.

92. Ibid., 190.

93. Ibid., 192.

94. Ibid., 192–93.

95. See especially the *Codex Mendoza* for information about tribute goods and also the *Matrícula de Tributos,* ed. Frances F. Berdan and Jacqueline de Durand-Forest (Graz, Austria: Akademische Druck-u. Verlagsanstalt, 1980). Frances Berdan informs me that there is no evidence that silver was a tribute item per se. Personal communication, November 3, 2014.

96. See, for example, Chimalpahin, *Chimalpahin's Conquest,* 124–26, for a sampling of some of the exquisite items that were among the Mexica treasures.

97. Durán, 206.

98. Ibid., 202.

99. Ibid., 208–11.

100. Ibid., 212–13.

101. Ibid., 212–22.

102. Ibid., 231.

103. Ibid., 231–32. Translator Heyden states that, in reference to the treasure, the descriptive phrasing was a Nahua metaphor "for the captured soldiers who will be sacrificial victims," 231n7.

104. Ibid., 233.

105. Ibid., 235.

106. Ibid., 236–37.

107. Ibid., 242–46; DC 1:267 reports the conquest of the Cuextlateca in Four Rabbit, 1470, a war that Moteuczoma Ilhuicamina began. Although there is some discrepancy regarding royal regimes and therefore dates of rule, an important scientific study of the translocation of the great-tailed grackle, *Quiscalus mexicanus,* from Cuextla and Totonacapan to central Mexico, reportedly during the regime of Ahuitzotl (r. 1486–1502), is by Paul D. Haemig, "Introduction of the Great-Tailed Grackle by Aztec Emperor Auitzotl: Four-Stage Analysis with New Information," *Ardeola* 58, no. 2 (2011) 387–97. Haemig's primary source of information is Sahagún, *Códice Florentino,* Manuscrito 218-20 de la Colección Palatina de la Biblioteca Medicea Laurenziana, ed. facs., 3 vols. (Mexico City: Archivo General de la Nación, n.d.), book 11, ff. 53v–54r. See also Haemig's "Introduction of the Great-Tailed Grackle (*Quiscalus mexicanus*) by the Aztec Emperor Auitzotl: Provenance of the Historical Account," *Auk* 129, no. 1 (2012): 70–75.

108. The annals furnish both Two Flint, 1468, and Three House, 1469, as the date of Moteuczoma Ilhuicamina's death. DC 1:267 qualifies the year 1469 by adding, "Nican ypan in mellahuac in momiquillico." ("In this year, in truth, [Moteuczoma

Ilhuicamina] died.") Durán, 245, furnishes 1469 as the date of his death. *CC* 1:133 has 1468.

109. Durán, 247.

110. *CC* 1:132.

111. DC 1:267, 2:99.

112. Ibid., 2:81; *CC* 1:51.

113. *CC* 1:135.

114. Durán, 247; *CC* 1:51; AT, 189–90, lists the titled officials who petitioned Tlacaelel to serve as tlatoani.

115. Elsewhere, the annals state that Axayacatl's selection was based on the decision of Moteuczoma Ilhuicamina, Tlacaelel, and Chimalpopoca, tlatoani of Tlacopan, although Chimalpopoca was not installed in office until Four Rabbit, 1470, *CC* 1: 137. Note, however, that *CC* 1:51 states that "the great president, Tlacaelel the Cihuacoatl, himself chose as emperor of Mexico the youngest grandson of the dead emperor, who was named Axayacatzin, or *CC* 1:135, "he ruled because Huehue Moteuczoma had said [so]."

116. DC 2:79; *CC* 1:50.

117. *CC* 1:135–37.

118. DC 2:101.

119. *CC* 1:137.

120. See pages 95–97.

121. *CC* 1:137–41.

122. Ibid., 1:139.

123. DC 1:267, 269; 2:103.

124. Ibid., 2:103; 1:267–69.

125. Ibid., 2:103–15, 271. As noted, among the sources, there is an occasional conflict regarding the place and occasion of Axayacatl's injuries. See also Durán, 267–71, who states that he was wounded in combat against the Matlatzinca.

126. DC 2:107–13. The annals record that the famous song stayed in the hands of Tezozomoctli Acolnahuacatl, a son of Axayacatl, and then passed to the king's grandson, don Diego de Alvarado Huanitzin (r. 1520–38, Ecatepec; 1538–41, San Juan Tenochtitlan), a distinguished Mexica ruler in the colonial era.

127. Durán, 267.

128. DC 2:105. As an example of the scale of Mexica warfare, the Poctepeca, the Cozcacuauhtenanca, the Icpatepeca, and the Metepeca were also conquered in this same year.

129. Durán, 272.

130. Ibid., 272–76.

131. Ibid., 276–77. See in this volume, pages 98–99, for the dedication of an earlier sun stone.

132. Ibid., 278; DC 2:103, states that Axayacatl "attacked those of Michoacan and the Mazahuaca in Five Reed, 1471."

133. The Mexica, of course, reckoned quantities by means of the vigesimal system.

134. Durán, 282.

135. Ibid., 289–90.

136. *CC* 1:141 states that Tlacaelel the Cihuacoatl died during Axayacatl's rule in Nine Reed, 1475.

137. DC 1:271, 2:105, 107.

138. Ibid., 1:273. However, once again attesting to possible confusion from a variety of sources, DC 2:115–17 furnishes a somewhat more complete list that includes the provenience and occasionally the names of some of the mothers of his children. Here, Moteuczoma Xocoyotl was the sixth son, and Cuitlahuac the fifth of nineteen children. The mother of both men was from Itztapalapan, and Cuitlahuac eventually ruled there before succeeding his brother on the throne in Mexico Tenochtitlan in 1520. But *CC* 1:149–50 lists thirteen children, with Moteuczoma Xocoyotl the eighth child, and Cuitlahuac the eleventh. *CC* 2:79 lists Moteuczoma as his first child and Cuitlahuac as his second. *CC* 2:97, lists only two legitimate sons: Moteuczoma Xocoyotl and Macuilmalinaltzin, who died in battle in Huexotzinco.

139. *CC* 1:51.

140. Durán, 296–98.

141. Ibid., 299.

142. Ibid., 300–301; AT, 438.

143. Durán, 303–4.

144. AT, 247–67; Durán, 306–8.

145. DC 2:123.

146. Durán, 307–8.

147. *CC* 1:51.

148. For example, *CC* 1:51, has five years, DC 1:281, has six years, and *CC* 1:153, has both four and six years for Tizoc's period of rulership.

149. *CC* 2:57. Durán's *History* reports many more battles and a longer period of rule for Ahuitzotzin.

150. DC 1:280.

151. Ibid.,1:281.

152. *CC* 2:115.

153. Ibid., 1:31, and as noted previously, page 52.

154. Ibid., 2:115.

155. Ibid., 1:149, lists a Tepehuatzin the Tlacochcalcatl and a Tlacahuepan the elder the Tlachochcalcatl, a Machimalle, and several more sons of Axayacatl. See also DC 1:281, 411; DC 2:123; *CC* 1:53–54, 153.

156. DC 1:411.

157. *CC* 2:115.

158. Tlatoani Itzcoatl, of course, was the exception.

159. Chimalpahin, *Chimalpahin's Conquest*, 375.

160. DC 2:200. *CC* 2:41, describes the office as that of tlatoani. For discussion of the images and the documents in which they appear, see Dennis Carr, "The Beinecke Map: Iconography and Physical Properties," in *Painting a Map of Sixteenth-Century*

Mexico City: Land, Writing, and Native Rule, ed. Mary E. Miller and Barbara E. Mundy (New Haven, Conn.: Yale University Press, 2012), 14; Barbara E. Mundy, "Pictography, Writing, and Mapping in the Valley of Mexico and the Beinecke Map," in *Painting a Map*, ed. Miller and Mundy, 44; and Barbara E. Mundy, "Crown and Tlatoque: The Iconography of Rulership in the Beinecke Map," in *Painting a Map*, ed. Miller and Mundy, 123.

161. *AHT*, 137.

162. For more information about don Diego's tenure as gobernador, see William F. Connell, *After Moctezuma: Indigenous Politics and Self-Government in Mexico City, 1524–1730* (Norman: University of Oklahoma Press, 2011), 44, 65; Gibson, *Aztecs*,169, and Gibson, *Tlaxcala in the Sixteenth Century* (Stanford: Stanford University Press, 1952), 120–21.

163. *CC* 1:65. Cited previously, pages 33–34. It would appear that Alvarado Tezozomoc and Tehuetzquititzin were distant cousins.

164. DC 2:172. Robert Ricard, *The Spiritual Conquest of Mexico: An Essay on the Apostolate and the Evangelizing Methods of the Mendicant Orders in New Spain, 1523–1572*, trans. Lesley Byrd Simpson (Berkeley: University of California Press, 1974), 110–16, states that the "first native marriages celebrated in Mexico" were in 1526. He claims that the friars felt a great urgency to eliminate polygyny and begin the administration of the sacrament of marriage.

165. *CC* 2:115–17. Different annals furnish different names for the sons of don Diego de San Francisco Tehuetzquititzin the Tlacateccatl. He had several wives and various offspring.

166. *CC* 2:105.

167. Ibid.

168. *CC* 2:105, 115–17.

169. See pages 138–41 and 143–44 for information about the Tlacaelels in Acatlan.

170. *CC* 2:117.

171. Durán, 309–43, treats these events in considerable detail.

172. *CC* 2:35 states that Nezahualpilli was born in Eleven Flint, 1464, and succeeded his father on the throne in Six Flint, 1472, at the age of nine.

173. Durán, 311.

174. Ibid.

175. *CC* 1:215 adds that it was "on the day count Ten Rabbit, the fifteenth of April, and the eighth day of Toçoztontli in the ancient month count" in the year Seven Rabbit, 1486, that Ahuitzotl was installed on the throne.

176. Durán, 317.

177. Ibid., 322.

178. For information about indigenous women as intellectuals and professionals, see Elizabeth Hill Boone, "*In Tlamatinime:* The Wise Men and Women of Aztec Mexico," in *Painted Books and Indigenous Knowledge in Mesoamerica: Manuscript Studies in Honor of Mary Elizabeth Smith*, ed. Elizabeth Hill Boone (New Orleans: Tulane University, 2005), 9–25.

179. DC 2:125 states that Ahuitzotl fought in Tziuhcohuac in Eight Reed, 1487. The sources also describe his magnificent warrior attire.

180. See page 98 for discussion of a previous battle against the Huaxteca.

181. Durán, 328; AHT, 131.

182. AT, 301–5, furnishes details about the various deities that were also honored at the coronation.

183. DC 1:283; 2:125. Durán, 335, however, states that there were 80,400 men sacrificed. See also José Luis de Rojas, Tenochtitlan: Capital of the Aztec Empire (Gainesville: University Press of Florida, 2014), 34, who questions the accuracy of this number. It is interesting, too, that Rojas credits Tizoc with this sacrifice, although he states that it was carried out in Eight Reed, 1487, when Ahuitzotl was ruling.

184. AT, 302–8.

185. Durán, 355–60.

186. Ibid., 361.

187. It should be noted that Chimalpahin was also favorably inclined toward Ahuitzotl, since he restored the remaining rulerships in Chalco, most especially in Chimalphin's home altepetl, Tenanco. Ahuitzotl was also responsible for installing Tlacaelel's grandson, Miccacalcatl Tlaltecuintzin the Chichimecateuctli, in office as tlatoani of Tequanipan, Amecameca (r. 1492–1522). DC 1:283–89, 407; 2:321–25.

4. TLACAELEL'S SUCCESSORS IN THE COLONIAL ERA

Epigraph 1. Durán, 361.

Epigraph 2. Ibid.

Epigraph 3. CC 1:47.

Epigraph 4. AHT, 167.

1. CC 2:35–37. AT, 348–49, states that Tlacaelel the elder was more than 120 years old when he died. Note that a different set of annals records that Tlacaelel died in Nine Reed, 1475, during the reign of Axayacatl, CC 1:141.

2. Durán, 361–63.

3. Ibid. CC 2:35–37. See Sahagún, *Florentine Codex*, book 3, The Origin of the Gods, 62, possibly suggesting an exalted affiliation with a Toltec legendary figure, has a Topiltzin Quetzalcoatl Tlilpotonqui, but in book 11, Earthly Things, 168, he states that Tlilpotonqui is a type of forest herb that was used to treat fever either as a poultice or as a solution to be drunk. CC 1:181 has a Topiltzin Nacxitl Quetzalcoatl Tlilpotonqui. Durán, 361, defines Tlilpotonqui as "The Black One, or more exactly, He Who Smells of Black Pitch."

4. Durán, 361; CC 1:141–43; 2:99. Capt. Rodríguez took doña Juana as his concubine, not as his wife. Note that Gabriel de Villafuerte reportedly had two daughters of the same name who married men with similar names. This may be the result of Chimalpahin consulting two different sources. See CC 1:155, which states that King Ahuitzotl's fourth child was named Tlacaelel Xocoyotl, which indeed suggests a possible confusion of annals again.

5. AT, 120.

6. *CC* 1:47–9, 55.

7. Ibid., 1:145.

8. Durán, 361.

9. AT, 358.

10. AT, 363; Durán, 388–89; *CC* 1:55. Fig. 12 indicates that Moteuczoma Xocoyotl was the great-grandson of Moteuczoma Ilhuicamina, not the grandson.

11. *CC* 1:55.

12. Sahagún, *Florentine Codex*, book 12, The Conquest, 9, observed that when Moteuczoma Xocoyotl called his council, in his documents the Cihuacoatl was the first man listed; see also Durán, 394.

13. For a present-day example of how polygyny can enlarge a royal court, see Hugh Eakin, "Will Saudi Arabia Ever Change?" *New York Review of Books* 60, no. 1 (January 10, 2013): 37–39, who speaks of Saudi Arabia's "founding king's thirty-seven sons by more than twenty wives" and says that "there are now some seven thousand princes in the ever-growing royal family."

14. Durán, 395–96.

15. Ibid.

16. Ibid., 395–98.

17. Ibid., 398.

18. Ibid.

19. For just a few examples, see AT, 367–68, 417, 428, 438.

20. Ibid., 375.

21. Ibid., 387, 438; Durán, 411. Moreover, on one occasion Moteuczoma Xocoyotl sent the Cihuacoatl home from the battlefield to take care of governing and to execute the tutors and women attending his wives.

22. Durán, 423–24.

23. AT, 418, and "*los dos reyes, Moteucçoma y Çihuacoatl.*"

24. Durán, 424.

25. Ibid., 279, 424, 434–36.

26. Ibid., 435.

27. Ibid., 436.

28. Ibid., 440.

29. *CC* 1:153; 2:89. A quauhtlatoani was not typically a member of the royal lineage but still enjoyed authority. See Pedro Carrasco, "Royal Marriages in Ancient Mexico," in *Explorations in Ethnohistory: Indians of Central Mexico in the Sixteenth Century*, ed. H. R. Harvey and Hanns J. Prem (Albuquerque: University of New Mexico Press, 1984), 71, for a somewhat different succession pattern for the "Cihuacoatl of Tenochtitlan."

30. In Amecameca, the illustrious title and office of the Chichimecateuctli had been specific to the head altepetl tlayacatl, Itztlacoçauhcan. The titles for kings of the other tlayacatl in Tequanipan were the Tzompanhuacateuctli in Tzompanhuacan and the Teohuateuctli in Pochtlan Tequanipan. See Schroeder, *Chimalpahin and the Kingdoms*, 50–51, 62–63; DC 2:191, 207, 213.

31. *CC* 1:153, 157; 2:89, 109; DC 2:97, 133, 151, 163, 333.

32. *CC* 1:153.

33. Schroeder, *Chimalpahin and the Kingdoms*, 51.

34. Not all of the names of Tlilpotonqui's children were known to Chimalpahin. Nevertheless, other Nahuas knew them, and a Quauhpiaztzin, along with his sister Quetzalpetlatzin, were mentioned in a late Nahua catechism. See page 148.

35. *CC* 1:55, 143, 161–63; 2:109. By the fifth generation, all the descendants were considered to be Spaniards. There were an additional five children in this last group, names unknown, who were living with their father in Michoacan in 1619. See also Villella, *Indigenous Elites and Creole Identity*, chapter 2, and Donald E. Chipman, *Moctezuma's Children, Aztec Royalty under Spanish Rule* (Austin: University of Texas Press), 53–74, for more about the Valderrama and Cano families.

36. *CC* 1:143, 163.

37. *CC* 2:111.

38. *CC* 1:55.

39. Durán, 466.

40. Ibid., 467. AT, 443–44, *y para esto enbío allá al hermano y compañero mío, que le ponga el señorío, trono y asiento, Çihuacoatl.*

41. Sahagún, *Florentine Codex*, book 12, The Conquest, 45. Fray Bernardino does mention a Totomotzin but does not associate him with Tlacaelel or the office of the Cihuacoatl.

42. *Chimalpahin's Conquest*, 182–83.

43. AT, 400–402, 417–18, 438, passim.

44. Unfortunately, his mother's name is unknown, *CC* 1:141. Of the five candidates for the Tetzcoca rulership, however, Cacamatzin was not the first choice.

45. *CC* 2:37.

46. Ibid.

47. Sahagún, *Florentine Codex*, book 12, The Conquest, 9.

48. Durán, 545. However, "La historia de Tlatelolco," 65, states that when the Spaniards were settled in Tetzcoco, the Mexica began to kill each other, and in the year Three House a Tziuacpopocatzin Cihuacoatl along with Moteuczoma Xocoyotl's sons were killed. "*Cuando ellos se hubieron establecido en Tetzcoco, entonces los tenochca empezaron a matarse mutuamente. En el año 3 Calli mataron a sus príncipes, Ciuacóuatl Tziuacpopocatzin y Cipactzin Tencuecuenotzin; mataron a Axayaca y Xoxopeúaloc, los hijos de Motecuzomatzin.*" Later, there is a reference to a "Ciuacóatl Motelchiuh," 66, a unique instance of this title for Motelchiuhtzin, since he was not even of noble birth. *CC* 1:167 notes that a Tzihuacpopoca was among the six sons of Moteuczoma who were killed on Quauhtemoc's command. It is likely that the "Ciaucoatl" [*sic*] in the Tlatelolco annals was one among several men murdered at that time.

49. *CC* 2:37–39; *AHT*, 145–47.

50. *CC* 1:47.

51. *CC* 1:137–39. Chimalpahin added, "The Tlatelolca were no more because of concubines." For more about this event, see Schroeder, "First American Valentine."

52. *CC* 1:139. And see pages 95–97 for more about the war against Tlatelolco.

53. *CC* 1:140–41. Note particularly the distinguishing Nahuatl terminology for when a quauhtlatoani took office, *yn conpehuatli, yn ye quauhtlatohua yn tlacatl ytzquauhtzin tlacochcalcatl* (the lord Itzquauhtzin the Tlacochcalcatl began to be interim ruler).

54. *CC* 2:79.

55. Ibid., 2:57.

56. For abundant examples of sons who succeeded to the throne in their mothers' home polities, see Schroeder, "Why Women Matter in History," and Schroeder, "The Noblewomen of Chalco."

57. *CC* 2:39. Tlacotzin is listed as the son of Tlacaelel's tenth child, Tezcatl-teuctli. See fig. 16, and *CC* 1:145. See also William F. Connell, "Alliance Building and the Restoration of Native Government in the Altepetl of Mexico Tenochtitlan, 1521–1565," in *City Indians in Spain's American Empire: Urban Indigenous Society in Colonial Mesoamerica and Andean South America, 1530–1810*, ed. Dana Velasco Murillo, Mark Lentz, and Margarita R. Ochoa (Brighton, UK: Sussex Academic Press, 2012), 8–31, who treats Tlacotzin at some length.

58. *CC* 2:38. Chimalpahin notes that it was not until later that Tlacotzin became a Christian: *Eligieron los grandes de Mexico Por capitan general a tlacotzin que despues fue christiano y se llamo Don Juan Velazquez. que fue el mas valeroso hombre lo hizieron cihuacohuatl y vltimo cihuacohuatl de Mexico, CC* 1:56.

59. Hernando Cortés, *Letters from Mexico*, 263.

60. Sahagún, *Florentine Codex*, book 12, The Conquest, 115–17; James Lockhart, ed. and trans., *We People Here: Nahuatl Accounts of the Conquest of Mexico* (Berkeley: University of California Press, 1993), 234.

61. Sahagún, *Florentine Codex*, book 12, The Conquest, 117–18; Lockhart, *We People Here*, 240. "La historia de Tlatelolco," 75, corroborates the conversations among Cortés, Quauhtemoc, and his Cihuacoatl.

62. Sahagún, *Florentine Codex*, book 12, The Conquest, 118. See also *Anales de Tlatelolco*, ed. and trans. Rafael Tena (Mexico City: CONACULTA, 2004), 106.

63. Sahagún, *Florentine Codex*, book 12, The Conquest, 119–20, 123.

64. Ibid., 12:125–26; Lockhart, *We People Here*, 255.

65. Traditionally, the two figures on the left were thought to be Cortés and his interpreter Malintzin. Art historian Lori Diel believes that the "Malintzin" figure is actually a Franciscan friar wearing a hooded habit (or an executioner), with the fire glyph in the center an indication of the torture of the captives, personal communication, June 16, 2015, and see Lori B. Diel, "Codex Mexicanus: Information Essential to Know in Late Sixteenth-Century New Spain," in progress. See also *Codex Mexicanus*. Paris: Société des Américanistes, 1952; and Ernest Mengin, "Commentaire du Codex mexicanus nos. 23–24 de la Bibliothèque Nationale de Paris," *Journal de la Société des Américanistes*, 41:2, 1952, 387–498.

66. *DC* 2:157–59.

67. Cortés, *Letters from Mexico*, 321. Cortés appears to be associating Tlacotzin with the rule of Moteuczoma Xocoyotl, which surely would not have been the case since Tlacaelel the younger was serving as the Cihuacoatl at that time. Tlacotzin was not elected as the Cihuacoatl until Quauhtemoc was installed as ruler in 1521. However, Tlacotzin may have already attended Moteuczoma's royal council in some prestigious capacity, as well as being an eagle warrior.

68. Ibid.

69. *Chimalpahin's Conquest*, 362. Don Pedro was surely another of Cortés's favorites. He was lord of Tula and then part of the conqueror's entourage when he returned to Spain in 1528, 420.

70. *CC* 2:38.

71. Barbara E. Mundy, *The Death of Aztec Tenochtitlan, the Life of Mexico City* (Austin: University of Texas Press, 2015), does not furnish the dates of the Spanish cabildo *actas* regarding the establishment of the market, 80.

72. *Chimalpahin's Conquest*, 375, 381–82.

73. *CC* 1:59; 2:39; *Chimalpahin's Conquest*, 390. See also Kevin Terraciano, "Three Views of the Conquest of Mexico from the *Other* Mexica," in *The Conquest All Over Again: Nahuas and Zapotecs Thinking, Writing, and Painting Spanish Colonialism*, ed. Susan Schroeder (Brighton, UK: Sussex Academic Press, 2010), 15–40. Departing from other credible historical sources, Bernal Díaz del Castillo, *True History*, 404–5, asserted that Tlacotzin the Cihuacoatl told Cortés that Quauhtemoc was plotting to fight and overthrow the Spaniards. The notion is improbable, considering that they were all in a region now known as Honduras, comprising hamlets of Maya-speaking peoples and certainly beyond the imperial reach of the Aztecs. Nevertheless, Paul Gillingham, *Cuauhtemoc's Bones: Forging National Identity in Modern Mexico* (Albuquerque: University of New Mexico Press, 2011), 36, 41, goes so far as to describe Tlacotzin as "Cortés's puppet" and a "quisling." He consistently misrepresents Tlacotzin as more of a sycophant and opportunist than as the Cihuacoatl, a brave warrior and stalwart ally of the king. His source for this particular information is unclear and other information is incorrect. However, Robert H. Barlow, *Obras de Robert H. Barlow: Los mexicas y la triple alianza*, ed. Jesús Monjarás-Ruiz, Elena Limón, and María de la Cruz Paillés H. (Mexico City: Instituto Nacional de Antropología e Historia, 1990), 3:227–31, suggests that Tlacotzin, or "Juan Velázquez, la serpiente femenina," falsely accused Quauhtemoc, since he would likely be the man to benefit from his death.

74. *Chimalpahin's Conquest*, 391. Note, however, that *CC* 2:38 states that Quauhtemoc was killed in Six Flint, 1524, and that Tlacotzin was already baptized.

75. *CC* 1:168; or *quihuallahtocatlallica capitan don hernando cortes Marques yn ye yc oquaatequilloc don Juan Velazquez tlacotzin cihuacoatl tlahtohuani yezqui tenuchtitlan*, *CC* 2:38.

76. There has been considerable disparaging of Tlacotzin as a legitimate tlatoani. J. Rounds, "Dynastic Succession, 63–89, maintains that the Cihuacoatl

never ruled; and Richard Townsend, "Coronation at Tenochtitlan," in *The Imagination of Matter: Religion and Ecology in Mesoamerican Traditions*, ed. David Carrasco (Oxford: British Archaeological Reports, 1989), 155–88, believes that there had to be a royal coronation before one could officially be recognized as a tlatoani, with enthronement, crowns, piercings, and the like. Indeed, there is an occasional description of such procedures, but in the hundreds of mentions of installations in office in the Nahuatl record, the phrase *motlatocatlalli yn tlacatl yn . . . tlatoani Tenochtitlan* is standard, and nothing else is necessary to explain the significance of a man (or woman) assuming the throne. Lori Boornazian Diel, *The Tira de Tepechpan: Negotiating Place under Aztec and Spanish Rule* (Austin: University of Texas Press, 2008), 79, 95, 141n12, believes an eagle image with a speech scroll indicates quauhtlatoani status for Tlacotzin, which more likely referred to his successors, who are described in both the Nahuatl and Spanish records as interim rulers. In addition, Barnes, "Secularizing for Survival, 319–44, implies an impropriety in succession, writing that Tlacotzin was installed "in the field . . . without the 'proper' ceremony." It is likely that Cuitlahuac, Quauhtemoc, and Tlacotzin, in spite of being scions of Mexica royalty and the dynastic lineage, all experienced makeshift formalities when it came to assuming office, considering the chaos, battles, and subsequent domination by Cortés. The Nahuatl in reference to their installations was consistent throughout, as doubtless was the Nahuas' understanding and appreciation of their kings in such times of crisis. *CC* 2:36, 38. See also Sahagún, *Florentine Codex*, book 8, Kings and Lords, illustrations, n.p., which are noteworthy since even though Tlacotzin is omitted, the images of his successors, Motelchiuhtzin and Xochiquen, known as quauhtlatoque, are both depicted on thrones with xiuhhuitzolli like their predecessors, the dynastic kings.

77. DC 2:169–71; *CC* 1:169. The location of Tlacotzin the Cihuacoatl's death varies: Huehuetlan, *CC* 2:38; Nochiztlan, *CC* 1:168; and Achiyotlan, *CC* 1:58.

78. *AHT*, 135; DC 2:169–71.

79. *CC* 1:168.

80. Ibid., 1:57–59; 2:39; *Chimalpahin's Conquest*, 391.

81. There is a possible discrepancy regarding the date of Tlacotzin's death. See *CC* 2:38, which notes a date of Seven House, 1525.

82. *Geschichte der Azteken: Der Codex Aubin und verwandte Dokumente*, ed. and trans. Walter Lehmann and Gerdt Kutscher (Berlin: Gebr. Mann Verlag, 1981), 34, 73, 259 (fol. 45r). See also *Historia de la nación mexicana: Códice de 1576 (Códice Aubin)*, ed. and trans. Charles E. Dibble (Madrid: Ediciones José Porrúa Turanzas, 1963), for a Spanish translation. There are errors in the dates associated with the images of both Quauhtemoc and Tlacotzin in the Codex Aubin. The image of Tlacotzin the Cihuacoatl in the codex shows that he was installed in [Five Acatl], 1523, an obvious error since it also shows Quauhtemoc, installed in [Three House], 1521, and not dying until [Seven House], 1525.

83. See Eduard Seler, "Alexander von Humboldt's Picture Manuscripts in the Royal Library at Berlin," *Mexican and Central American Antiquities, Calendar*

Systems, and History (Washington, D.C.: Smithsonian Institution, Government Printing Office, 1904), 154–76, for a discussion of the content of Humboldt Fragment II.

84. I am most grateful to Professor Edward Calnek for sharing his research notes regarding the locations of Xoloco, Acatlan, and Moyotlan. Much effort is being expended to elucidate the Nahuatl sociopolitical terminology and organization of Mexico Tenochtitlan. *CC* 2:69, 83.

85. Alfonso Caso, *Los barrios antiguos de Tenochtitlan y Tlatelolco* (Mexico City: Memorias de la Academia Mexicana de la Historia, 1956), insert, plano 1.

86. Caso, insert, plano 2. For more about Nahuatl place-names and locations, see Barbara E. Mundy, "Place-Names in Mexico Tenochtitlan," *Ethnohistory* 61, no. 2 (2014): 329–58.

87. *Chimalpahin's Conquest*, 362.

88. See Schroeder, *Chimalpahin and the Kingdoms*, passim, for how Chimalpahin reveals the sociopolitical structure and operation of three different levels of altepetl in the confederated altepetl of Chalco. Although he is not entirely consistent, most often as Chimalpahin identifies and discusses sociopolitical entities, the smallest unit is first, indicating that it is a district within the unit that he mentions next, and so forth. For just one example, Itztlacoçauhcan Amecameca Chalco identifies three levels of altepetl, from the smallest to the largest, and of course there were subdistricts within Itztlacoçauhcan.

89. *CC* 2:105. However, it appears that Xoloco also had its nobility. Consider *"yn ce cihuapilli xulloco chane"* (a noblewoman and resident of Xoloco), *CC* 2:115.

90. See pages 112–15.

91. *CC* 2:105.

92. Ibid., 2:117.

93. See Robert Haskett, *Indigenous Rulers: An Ethnohistory of Town Government in Colonial Cuernavaca* (Albuquerque: University of New Mexico Press, 1991), 95, and Laura E. Matthew, *Memories of Conquest: Becoming Mexicano in Colonial Guatemala* (Chapel Hill: University of North Carolina Press, 2012), 84–85, 92.

94. Haskett, *Visions of Paradise: Primordial Titles and Mesoamerican History in Cuernavaca* (Norman: University of Oklahoma Press, 2005), 59. Supporting this theory, in the hall dedicated to Aztec sculpture at Mexico City's Museo Nacional de Antropología there is a stone statue in the round of approximately one meter in height with traces of red paint with a finely carved image of Cihuacoatl ("Cihuacoatl con Atributos del Maíz) from Morelos.

95. See Ruiz de Alarcón, *Treatise on the Heathen Superstitions*.

96. *Chimalpahin's Conquest*, 444; *DC* 1:287.

97. Peter Gerhard, *A Guide to the Historical Geography of New Spain* (Cambridge: Cambridge University Press, 1972), 445.

98. *Chimalpahin's Conquest*, 420.

99. For example, *AHT*, 29, 85, 173, 251, 257, 259.

100. One cannot help but wonder if, writing in Nahuatl, Castillo was not being literal, *acalotenco* possibly signifying "at the edge of the canoe road (canal)," a landing or port of sorts, since Xoloco was adjacent to the water.

101. Cristóbal del Castillo, *Historia de la venida de los mexicanos*, 193.

102. AT, 339.

103. Bustamante, *Necesidad de la unión*, 29n1.

104. Sahagún, *Florentine Codex*, book 12, The Conquest, 43–44; DC 2:257.

105. Durán, *History*, 155. And see DC 1:302. Castillo, *Historia de la venida de los mexicanos*, 193–94, too, speaks of Acachinanco and the causeway in Xoloco.

106. Sahagún, *Florentine Codex*, book 12, in Lockhart, *We People Here*, 186–87.

107. Sahagún, *Florentine Codex*, book 12, The Conquest, n.p., illustrations 120, 121, 122, 124, and 127.

108. CC 1:216; DC 1:157. Historically—and adding to the prime importance of the location in Xoloco—Acachinanco was also the site of the main culvert transporting spring water from Coyoacan to Mexico Tenochtitlan. There it flowed into a reservoir of sorts, or at least an island headwater, where residents of the capital could come by way of canoe for their fresh water needs. On at least one occasion the waters from Coyoacan caused serious flooding of the Mexica capital and led to the killing of the king of Coyoacan. See Durán, *History*, 369, and previous fig. 10.

109. DC 2:257.

110. Gerhard, *Guide*, 181–82.

111. Villella, *Indigenous Elites and Creole Identity*, chapter 8.

112. Durán, 560–61.

113. *Códice Osuna: Reproducción facsimilar de la obra del mismo título, editada en Madrid, 1878* (Mexico City: Instituto Indigenista Interamericano, 1947), 57, 131, 137. Xoloco and Acatlan are described as barrios, 137.

114. Luis Reyes García, ed. and trans., *Como te confundes? Acaso no somos conquistados? Anales de Juan Bautista* (Mexico City: Centro de Investigaciones y Estudios Superiores en Antropología Social; Biblioteca Lorenzo Boturini, Insigne y Nacional Basílica de Guadalupe, 2001), 295n149.

115. *Historia de la nación mexicana*, 65, 91.

116. See page 22.

117. Reyes García, *Como te confundes?*, 237.

118. Susan Kellogg, *Law and the Transformation of Aztec Culture, 1500–1700* (Norman: University of Oklahoma Press, 1995), 53–54.

119. By the seventeenth century, other than the Moctezumas, it is rare to find a Nahuatl surname. Being a Tlacaelel was obviously still important. Other references to the Tlacaelel family in the colonial era have yet to be located.

120. *AHT*, 155, 167.

121. Ibid., 61. In don Gabriel de Ayala's annals it is noted in Four Reed, 1535, that Viceroy don Antonio de Mendoza granted offices to high-ranking Nahuas along with the privilege of owning and presumably riding horses (*cavolloti*). It is expected that the alcaldes and regidores of San Juan Tenochtitlan enjoyed these same honors.

122. *AHT*, 231.

123. Ibid., 239. For additional information regarding continuity of authority, prestige, and lifestyle among Nahua nobles in the colonial era, see Charles Gibson, "The Aztec Aristocracy in Colonial Mexico," *Comparative Studies in Society and History* 2 (1960): 169–96.

CONCLUSION:
A Legend

Epigraph. DC 1:207.

1. DC 2:370; Kagan, *Clio and the Crown*, 19; Peggy K. Liss, *Isabel the Queen: Life and Times* (Philadelphia: University of Pennsylvania Press, rev. ed., 2004).

2. DC 2:270–381, and see Schroeder, "Why Women Matter in History," where Chimalpahin lauds the rulership of women and uses Christianity to justify their succession. For additional information about Queen Juana, see Bethany Aram, *Juana the Mad: Sovereignty and Dynasty in Renaissance Europe* (Baltimore, Md.: Johns Hopkins University Press, 2005).

3. *AHT*, 35, 39–41, 65, 139.

4. Ibid., 65

5. Ibid. People in New Spain knew how to host a funeral on a grand scale, though, and Chimalpahin devotes many pages to the topic when fray García Guerra, viceroy and archbishop of New Spain (r. 1611–12), died in Three Flint, 1612. Guerra had had an ominous time in office, and it was observed by Spaniards and natives alike, *AHT*, 199–215.

6. *AHT*, 87, 89.

7. Ibid., 91. Her funeral was said to be as lavish as that for García Guerra and brought out everyone in the capital, either as participants or as observers, 211, 213–15, 231, 273.

8. Ibid., 113, 161.

9. Bibliothèque Nationale, France, Fonds mexicains 399, 20v. Here, his name is spelled Tlacayelel. See David Tavárez, "Mutable Memories: The Moteuczomas and Nahua Nobility in the Atzaqualco Catechism," in *Painted Words: Nahua Catholicism, Politics, and Memory in the Atzaqualco Pictorial Catechism*, ed. Louise Burkhart, Elizabeth H. Boone, and David Tavárez (Washington, D.C.: Dumbarton Oaks, 2016).

10. Louise Burkhart has contributed much to the topic, for example, Louise M. Burkhart, "The 'Little Doctrine' and Indigenous Catechesis in New Spain," *Hispanic American Historical Review* 94, no. 2 (2014): 167–206.

11. CC 1:60.

BIBLIOGRAPHY

Acosta, José de. *Natural and Moral History of the Indies*. Edited by Jane E. Mangan. Translated by Frances López Morillas. Durham, N.C.: Duke University Press, 2002.

Acosta Saignes, Miguel. "Los teopixque." *Revista Mexicana de Estudios Antropológicos* 8 (1946): 147–205.

Alva Ixtlilxochitl, don Fernando de. *Obras históricas*. Edited by Edmundo O'Gorman. 2 vols. Mexico City: Universidad Nacional Autónoma de México, 1975, 1977.

Alvarado Tezozomoc, don Hernando de. *Crónica mexicana*. Edited by Gonzalo Díaz Migoyo and Germán Vázquez Chamorro. Madrid: Dastin, 2001.

Anales de Cuauhtitlan. Edited and translated by Rafael Tena. Mexico City: Cien de México, 2011.

Anales de Tlatelolco. Edited and translated by Rafael Tena. Mexico City: CONACULTA, 2004.

Anales de Tlatelolco: Unos anales históricos de la nación mexicana y Códice de Tlatelolco. Edited by Heinrich Berlin. Mexico City: Editorial y Litografía Regina de los Ángeles, 1980.

Anónimo mexicano. Edited and translated by Richley H. Crapo and Bonnie Glass-Coffin. Logan: Utah State University Press, 2005.

Arram, Bethany. *Juana the Mad: Sovereignty and Dynasty in Renaissance Europe*. Baltimore, Md.: Johns Hopkins University Press, 2005.

Barlow, Robert H. "La Crónica X: Versiones coloniales de la historia de los mexica tenochca." *Revista Mexicana de Estudios Antropológicos* 7 (1945): 65–87.

———. *Obras de Robert H. Barlow: Los mexicas y la Triple Alianza*. Edited by Jesús Monjarás-Ruiz, Elena Limón, and María de la Cruz Paillés H. Mexico City: Instituto Nacional de Antropología e Historia, 1990.

Barnes, William L. "Secularizing for Survival: Changing Depictions of Central Mexican Native Rule in the Early Colonial Period." In *Painted Books and Indigenous Knowledge in Mesoamerica: Manuscript Studies in Honor of Mary Elizabeth Smith*, edited by Elizabeth Hill Boone, 319–44. Middle American Research Institute 69. New Orleans: Tulane University, 2005.

Berdan, Frances F. *Aztec Archaeology and Ethnohistory.* New York: Cambridge University Press, 2014.

———. "The Economics of Aztec Luxury Trade and Tribute." In *The Aztec Templo Mayor*, edited by Elizabeth Hill Boone, 161–83. Washington, D.C.: Dumbarton Oaks Research Library and Collection, 1983.

Bernal, Ignacio. "Los calendarios de Durán: Más confusión alrededor de la Crónica X." *Revista Mexicana de Estudios Antropológicos* 9 (1947): 125–34.

———. "Durán's *Historia* and the *Crónica X.*" In Diego Durán, *The History of the Indies of New Spain*, edited and translated by Doris Heyden. Norman: University of Oklahoma Press, 1994.

Beyer, Hermann. *Mito y simbología del México antiguo.* Special edition of *El México Antiguo: Revista Internacional de Arqueología, Etnología, Folklore, Historia, Historia Antigua y Lingüística Mexicanas.* Edited by Carmen Cook de Leonard. Mexico City: Sociedad Alemana Mexicanista, 1965.

Boone, Elizabeth Hill. "Coatlicues at the Templo Mayor." *Ancient Mesoamerica* 10 (1999): 189–206.

———. *Cycles of Time and Meaning in the Mexican Books of Fate.* Austin: University of Texas Press, 2007.

———. "The Image of Huitzilopochtli: Changing Ideas and Visual Manifestations of the Aztec God." In *The Imagination of Matter: Religion and Ecology in Mesoamerican Traditions*, edited by David Carrasco, 51–82. BAR International Series 515. Oxford: British Archaeological Reports, 1989.

———. "*In Tlamatinime*: The Wise Men and Women of Aztec Mexico." In *Painted Books and Indigenous Knowledge in Mesoamerica: Manuscript Studies in Honor of Mary Elizabeth Smith*, edited by Elizabeth Hill Boone, 9–25. Middle American Research Institute 69. New Orleans: Tulane University, 2005.

———. "The Nature and Earlier Versions of Diego Durán's 'Historia de las Indias' in Madrid." Unpublished manuscript. Summer 1978.

Burkhart, Louise M. "The 'Little Doctrine' and Indigenous Catechesis in New Spain." *Hispanic American Historical Review* 94, no. 2 (2014): 167–206.

Bustamante, Carlos María de. *Necesidad de la unión de todos los mexicanos contra las asechanzas de la nación española y liga europea comprobada con La historia de la antigua república de Tlaxcallan.* Mexico City: Imprenta del Águila, 1826.

Carr, Dennis. "The Beinecke Map: Iconography and Physical Properties." In *Painting a Map of Sixteenth-Century Mexico City: Land, Writing, and Native Rule*, edited by Mary E. Miller and Barbara E. Mundy, 9–30. New Haven, Conn.: Yale University Press, 2012.

Carrasco, David. *City of Sacrifice: The Aztec Empire and the Role of Violence in Civilization.* Boston: Beacon Press, 1999.

———, ed. *To Change Place: Aztec Ceremonial Landscapes.* Boulder: University Press of Colorado, 1991.

Carrasco, Pedro. "Royal Marriages in Ancient Mexico." In *Explorations in Ethnohistory: Indians of Central Mexico in the Sixteenth Century*, edited by H. R. Harvey and Hanns J. Prem, 41–81. Albuquerque: University of New Mexico Press, 1984.

Casas, fray Bartolomé de las. *Apologética historia sumaria.* Edited by Edmundo O'Gorman. 2 vols. Mexico City: Instituto de Investigaciones Históricas, Universidad Nacional Autónoma de México, 1967.

Caso, Alfonso. *Los barrios antiguos de Tenochtitlan y Tlatelolco.* Mexico City: Memorias de la Academia Mexicana de la Historia, 1956.

———. "Una fecha en el Códice Ramírez." *Revista Mexicana de Estudios Antropológicos* 7 (1945): 82–83.

Castillo, Cristóbal del. *Historia de la venida de los mexicanos y otros pueblos e Historia de la conquista.* Edited by Federico Navarrete Linares. Mexico City: Instituto Nacional de Antropología e Historia, 1991.

Chimalpáhin, Domingo. *Las ocho relaciones y El memorial de Colhuacan.* Translated by Rafael Tena. 2 vols. Mexico City: Cien de México, 1998.

Chimalpahin Quauhtlehuanitzin, don Domingo de San Antón Muñón. *Annals of His Time.* Edited and translated by James Lockhart, Susan Schroeder, and Doris Namala. Stanford: Stanford University Press, 2006.

———. *Chimalpahin's Conquest: A Nahua Historian's Rewriting of Francisco López de Gómara's Conquista de México.* Edited and translated by Susan Schroeder, Anne J. Cruz, Cristián Roa-de-la-Carrera, and David E. Tavárez. Stanford: Stanford University Press, 2010.

———. *Codex Chimalpahin: Society and Politics in Mexico Tenochtitlan, Tlatelolco, Texcoco, Culhuacan, and Other Nahua Altepetl in Central Mexico. The Nahuatl and Spanish Annals and Accounts collected and recorded by don Domingo de San Antón Muñón Chimalpahin Quauhtlehuanitzin.* Edited and translated by Arthur J. O. Anderson and Susan Schroeder. 2 vols. Norman: University of Oklahoma Press, 1997.

———. "Exercicio quotidiano." In *Codex Chimalpahin,* 2:130–83.

Chipman, Donald E. *Moctezuma's Children: Aztec Royalty under Spanish Rule, 1520–1700.* Austin: University of Texas Press, 2005.

Clavigero, Francisco J. *Historia antigua de México.* Translated by J. Joaquín de Mora. 2 vols. Mexico City: Editorial Delfín, 1944.

Codex Mendoza. Edited by Frances F. Berdan and Patricia Rieff Anawalt. 4 vols. Berkeley: University of California Press, 1992.

Codex Mexicanus. Paris: Société des Américanistes, 1952.

Codex Telleriano-Remensis: Ritual, Divination, and History in a Pictorial Aztec Manuscript. Edited by Eloise Quiñones Keber. Austin: University of Texas Press, 1995.

El Códice de Huichapan. Mexico City: Telecomunicaciones de México, 1992.

El Códice de Huichapan: Paleografía y traducción. Edited by Yolanda Lastra and Doris Bartholomew. Mexico City: Universidad Nacional Autónoma de México, 2001.

El Códice de Huichapan. Vol. 1, *Relato otomí del México prehispánico y colonial.* Edited by Manuel Alvarado Guinchard. Mexico City: Departamento de Lingüística, Instituto Nacional de Antropología e Historia, 1976.

Códice Osuna: Reproducción facsimilar de la obra del mismo título, editada en Madrid, 1878. Mexico City: Instituto Indigenista Interamericano, 1947.

Colston, Stephen A. "Tlacaelel's Descendants and the Authorship of the 'Historia Mexicana.'" *Indiana* 2 (1974): 69–72.

Connell, William F. *After Moctezuma: Indigenous Politics and Self-Government in Mexico City, 1524–1730.* Norman: University of Oklahoma Press, 2011.

———. "Alliance-Building and the Restoration of Native Government in the Altepetl of Mexico Tenochtitlan, 1521–1565." In *City Indians in Spain's American Empire: Urban Indigenous Society in Colonial Mesoamerica and Andean South America, 1530–1810,* edited by Dana Velasco Murillo, Mark Lentz, and Margarita R. Ochoa, 8–31. Brighton, UK: Sussex Academic Press, 2012.

Conway, Richard. "Lakes, Canoes, and the Aquatic Communities of Xochimilco and Chalco, New Spain." *Ethnohistory* 59, no. 3 (2012): 541–68.

Cortés, Hernando. *Letters from Mexico.* Edited and translated by Anthony Pagden. New Haven, Conn.: Yale University Press, 1986.

Couch, N. C. Christopher. "Fragments of History: The Durán Paste-Over Illustrations." Paper presented at the American Society for Ethnohistory conference, November 4, 1983.

———. "Style and Ideology in the Durán Illustrations: An Interpretive Study of Three Early Colonial Mexican Manuscripts." Ph.D. diss., Columbia University, 1987.

Cummins, Tom. "The Indulgent Image: Prints in the New World." In *Contested Visions in the Spanish Colonial World,* edited by Ilona Katzew, 203–25. Los Angeles: Los Angeles County Museum of Art, 2011.

Cushman, Ellen. *The Cherokee Syllabary: Writing the People's Perseverance.* Norman: University of Oklahoma Press, 2011.

Díaz del Castillo, Bernal. *The Discovery and Conquest of Mexico.* Translated by A. P. Maudslay. New York: Da Capo Press, [1908] 1996.

———. *The True History of the Conquest of Mexico.* Translated by Maurice Keatinge. La Jolla, Calif.: Renaissance; Press, [1568] 1979.

Diel, Lori Boornazian. "The *Codex Mexicanus* Genealogy: Binding the Aztec Past to the Colonial Present." *Latin American Colonial Review* 24, no. 2 (2015): 120–46.

———. *The Tira de Tepechpan: Negotiating Place under Aztec and Spanish Rule.* Austin: University of Texas Press, 2008.

Douglas, Eduardo de Jesús. "Our Fathers, Our Mothers: Painting an Indian Genealogy in New Spain." In *Contested Visions in the Spanish Colonial World,* edited by Ilona Katzew, 117–31. Los Angeles: Los Angeles County Museum of Art, 2011.

Durán, fray Diego. *Book of the Gods and Rites and the Ancient Calendar.* Edited and translated by Fernando Horcasitas and Doris Heyden. Norman: University of Oklahoma Press, 1975.

———. *Historia de las Indias de Nueva España e Islas de la Tierra Firme.* Transcribed by Francisco González Varela. 2 vols. Mexico City: Banco Santander, 1990, 1991.

———. *The History of the Indies of New Spain.* Edited and translated by Doris Heyden. Norman: University of Oklahoma Press, 1994.

Eakin, Hugh, "Will Saudi Arabia Ever Change?" *New York Review of Books* 60, no. 1 (January 10, 2013): 37–39.

Gerhard, Peter. *A Guide to the Historical Geography of New Spain.* Cambridge: Cambridge University Press, 1972.

Geschichte der Azteken: Der Codex Aubin und verwandte Dokumente. Edited and translated by Walter Lehmann and Gerdt Kutscher. Berlin: Gebr. Mann Verlag, 1981.

Gibson, Charles. "The Aztec Aristocracy in Colonial Mexico." *Comparative Studies in Society and History* 2 (1960): 169–96.

———. *The Aztecs under Spanish Rule: A History of the Indians of the Valley of Mexico, 1519–1810.* Stanford: Stanford: University Press, 1964.

———. *Tlaxcala in the Sixteenth Century.* Stanford: Stanford University Press, 1952.

Gillingham, Paul. *Cuauhtemoc's Bones: Forging National Identity in Modern Mexico.* Albuquerque: University of New Mexico Press, 2011.

Graulich, Michel. *Myths of Ancient Mexico.* Translated by Bernardo R. Ortiz de Montellano and Thelma Ortiz de Montellano. Norman: University of Oklahoma Press, 1997.

Greenblatt, Stephen. *Will in the World: How Shakespeare Became Shakespeare.* New York: W.W. Norton, 2004.

Haemig, Paul D. "Introduction of the Great-Tailed Grackle by Aztec Emperor Auitzotl: Four-Stage Analysis with New Information." *Ardeola* 58, no. 2 (2011): 387–97.

———. "Introduction of the Great-Tailed Grackle (*Quiscalus mexicanus*) by Aztec Emperor Auitzotl: Provenance of the Historical Account." *Auk* 129, no. 1 (2012): 70–75.

Hajovsky, Patrick Thomas. *On the Lips of Others: Moteuczoma's Fame in Aztec Monuments and Rituals.* Austin: University of Texas Press, 2015.

Haskett, Robert. *Indigenous Rulers: An Ethnohistory of Town Government in Colonial Cuernavaca.* Albuquerque: University of New Mexico Press, 1991.

———. *Visions of Paradise: Primordial Titles and Mesoamerican History in Cuernavaca.* Norman: University of Oklahoma Press, 2005.

Hassig, Ross. *Aztec Warfare: Imperial Expansion and Political Control.* Norman: University of Oklahoma Press, 1988.

———. *War and Society in Ancient Mesoamerica.* Berkeley: University of California Press, 1992.

Higuera, Salvador Mateo. *Los dioses supremos: Enciclopedia gráfica del México antiguo.* Mexico City: Secretaría de Hacienda y Crédito Público, 1992.

Historia de la nación mexicana: Códice de 1576 (Códice Aubin). Edited and translated by Charles E. Dibble. Madrid: Ediciones José Porrúa Turanzas, 1963.

"La historia de Tlatelolco desde los tiempos más remotos." In *Anales de Tlatelolco: Unos anales históricos de la nación mexicana y Códice de Tlatelolco*, edited by Heinrich Berlin, 29–76. Mexico City: Editorial y Litografía Regina de los Ángeles, 1980.

Johansson K., Patrick. "Tlahtoani y cihuacóatl: Una dualidad teocrática en México-Tenochtitlan." *Arqueología Mexicana* 23, no. 133 (2015): 22–29.

———. "Tlatoani y Cihuacoatl: Lo diestro solar y lo siniestro lunar en el alto mando mexica." *Estudios de Cultura Náhuatl* 28 (1998): 39–75.

Kagan, Richard L. *Clio and the Crown: The Politics of History in Medieval and Early Modern Spain*. Baltimore, Md.: Johns Hopkins University Press, 2009.

Kellogg, Susan. *Law and the Transformation of Aztec Culture, 1500–1700*. Norman: University of Oklahoma Press, 1995.

Klein, Cecelia F. "Rethinking Cihuacoatl: Aztec Political Imagery of the Conquered Woman." In *Smoke and Mist: Mesoamerican Studies in Memory of Thelma D. Sullivan*, edited by J. Kathryn Josserand and Karen Kavin, 237–77. BAR International Series 1. Oxford: British Archaeological Reports, 1988.

———. "The Shield Women: Resolution of an Aztec Gender Paradox." In *Current Topics in Aztec Studies: Essays in Honor of Dr. H. B. Nicholson*, edited by Alana Cordy-Collins and Douglas Sharon, 39–64. San Diego Museum Papers 30. San Diego, Calif.: San Diego Museum of Man, 1993.

Kubler, George, and Charles Gibson. *The Tovar Calendar*. New Haven: Memoirs of the Connecticut Academy of Arts and Sciences, 1951.

Lateiner, Donald. *The Historical Method of Herodotus*. Toronto: University of Toronto Press, 1989.

León-Portilla, Miguel. *The Aztec Image of Self and Society: An Introduction to Nahua Culture*. Edited by J. Jorge Klor de Alva. Salt Lake City: University of Utah Press, 1992.

———. "Motecuhzoma Ilhuicamina." In *The Oxford Encyclopedia of Mesoamerican Cultures: The Civilizations of Mexico and Central America*, edited by David Carrasco, 2:343–44. 3 vols. New York: Oxford University Press, 2001.

Lepore, Jill. *The Story of America: Essays on Origins*. Princeton, N.J.: Princeton University Press, 2012.

El libro del Ciuacoatl: Homenaje para el año del Fuego Nuevo, Libro explicativo del llamado Códice Borbónico. Edited by Ferdinand Anders, Maarten Jansen, and Luis Reyes García. Spain, Austria, and Mexico City: Sociedad Estatal Quinto Centenario, Akademische Druck- u. Verlagsanstalt, and Fondo de Cultura Económica, 1991.

Liebsohn, Dana. *Script and Glyph: Pre-Hispanic History, Colonial Bookmaking, and the* Historia Tolteca-Chichimeca. Washington, D.C.: Dumbarton Oaks Research Library and Collection, 2009.

Liss, Peggy K. *Isabel the Queen: Life and Times*. rev. ed. Philadelphia: University of Pennsylvania Press, 2004.

Lockhart, James. Introduction to *Annals of His Times*, edited by James Lockhart, Susan Schroeder, and Doris Namala, 3–23. Stanford: Stanford University Press, 2006.

———. *The Nahuas after the Conquest: A Social and Cultural History of the Indians of Central Mexico, Sixteenth through Eighteenth Centuries*. Stanford: Stanford University Press, 1992.

———. *We People Here: Nahuatl Accounts of the Conquest of Mexico*. Berkeley: University of California Press, 1993.

López Austin, Alfredo. *The Human Body and Ideology: Concepts of the Ancient Nahuas*. Translated by Thelma Ortiz de Montellano and Bernardo Ortiz de Montellano. 2 vols. Salt Lake City: University of Utah Press, 1988.

López de Gómara, Francisco. *Historia de las Indias y Conquista de México*. Zaragoza: Agustín Millán, 1552.

Magaloni Kerpel, Diana. *The Colors of the New World: Artists, Materials, and the Creation of the* Florentine Codex. Los Angeles: Getty Research Institute, 2014.

Martínez, Henrico. *Reportorio de los tiempos e Historia natural de Nueva España*. Mexico City: Secretaría de Educación Pública, [1606] 1948.

Matos Moctezuma, Eduardo. "Symbolism of the Templo Mayor." In *The Aztec Templo Mayor*, edited by Elizabeth Hill Boone, 185–209. Washington, D.C.: Dumbarton Oaks Research Library and Collection, 1983.

Matrícula de Tributos. Edited by Frances F. Berdan and Jacqueline de Durand-Forest. Graz, Austria: Akademische Druck-u. Verlagsanstalt, 1980.

Matthew, Laura E. *Memories of Conquest: Becoming Mexicano in Colonial Guatemala*. Chapel Hill: University of North Carolina Press, 2012.

Medina, Cuauhtémoc. "Beyond Sources." In *The Colors of the New World: Artists, Materials, and the Creation of the* Florentine Codex, by Diana Magaloni Kerpel, ix–xi. Los Angeles: Getty Research Institute, 2014.

Megged, Amos, and Stephanie Wood, eds. *Mesoamerican Memory: Enduring Systems of Remembrance*. Norman: University of Oklahoma Press, 2012.

Mendieta, fray Gerónimo de. *Historia eclesiástica indiana*. Mexico City: Editorial Porrúa, 1980.

Mengin, Ernest. " Commentaire du Codex Mexicanus nos. 23–24 de la Bibliothèque Nationale de Paris." *Journal de la Société des Américanistes* 41, no. 2 (1952): 387–498.

Molina, fray Alonso de. *Vocbulario en lengua castellana y mexicana y mexicana y castellana*. Mexico City: Editorial Porrúa, 1970.

Mundy, Barbara E. "Crown and Tlatoque: The Iconography of Rulership in the Beinecke Map." In *Painting a Map of Sixteenth-Century Mexico City: Land, Writing, and Native Rule*, 111–36. New Haven, Conn.: Yale University Press, 2012.

———. *The Death of Aztec Tenochtitlan, the Life of Mexico City*. Austin: University of Texas Press, 2015.

———. "Pictography, Writing, and Mapping in the Valley of Mexico and the Beinecke Map." In *Painting a Map of Sixteenth-Century Mexico City: Land, Writing, and Native Rule*, 31–52. New Haven, Conn.: Yale University Press, 2012.

———. "Place-Names in Mexico Tenochtitlan." *Ethnohistory* 61, no. 2 (2014): 329–58.

Nesvig, Martin Austin. "The Epistemological Politics of Vernacular Scripture in Sixteenth-Century Mexico." *Americas* 70, no. 2 (2013): 165–201.

Nicholson, H. B. "The Aztecs." Book review. *American Anthropologist* 66, no. 6 (1964): 1408–11.

———. "Hugh Thomas' *Conquest*: Observations on the Coverage of the Indigenous Cultures." In *In Chalchihuitl in Quetzalli, Precious Greenstone, Precious Quetzal Feather: Mesoamerican Studies in Honor of Doris Heyden*, edited by Eloise Quiñones Keber, 129–36. Culver City, Calif.: Labyrinthos, 2000.

Nuttall, Zelia. *The Fundamental Principles of the Old and New World Civilizations: A Comparative Research Based on a Study of the Ancient Mexican Religious, Sociological and Calendrical Systems*. Archaeological and Ethnological Papers of the Peabody Museum 2. Cambridge, Mass.: Harvard University, 1901.

Olko, Justyna. *Insignia of Rank in the Nahua World, from the Fifteenth to the Seventeenth Century*. Boulder: University Press of Colorado, 2014.

Padden, R. C. *The Hummingbird and the Hawk: Conquest and Sovereignty in the Valley of Mexico, 1503–1541*. New York: Harper Torchbooks, 1970.

Peperstraete, Sylvie. *La "Chronique X": Reconstitution et analyse d'une source perdue fondamentale sur la civilisation Aztèque, d'après l'Historia de las Indias de Nueva España de D. Durán (1581) et la Crónica Mexicana de F. A. Tezozomoc (ca. 1598)*. BAR International Series 1630. Oxford: British Archaeological Reports, 2007.

Prescott, William H. *History of the Conquest of Mexico*. Edited by John Foster Kirk. 2 vols. Philadelphia: J. B. Lippincott, 1873.

Pritchett, W. Kendrick. *The Liar School of Herodotos*. Amsterdam: J. C. Geiben, 1993.

Read, Kay A. "More than Earth: Cihuacoatl as Mother, Warrior, and Inside Ruler." In *Códices y documentos sobre México: Tercer Simposio Internacional*, edited by Constanza Vega Sosa, 407–26. Mexico City: Instituto Nacional de Antropología e Historia, 2000.

Restall, Matthew, Lisa Sousa, and Kevin Terraciano, eds. *Mesoamerican Voices: Native-Language Writings from Colonial Mexico, Oaxaca, Yucatan, and Guatemala*. New York: Oxford University Press, 2005.

Reyes García, Luis, ed. and trans. *Como te confundes? Acaso no somos conquistados? Anales de Juan Bautista*. Mexico City: Centro de Investigaciones y Estudios Superiores en Antropología Social; Biblioteca Lorenzo Boturini, Insigne y Nacional Basílica de Guadalupe, 2001.

Ricard, Robert. *The Spiritual Conquest of Mexico: An Essay on the Apostolate and the Evangelizing Methods of the Mendicant Orders in New Spain, 1523–1572*. Translated by Lesley Byrd Simpson. Berkeley: University of California Press, 1974.

Robertson, Donald. "Paste-Over Illustrations in the Durán Codex of Madrid." *Tlalocan* 5, no. 4 (1968): 340–48.

Rojas, José Luis de. *Tenochtitlan: Capital of the Aztec Empire.* Gainesville: University Press of Florida, 2014.

Romero Galván, José Rubén. *Los privilegios perdidos: Hernando Alvarado Tezozomoc, su tiempo, su nobleza, y su Crónica mexicana.* Mexico City: Universidad Nacional Autónoma de México, 2003.

Rounds, J. "Dynastic Succession and the Centralizing of Power in Tenochtitlan." In *The Inca and Aztec States, 1400–1800,* edited by George A. Collier, Renato I. Rosaldo, and John D. Wirth, 63–89. New York: Academic Press, 1982.

Ruiz de Alarcón. *Treatise on the Heathen Superstitions That Today Live among the Indians Native to This New Spain, 1629.* Edited and translated by J. Richard Andrews and Ross Hassig. Norman: University of Oklahoma Press, 1984.

Ruiz Medrano, Ethelia. *Mexico's Indigenous Communities: Their Lands and Histories, 1500–2010.* Translated by Russ Davidson. Boulder: University Press of Colorado, 2010.

Sahagún, fray Bernardino de. *Códice Florentino.* Manuscrito 218-20 de la Colección Palatina de la Biblioteca Medicea Laurenziana. ed. facs. 3 vols. Mexico City: Archivo General de la Nación, 1979.

———. *Florentine Codex: General History of the Things of New Spain.* Edited and translated by Arthur J. O. Anderson and Charles E. Dibble. 12 vols. Santa Fe, N.M., and Salt Lake City, Utah: School of American Research and University of Utah Press, 1950–82.

———. *Primeros memoriales,* facs. ed. Norman and Madrid: University of Oklahoma Press and Patrimonio Nacional and Real Academia de la Historia, 1993.

———. *Primeros memoriales.* Translated by Thelma D. Sullivan. Edited by H. B. Nicholson, Arthur J. O. Anderson, Charles E. Dibble, Eloise Quiñones Keber, and Wayne Ruwet. Norman and Madrid: University of Oklahoma Press and Patrimonio Nacional and Real Academia de la Historia, 1997.

Sahlins, Marshall. *Apologies to Thucydides.* Chicago: University of Chicago Press, 2004.

Schama, Simon. *The Story of the Jews: Finding the Words, 1000 BC–1492 AD.* New York: Harper Collins, 2013.

Schroeder, Susan. *Chimalpahin and the Kingdoms of Chalco.* Tucson: University of Arizona Press, 1991.

———. "Chimalpahin Rewrites the Conquest: Yet Another Epic History?" In *The Conquest All Over Again: Nahuas and Zapotecs Thinking, Writing, and Painting Spanish Colonialism,* edited by Susan Schroeder, 101–23. Brighton, UK: Sussex Academic Press, 2010.

———. "The First American Valentine: Nahua Courtship and Other Aspects of Family Structuring in Mesoamerica." *Journal of Family History* 23, no. 4 (1998): 341–54.

———. "Introduction: The Genre of Conquest Studies." In *Indian Conquistadors: Indigenous Allies in the Conquest of Mesoamerica*, edited by Laura Matthew and Michel R. Oudijk, 5–27. Norman: University of Oklahoma Press, 2007.

———. "The Noblewomen of Chalco." *Estudios de Cultura Náhuatl* 22 (1992): 45–86.

———. "The Truth about the *Crónica Mexicayotl*." *Colonial Latin American Review* 20, no. 2 (2011): 233–47.

———. "Why Women Matter in History." In *Indigenous Intellectuals: Knowledge, Power, and Colonial Culture in Mexico and the Andes*, edited by Gabriela Ramos and Yanna Yannakakis, 107–31. Durham, N.C.: Duke University Press, 2014.

Seler, Eduard. "Alexander von Humboldt's Picture Manuscripts in the Royal Library at Berlin." In *Mexican and Central American Antiquities, Calendar Systems, and History*, 123–229. Washington, D.C.: Smithsonian Institution, Government Printing Office, 1904.

Sell, Barry D., and Larissa Taylor. "'He Could Have Made Marvels in This Language': A Nahuatl Sermon by Father Juan de Tovar, S.J." *Estudios de Cultura Náhuatl* 26 (1996): 211–44.

Shakespeare, William. *The Unabridged Shakespeare*. Edited by William George Clark and William Adis Wright. Philadelphia: Courage Books, 1989.

Sigal, Pete. "Imagining Cihuacoatl: Masculine Rituals, Nahua Goddesses and the Texts of the Tlacuilos." *Gender and History* 22, no. 3 (2010): 538–63.

Suetonius Tranquillus, Gaius. *Lives of the Caesars*. Translated by Catharine Edwards. New York: Oxford University Press, 2000.

———. *The Twelve Caesars*. Translated by Robert Graves. Baltimore, Md.: Penguin Books, 1957.

Tacitus, Cornelius. *Tacitus: The Annals*. Translated by A. J. Woodman. Indianapolis, Ind.: Hackett, 2004.

Tavárez, David. "Mutable Memories: The Moteuczomas and Nahua Nobility in the Atzaqualco Catechism." In *Painted Words: Nahua Catholicism, Politics, and Memory in the Atzaqualco Pictorial Catechism*. Washington, D.C.: Dumbarton Oaks, 2016.

———. "Nahua Intellectuals, Franciscan Scholars, and the *Devotio moderna* in Colonial Mexico." *Americas* 70, no. 2 (2013): 203–35.

Tena, Rafael. *La religión mexica*. 2nd ed. Mexico City: Instituto Nacional de Antropología e Historia, 2012.

———. "Revisión de la hipótesis sobre 'La Crónica X.'" In *Códices y documentos sobre México*, edited by Salvador Rueda Smithers, Constanza Vega Sosa, and Rodrigo Martínez Baracs, 2:163–78. 2 vols. Mexico City: Instituto Nacional de Antropología e Historia, 1997.

Terraciano, Kevin. "Three Views of the Conquest of Mexico from the *Other Mexica*." In *The Conquest All Over Again: Nahuas and Zapotecs Thinking, Writing, and Painting Spanish Colonialism*, edited by Susan Schroeder, 15–40. Brighton, UK: Sussex Academic Press, 2010.

Torquemada, fray Juan de. *Monarquía indiana*. 3 vols. Mexico City: Editorial Porrúa, 1975.

Tovar, Juan de. *Codex Ramírez: Relación del origen de los indios que habitan esta Nueva España, según sus historias*. Edited by Manuel Orozco y Berra. Mexico City: Editorial Leyenda, 1980.

———. *Manuscrit Tovar*. Edited by Jacques Lafaye. Graz, Austria: Akademische Druck- u. Verlagsanstalt, 1972.

Townsend, Camilla. "From Old Worlds to New: The Creation of the *Historia Tolteca-Chichimeca*." Paper presented at the American Society for Ethnohistory conference, New Orleans, September 2013.

Townsend, Richard. "Coronation at Tenochtitlan." In *The Imagination of Matter: Religion and Ecology in Mesoamerican Traditions*, edited by David Carrasco, 155–88. BAR International Series 515. Oxford: British Archaeological Reports, 1989.

Velazco, Salvador. *Visiones de Anáhuac: Reconstrucciones historiográficas y etnicidades emergentes en el México colonial: Fernando de Alva Ixtlilxochitl, Diego Muñoz Camargo y Hernando Alvarado Tezozomoc*. Guadalajara: Universidad de Guadalajara, 2003.

Villella, Peter B. "Indian Lords, Hispanic Gentlemen: The Salazars of Colonial Tlaxcala." *Americas* 69, no. 1 (2012): 1–36.

———. *Indigenous Elites and Creole Identity in Colonial Mexico, 1500–1800*. Cambridge: Cambridge University Press, 2016.

Winning, Hasso von. "Tlacaelel, Aztec General and Statesman." *Masterkey* 38, no. 2 (1964): 44–53.

INDEX

Index entries are listed in the categories of
Individuals, Locales and Ethnic Groups, and Subjects.

INDIVIDUALS

LOCALES AND ASSOCIATED ETHNIC GROUPS

alcalde, 145, 146

altar, 54; temple, 99, 100, 108

altepetl, 5, 11–12, 13, 14, 15, 16, 18, 19, 20, 29, 30, 31, 32, 36, 37, 39, 53, 54, 55, 56, 57, 59, 60, 61, 62, 63, 66, 67, 68, 70, 71, 72, 73, 76, 78, 80, 81, 82, 87, 88, 93, 96, 98, 99, 103, 104, 107, 110, 112, 118, 120, 121, 124, 129, 134, 139, 148; confederation, 22, 23, 60, 63, 67, 68, 72; interaltepetl relations, 19; micropatriotism, 14. See also *tlayacatl*

annals, Nahuatl, 5, 7, 10, 11, 12, 14, 15, 16, 18, 19, 20, 34, 35, 36, 37, 40, 43, 44, 45, 47, 49, 51, 52, 54, 55, 57, 58, 59, 62, 63, 64, 68, 73, 74, 80, 81, 83, 85, 86, 88, 90, 96, 97, 105, 107, 109, 112, 113, 115, 119, 120, 125, 129, 131, 134, 140, 142, 143, 144, 145, 147, 148, 149; of Juan Bautista, 144. *See also* pictorial account(s)

Apologética historia sumaria, 39

aqueduct, 61, 82, 175n3

arrow(s), 54, 64, 71, 72, 75, 81, 85, 91, 127

Atempanecatl, 22, 24, 25, 34, 62, 144, 161n7; image, 24. *See also* Atenpanecatl, Bartolomé *in index of individuals*

atlatl, 54, 75

Augustinian(s), 10, 146

aviary, 100

banquet(s), 20, 30, 65, 70, 72, 96

bastard, 59, 116, 140

batten, 16, 30

Biblioteca Nacional de Madrid, 40

bird(s), 53, 72. *See also* eagle; grackle, great-tailed; hummingbird; quail; quetzal

black(s), 9

bow(s), 54, 75

brigantines, 143

cabildo, 145, 146

cactus (tuna), 15; stone, 53; vessel, 87

calendar: Christian, 14–15; cycle, 14, 30; Mesoamerican, 14, 15

calpolli, 11, 65

Camaxtli (deity), 89, 91

cannibalism, 19, 22, 32, 64, 75, 100, 103, 104, 108, 121

canoe(s), 68, 72–73, 82, 87, 88, 93, 135

carrying bag, net, 75

Casa de Aguilas, 19

catechism, 148

cathedral, 53

Chalca yaocihuacuicatl, 108

chinampa(s), 55, 71, 85

chocolate, 30, 100, 118

ciénaga, 140

Cihuacoatl (deity), 6, 18, 26–32, 33, 38, 39, 40, 47, 48, 127, 140; attire, 26, 30, 127; as cannibal, 32; depiction, 21, 25, 30–31; images, 27, 29, 31; *patrona*, 32; temple (Tlillan), 29, 31, 39

Cihuacoatl (office), 3, 20, 22, 24, 37, 38, 39, 40–41, 43, 47, 95, 102, 103, 122, 123, 124, 126, 127, 132, 133, 134, 135, 137, 140, 146; definition, 21, 22; end of title and office, 139; glyph, 59, 139; perpetual, 22; prestige, 38; Tlacaelel the elder as, 6, 7, 17, 18, 20, 22, 23, 24, 32, 33, 37, 38, 42, 43, 44, 45, 47, 59, 62, 66, 76, 80, 82, 83, 89, 91, 94, 98, 104, 107, 116, 117, 120, 122–25, 136, 140, 145; Tlacaelel Xocoyotl as, 131–32; Tlacotzin as, 133–39; Tlilpotonqui as, 124–31; wealth, 137

cihuapilli, 52, 125, 129

Cihuatlatoani, 33

cloak, 25, 42, 48, 71, 82, 139, 147. See also *manta(s)*

Printed in the USA
CPSIA information can be obtained
at www.ICGtesting.com
CBHW032320010424
6237CB00004B/249

9 780806 192222